BROTHERS
IN ARMS

ALSO BY GERAINT JONES

Blood Forest
Siege

AS CO-AUTHOR
No Way Out by Adam Jowett

ALSO WITH JAMES PATTERSON AS REES JONES
Private Princess
Private Royals
Heist

BROTHERS IN ARMS

GERAINT JONES

MACMILLAN

First published 2019 by Macmillan
an imprint of Pan Macmillan
20 New Wharf Road, London N1 9RR
Associated companies throughout the world
www.panmacmillan.com

ISBN 978-1-529-00040-5 HB
ISBN 978-1-529-00041-2 TPB

1 3 5 7 9 8 6 4 2

A CIP catalogue record for this book is available from the British Library.

Typeset by Jouve (UK), Milton Keynes
Printed and bound by CPI Group (UK) Ltd, Croydon, CR0 4YY

Visit **www.panmacmillan.com** to read more about all our books
and to buy them. You will also find features, author interviews and
news of any author events, and you can sign up for e-newsletters
so that you're always first to hear about our new releases.

To that rare breed of man, the infantry soldier.

Contents

Map A

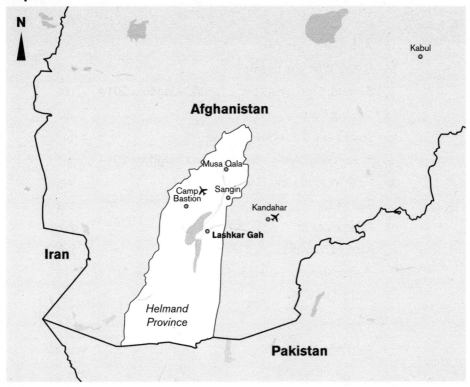

Map B

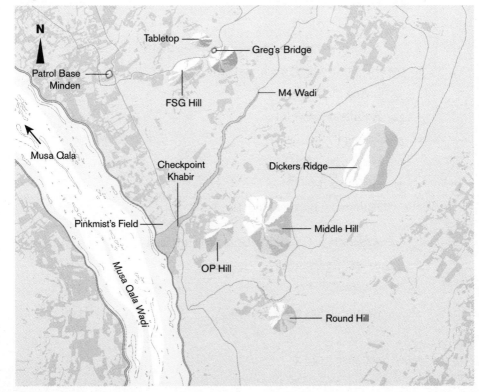

AUTHOR'S NOTE

I never thought that I would become a drug addict. I never thought that I would want to take my own life.

That all changed after Afghanistan, and this book is based on the journals that I kept during my time there. Maybe my opinions here seem raw and angry, but I have been true to how we felt at the time. Almost a decade has passed since our tour and I have softened with hindsight, but this book is about our experiences on the ground, and so it would be wrong of me to moderate our behaviour and attitudes for the sake of people's feelings now that I am safe from harm, and free of bullshit.

That being said, I'll be the first to admit that my own knowledge of war is severly limited. I did not climb trench ladders at Ypres. I did not storm the beaches in Normandy. I did not fight in the cities of Hué, Grozny, or Fallujah. I did serve in Basra and in Helmand Province, but there are a lot of others who did more than me – bearded men of the SAS who killed the enemy where they slept. Young riflemen who lost friends and limbs to IEDs on a horrifyingly regular basis. However, my own experience is the only prism through which I can offer an insight into that which I hold most sacred: my comrades. This story is for them, because they deserve to be remembered forever.

Though I know little of war, I feel as though I know a great deal about soldiers and the comradeship that exists between them. I have written this book so that those who have never had the honour of experienceng the camaraderie can look from afar and be touched by it, and so those of you who have known the bond – a bond so special that it can only be forged on the anvil of shared danger and loss – can find in these pages memories of your own comrades, for the spirit of the soldier is constant, timeless, and universal.

Finally, I have written this book for myself, so that I can open its pages and be taken back to the greatest days of my life. I lived among heroes, and this is their story.

INTRODUCTION

You Weren't There, Man

Somebody wants you dead.

Just think about that for a minute. Somebody in your town, your neighbourhood, wants you dead.

You know this, because of what you just found. It was waiting for you, buried, and buried quickly. They hadn't put it there until they saw you coming. This was meant for you. Nobody else.

You.

And now you look across the cornfield and see the farmer, squatting, watching, his face giving you nothing. Was it him? How about the policeman who's smiling, asking you for a cigarette? Could he have something to do with it? He seems sure of where to put his feet. You haven't trusted yours for months.

What about the kid, the one you gave the chocolate bars to the last time you left your place? Hadn't he asked when you'd be coming out again? Maybe he was the one who threw that grenade over your wall last week, when you were sitting down to dinner?

You look around at these people, your neighbours for the past six months. You look around at them, and you know that one of them wants you dead – and that those who don't, know who does.

And you're only 200 metres into your journey. Two miles to go. You know that whoever wants you dead won't stop. The people around you know it too, and they smile, and ask for cigarettes and chocolate. You let them. While they're here, you're safe. Probably.

But you can't stay for long. You have work to do, and now you're spooked. You know that this dusty track holds surprises. The kind of surprises that will send your legs in one direction, and your head in another. And so you ask the Boss's permission to make a new track, through the farmer's field.

And you're told no, you're not to upset the neighbours.

You argue. You make good points. But the answer is the same: *No*. Follow the track. Follow the track, and pray you don't find its surprises.

And this is when you realize what your life is worth.

Less than a few hundred stems of corn.

And so you walk on, hating. Hating the people who send you down the track. Hating the people who want you dead. And hating the people who hide them.

Can you picture this? That it's you on the track? Maybe.

Can you feel it? Can you know how it feels, to see the smiling faces that want you dead, a life that's worth less than a few bags of corn?

No. You can't.

So don't judge too harshly.

1

The Church

July 2009

There was no room inside, but it was the kind of beautiful day that can only be found in an English summer, the dappled sunshine suggestive of comfort and nostalgia, and so I found myself a place in the crammed churchyard. The crowd was a mixture of civilian suits and dresses shot through with uniforms from every branch and arm of the services. Hanging back at the edges were the curious onlookers, drawn in by the regimented pomp of a military funeral.

I felt eyes on me and looked to my left. A short, sallow-skinned man in the blue of the RAF took it as an invitation to approach. He was a southerner, and spoke to me as if I was a long-lost friend.

'Alright mate. You were in Iraq, weren't you? Two years ago? I never forget a boat race.'

He was an RAF Regiment gunner, and like all infantry soldiers I despised his type, thinking of them as blaggers and posers. I also disapproved of his use of rhyming slang – we were at a funeral, not on the set of a Guy Ritchie movie – but the man had come to pay respects to my friend, and so after the pause to assess him, I put out a grudging hand.

'I was, yeah.'

'You knew him?' he asked, his head bobbing towards the church. I nodded. 'You with him when he died?'

I hadn't been. Jamie had become a friend as we went through pre-deployment training together. You can get to know anybody fast when you live in each other's pockets for a few weeks, and Jamie's infectious enthusiasm and outlook on life had left me with a big soft spot for the kid. His unit had deployed just a few weeks earlier, and now he was dead. Killed by a single shot from a sniper, as he called from a rooftop about his choice of ration pack for dinner.

I'd found out about his death on Facebook. I'd been excited when I saw him login to the chat application.

> **Gez:**
> Hiya mate! How you doing?

> **Jamie:**
> Hi. James was killed this morning.

I didn't have the sense to put it together.

> **Gez:**
> Sorry to hear that mate :(Was he a pal?

> **Jamie:**
> Sorry. This is James's mum. He was killed this morning.

And now I watched as his flag-draped coffin was carried towards the church doors by the rigid guardsmen.

But I wasn't watching my friend.

I was watching his mother.

There was no sobbing. No sign of frailty. She carried herself like a queen, and my eyes threatened to leak for the first time as I saw that courage. I'd see it in other mothers of the fallen, and that strength breaks your heart and fills you with purpose in the same moment.

The service was held. Jamie would be buried elsewhere, a closed ceremony. I left the churchyard, changing out of my dress uniform in the alley behind a hair salon. Some of the girls saw me and smiled. I smiled back.

I pulled my car over to the side of the main road, watching as the dark fleet of Jamie's cortege approached. The streets were lined. Afghanistan was the kind of shooting war the public could pretend to understand, not like the poisoned chalice of Iraq, and now our dead soldiers were revered, Kipling's verse on the 'thin red line of heroes' as true as it ever was.

I looked again for Jamie's mother. I didn't know why. Perhaps I was thinking of my own. How she'd look if it was me in the ground. I didn't see her, and traffic resumed. The people of the town dispersed, the war for them over until the next reel of grainy combat footage on the six o'clock news.

I headed west, to my unit. On the drive, I thought about Jamie, his family, and my own. I thought about how his child was without a father, his mother without a son. I thought about how we had both volunteered for a war that we knew nothing about. A war that had taken his life.

That night, I flew to Helmand.

AFGHAN

2

Summer Camp

For the infantryman, Camp Bastion was soldiering purgatory. The hot air here was thick with the smell of fuel, and tangy dust kicked up by scores of beat-up Land Rovers, these belonging to the base-rats who inhabited air-conditioned accommodation for the entirety of their deployments. Though the population was that of a British village, the sprawling camp had grown since 2006 to become the size of a town, and like all troops new to theatre, we had come here to acclimatize, receive last-minute training, and to take over the vehicles that A Company would use for the duration of our tour – or at least until they were blown up. The mangled wreck of the Jackal patrol vehicle beside our tent was a daily reminder of what awaited us.

A Company was accommodated in part of a tented city, segregated into three platoons and bands of friends. My own clique in Three Platoon was made up of other junior NCOs like me, corporals and lance corporals, veterans of Iraq and mostly members of the battalion's Anti-Tank and Reconnaissance platoons, which prided themselves on a laid-back but professional approach to soldiering. In conventional warfare, 'Recce' would go ahead of the battalion to find the enemy, but here they would act as footsloggers, the same as any other bayonet in the company. The Anti-Tank men had brought their Javelin missiles along, but we weren't expecting to see any Taliban tanks coming over the horizon, and so for the most part these specialists would also be going back to their bread and butter as riflemen.

Toby was one of these anti-tankers. He was the battalion scrum half, and like most who had played the position, he was short, squat, and could argue with himself over the colour of the sky. A true old sweat, he was a career soldier, this his fourth tour at the ripe old age of twenty-six. It was no adventure to him, just another deployment in the long list of operations and overseas exercises. At home were Toby's two girls, and he was putting his life at risk to provide for them. The short-fused soldier was also the man responsible for naming our clique 'The Firm', after a cheesy British gangster flick that he'd been watching.

With kind eyes but a lashing tongue, Jay was a full corporal, and had been a rising star in the battalion until the green had leaked out of him after a few years of service. He was literally The Firm's most laid-back member, his primary focus in life being sleep. Men of this disposition were known as being a 'mantress'; half man, half mattress. When conscious, Jay was constantly batting away questions about how he held on to a fiancée who was well out of his league. Like most of The Firm, he was in his mid-twenties, with the build so common to those enlisted into Support Company – average height, with a thick back and shoulders. The perfect design for humping machine guns, anti-tank missiles or mortars.

Danny was the oldest of our group. Pushing twenty-eight and in his twelfth year of service, he was as bitter as the dregs of a guard room coffee pot, his handsome features often made ugly with the contempt-filled looks he shot at those he thought inept – which, most of the time, was everyone that he came into contact with. During our first encounter, Danny had asked a mutual friend about the 'big-headed TA cunt' who'd just joined the company. It was me, and the disdain was mutual. The same day, I'd asked my own comrades from Iraq about the 'big-headed prick from "Recce"'. But then, thrown into the melting pot of our pre-deployment training, we soon found common ground – a hatred of the army's inflexible and often archaic rules, and a disdain for those who we regarded as slovenly and unbefitting of the mantle of 'soldier' – and we became great friends. Danny's disparaging view of humanity was not without grounds, however. He'd brought a native wife back with him from when the battalion had been stationed in Germany but the marriage had broken down under the fascinated gaze of the regiment. A single man now, we didn't ease up on letting him know about it, and he responded with the kind of inventive insults that would shame a short-changed crack whore.

Jake had missed out on the battalion's most volatile tour of Iraq, and came into this operation with more nerves than the rest of us – we knew enough to be scared, but for him there was that greater fear of the unknown. The Swansea boy was a canvas for tattoos that looked as though they'd been inked by a drunken four-year-old. He was also an eternal pessimist, rising to the bait when we'd tease him about the limbless future that awaited him. 'Pinkmist' quickly stuck to him as a nickname, and maybe we tempted fate with that, because he'd certainly live up to it.

I was the unlikely member of the group. I was the tattoo-less middle-class boy who was doing this 'for fun', and not because it was a career plan. A twenty-five-year-old university graduate turned lance corporal, this would be my third tour in three years. By using the backdoor of the Territorial Army, I had become what some would call a 'war junkie', signing up for whatever operations I could, and always begging to be sent to the unit that was likely to see the most action. I was eager and I was naive. I still thought war was a sport. I recognized the stakes were high, but I played willingly, because I knew that there was nothing else in life that would fill my limbs with adrenaline and my head with stories. I was in love with the notion of the hero, and like almost every young man who has gone to war, I was determined to play the part.

Coming into Helmand, our small group had some fifteen tours to its name, and so we considered ourselves 'sweats', and we knew enough to know that we didn't know enough. Afghanistan was not Iraq, and we'd be learning many of the same lessons as the greenest private, but we hoped that our instincts would see us through.

•

July had welcomed us with a 45°C slap in the face, troops often heard grumbling that 'it was redders, and they were threaders'. A rare display of common sense gave us a couple of days to adjust to the heat before we began our training in the empty desert. We used this time to explore Bastion, finding luxuries such as a Pizza Hut, coffee shops, and gyms. The place was Butlin's surrounded by razor wire, and if it wasn't for one thing we could have been in the desert outside of Las Vegas.

The hospital.

Day and night, British and American helicopters ferried broken soldiers to its landing pad. We watched the Chinooks and Black Hawks come in with lumps in our throats, praying beneath our breath for those on board, and more loudly that we would not become future passengers.

Our training began, a final chance to brush up on skills that could keep us alive. IED clearance. Contact drills. Medical training. We were visited by a former member of our battalion, now an SAS trooper. He was serving with the Medical Emergency Response Team (MERT), and still covered in blood from his last mission. Two soldiers had died, their deaths preventable had their tourniquets been properly applied. He was angry, and blasted us as though we'd been the ones responsible. When he left, many of the younger soldiers were white despite the heat.

'It's been a bad month,' Danny observed as we lay on our cot beds, enjoying the meagre cool of the struggling air-conditioning unit. 'I got a lift back from the Danish PX by a dragoon. They lost a guy today. He was trapped inside his vehicle and bled to death. He knew what was happening and was shouting for help, but his blokes couldn't get to him.'

'Fuckin' hell,' someone finally uttered. We all thought the lightly armoured CVRTs that the dragoons were using were deathtraps, incapabable of standing up to the enemy's IEDs.

'Don't tell that to the younger lads,' Jay added.

Danny looked offended. 'I don't talk to the younger lads.'

'Yeah, but you do try and scare them. Don't say anything about that,' the softer man insisted.

'I'm not a dickhead.'

'You told Wayne his wife had the body of a dead sea lion washed up on the beach,' I put in, referring to a saggy-faced NCO in our company.

'That was different.'

'And that you hoped he died in front of his kids on Christmas Day,' Toby added, laughing at the memory of one of Danny's many unprovoked assaults on his long-time comrade.

'Yeah, well, that's Wayne.'

That was Wayne. Respected, but an outsider to The Firm. No one could say why. Like so many other members of the company, he was liked by all within our tight clique but was never invited into our intimate brotherhood. Five was the magic number. Whether this was by design or not, I don't know.

On many of our evenings in Bastion we attended vigils for those who had fallen in the previous few days. A friend for each one of the deceased spoke a few words on their comrade's behalf. Many struggled, just as those in the ranks of the parade struggled to choke back the lumps in their throats. For myself, it was a time to reflect on the flesh and blood nature of my body, my imagination taking flight as I pictured myself torn, limbless, and broken. I pictured how the dead men remembered at the vigil had looked in life, and at their end. Was it quick? Did they know that they were dying? Nothing terrified me more than the idea of bleeding to death, and knowing it. Nothing knotted my stomach like the thought of a young soldier dying in the arms of his friends and begging for his mother.

What the fuck was I doing here?

One particular vigil stuck in my mind. It was held for an infantryman, a Fijian, and the bond of these islanders transcended unit and cap badge. Between the Brits there was a tribal distance between regiments, but not the Fijians. All of those present at Bastion, including those of our own company, sang a hymn in their own language. Though none of us could understand the words, the meaning was obvious, as beautiful as it was tragic.

The last post was sounded by a bugler, and was followed by the familiar verse recited at all military funerals and services:

They shall not grow old, as we that are left grow old:
Age shall not weary them, nor the years condemn.
At the going down of the sun and in the morning
We will remember them.

The solemn reply echoed from the ranks. 'We will remember them.'

And then it was the turn of the bagpipes, a lament that faded into the evening's pink skies as the piper marched away. A shiver ran up my spine, and I pushed down the thought that it could be my name being read aloud to the sombre formation within a week's time. Which one of my friends would speak for me? Would he tell the truth, that I had come here with romantic visions of close combat and enemy dead at my feet? Or would he take the party line like all the others, and call me a consummate professional with a bright future in his beloved regiment?

As the service broke up a scuffle caught my eye. It was Jake, his hand around the throat of one of the younger soldiers.

'Fucking prick was laughin' and fidgetin' all the way through,' he snarled as he was pulled away. Jake's words earned the private a hard slap around the head from one of our sergeants. It took me a long time to realize why Jake had reacted so violently. It wasn't just about respect. It was the fear of knowing that some of us would be the focus of these services.

Having gathered up our friend, The Firm made its way back to the tents. Even Danny was silent, until we spotted a familiar face, a comrade of Iraq who served with a Scottish regiment; the Jocks had been used to fill the ranks of our own battalion before the recession had hit, and keeping a unit fully manned had become easier.

We swapped stories of mutual friends, learning that a former platoon commander, a well-liked leader in Basra, had been injured in an IED strike.

'What's it like compared to Iraq?' I asked the Black Watch soldier.

He shrugged, worn out by the summer's heavy fighting.

'It's all tha' same pish.'

I was lying face down on my cot bed, my nose in a book about another man's war. I'd served two tours of Iraq during the most violent years of the occupation and I'd come close to death, but I didn't feel as if I measured up to the warriors that I read about. It was a sense of inferiority that gripped me every day, and had done since childhood.

It was what compelled me to be here.

The writer Samuel Johnson said that 'every man thinks meanly of himself for not having been a soldier'. I had worn the uniform. Risked the IEDs, rockets, and gunfire. Lost comrades. And yet, reading about the generations of infantrymen before me, I felt like a fraud.

I didn't know why I wanted to be a soldier, I just knew that I had to be. I understood that I was in a minority. No matter how many people watched action movies, played shoot 'em up games, or pictured themselves mowing down hordes of bad guys before banging the hot damsel, the truth remained: armies struggled to recruit. Most people would hate to be soldiers.

As a kid, I played with plastic guns in the fields and woods. I know that some of my friends did this. I used to roll up my duvet at night so that it formed the edge of a trench. I don't think my friends did this. I remember, at eight years old, being gathered in class and told that the first Gulf War had started. I punched the air with glee, 'Yes!', and was immediately chastised by my teacher. At the time I hated her for her cowardice.

In my teens, I got my hands on as many personal accounts of war as I could. Vietnam was the most abundant source. I read about zapping, wasting, and raping. I wasn't too sure about the raping, but

I pictured myself doing the rest, emerging with a chest full of medals, and a necklace full of ears.

The week that I was old enough, I joined the cadets. This involved organized playing in the woods. The week that I turned seventeen I joined the Territorial Army, the Weekend Warriors. This was much the same, but the playing in the woods came with pay. It was the year 2000, twelve months before the world changed forever, as Americans are fond of saying.

It certainly changed for me.

During my A-level years, I chaffed as I watched British and American planes blow the shit out of Afghan mountainsides from my living room. As war-porny as it was, I could comfort myself that it was only really the special forces in action.

Then, in 2003, the invasion of Iraq began. These were British infantrymen on the ground. People my own age, from my own country, getting the chance to go to war. To do what soldiers do, and carry on the great traditions of our regiments. It gave me a war boner.

My mum had always wondered how they'd gotten young men to march off to the trenches, knowing that war awaited them. When she saw me practically drooling over the action on the TV, she had her answer: there was no answer. I'd had the same upbringing as my two brothers, but only one of us was losing sleep because he wasn't in a war zone.

The 'war phase' of Iraq was over in an instant, and as friends of mine began deploying there it sounded like a pretty mundane affair. A contact here. A riot there. I decided I could wait until university was done. The truth was, I just didn't want to get into trouble with my parents for dropping out. I was already showing great promise as a noble hero.

And then, in 2006, Iraq slid into a full-blown insurgency. Where soldiers had worn berets and sipped tea with the locals, now nothing less than tanks and armoured fighting vehicles could operate inside the city, and that at a cost of many lives.

I used the TA as the back door to my parent regular unit, the 2nd Battalion, The Royal Welsh, and hit the dusty streets, learning more in a few months as a team commander than I had ever done at university. There was no Firm then, though all of us except Jake were out there. There were other comrades. Other brothers. But their story is not the story of Afghanistan. It is enough to say that I had found my fraternity, was where I belonged, and in uniform I'd remain. When I returned from that deployment, my grandfather, a veteran of Bomber Command and its 75 per cent casualty rate, had told me that, 'I was going to get myself killed.' The words stuck in my head, but did little to dissuade me – I knew that my grandfather would not have taken his own advice had he been the one in uniform, because the battalion was my village now, the company my extended family, the platoon my home, and The Firm my brothers. We didn't talk about what we'd do for each other, but we all knew.

That didn't mean that we always got along, or couldn't enjoy a joke at each other's expense.

'You fucking wankers,' a red-faced Danny shouted as he entered the tent, enraged. 'Who the fuck did this?'

He was holding a letter in his hand, and Toby and I burst into uncontrollable laughter. We had written a love letter on Danny's behalf, sending it to our company's female clerk. She'd been good enough to take Danny aside and softly reject him.

He flung the paper at Toby, who read an extract. 'I know I sometimes seem angry, but I'm just putting on a front for the guys. I don't want them to know that I'm sensitive because of my st-st-stutter.'

'I hope you get your legs blown off. Both of you.' It was a regular insult of his, and all of ours.

Outsiders, listening in to our conversations, may have mistaken us for mortal enemies. In that tent, we joked about who would lose what limb, whose girlfriend would be first to be get fucked, whose would be the first to get gangbanged, and whose would leave us if we were sent home as cripples. It was friends airing their deepest fears under a cloak of dark humour, and it continued throughout the tour.

∙

Jay entered our tent, frowning as he announced that there would be cutting and changing between the platoons.

'We're not going anywhere,' he said, meaning The Firm, and we sagged, relieved. 'But the OC's taking sniper and javelin guys from us to put in the other platoons.'

Danny snorted. 'So now we have to sort out the teams all over again with blokes we don't know?'

'Fuck's sake, like,' Jake fumed. 'Who are we losing?'

'Grizzly, Foxpiss, Palin, and Fullback, among others.'

We were all especially aggrieved to lose Fullback, a sniper and good friend to us all. Later that day, he would tell us that that, 'I'm ninety-nine point nine per cent sure I'm gonna die in that platoon. They're shit.'

Being from Recce, Fullback was just upset at being pulled from his comfort zone. I doubted that the other platoons were shit, and they certainly weren't stupid. In return for our specialists, we were mostly sent the dross that they could not wait to be rid off.

'We've got all the mongs,' Danny spat.

'Johan is a top bloke,' I said, coming to the defence of the South African native I knew from Iraq. 'We've been lucky to get him.'

'Maybe they're alright,' Jake offered. 'You know what the rifle platoons are like. They just scream at the blokes. We can bring them along.'

'We don't have time to bring them along,' Danny insisted. 'They could have us killed in a few days.'

And some of the new private soldiers did everything to prove him right.

'Do I need my warm kit and Gore-Tex for the ranges?' the eighteen-year-old asked, leaving us too gobsmacked to reply. His name was Nacho, a private and one of the half dozen newcomers to our platoon. Perhaps the gormless, wire-haired idiot was immune to the sweltering heat of the desert.

'No, you daft cunt,' Danny finally said, rubbing at his temples.

'Are you sure? We had to take them in training.'

'Because your training was in fucking Yorkshire,' the NCO strained through gritted teeth.

I laughed at the exchange, in a good mood as I had just been issued a general purpose machine gun (GPMG, or gimpy), my belt-fed murder machine. I'd been lobbying my platoon sergeant about it since we arrived in theatre, making the case that we had an abundance of NCOs, and I was one of the stronger guys who could handle the weight of the gun and its ammunition, which would total 30kg, on top of which would come body armour, helmet, water, gun oil, med kit, and rations. In total, I could expect to patrol with the weight of a small man on my back.

'What are you gonna call her?' Jake asked as I cradled the weapon.

I looked down on the gun as though it were my child. 'The Widowmaker.' It was a wry answer, though I was already picturing Taliban fighters dropping by the dozen as we went about our honest work. In Iraq I had told myself that I wanted to emerge from the tour with at least five enemy dead to my name. Before deploying I had even planned out the tattoo I would get to celebrate my enemy's deaths – five hash marks. Above it, written in Arabic, a lyric from 'Raining Blood', my favourite Slayer track – 'Death will be their acquiescence' (not that I knew what acquiescence meant, but I thought it sounded cool). Instead, I had come home with a fat zero as my kill count. I would make up for it in Afghanistan, I promised myself.

'The Widowmaker?' Toby laughed. 'Danny's safe then. No one's gonna marry that stuttering fuck again.'

'You stutter yourself, you cunt!' Danny shot back, which was true. If anything, Toby's impediment was worse than Danny's, which only really came out when he was put under pressure from the higher ranks.

'How the fuck does the Boss have a stuttering radio operator?' Toby pressed on.

No one had an answer for him as we left the tents for the desert, spending that morning conducting ranges in soaring heat. The afternoon was given over to Op Barma, the task of finding IEDs. Something that none of us felt fully prepared for.

'They're fucking shit,' Toby said, watching our newest platoon members fuck up one drill after another. He moved off to take them aside and try once again to sink the lesson home with them.

'You cunts need to get a fucking grip!' he roared moments later, leaning down to shout into the face of a soldier of dwarf-like proportions. 'You fuck up like this on the ground, it means you fucking die! Do you understand that?'

Toby had wanted to simulate a casualty drill. As a standard operating procedure, we should all be carrying a tourniquet and field dressing in the left thigh pocket of our trousers. The stunted soldier wasn't, and Toby was right. Such a mistake could be the death of him in the field.

'What the fuck do they think they're seeing at the vigils?' Jay asked us that evening. 'Do they think they're invincible?'

'To be fair, I was like that,' I said in grudging defence of the teenagers. 'Wasn't until my mate lost his leg that I realized it could happen to me. I didn't even have insurance at that point.'

'What you got now?' Jake asked.

'As many units as I can with as many providers. I'd double it all if I could. My mate got a hundred and fifty grand off max units for his leg. How the fuck do you make that stretch from nineteen to ninety?'

'You'll be lucky to live ninety more days, you cunt,' Danny said happily.

'It's bullshit that we have to pay it ourselves anyway,' Jake put in, and no one disagreed with him. 'Civvies probably think it's all taken care of for us.'

A chorus of affirmative grunts met the statement, and then Danny was back on to the subject of the private soldiers.

'I couldn't give a fuck if they just got themselves killed,' he explained. 'But they'll be taking the rest of the team with them.'

Nobody objected to his logic, or took issue with his callous opinion.

'The head shed are fucking up just as much,' Jake muttered.

The company headquarters had failed to bring out a resupply of rations and water to the ranges that day, and as a result a number of soldiers were now hooked up to drips at the camp's hospital. The guys from One Platoon had to make it back from the desert on foot, only to find a sneering Sergeant Major waiting to greet them.

'Why are you sweating?' he'd asked men at the edge of collapse.

That night there was a Combined Services Entertainment show put on for the troops, a procession of well-meaning entertainers that we were obliged to watch, but The Firm sneaked out during the first interval. Entertainment like that may have been welcomed by those stationed for the duration of their tour at the base, but we knew that this place was only a stepping stone for us. Like ripping off a plaster, we wanted to get it over with as soon as possible. Each extra day in Bastion was a day in a fucked-up fairy tale that only delayed the coming of violence and action.

Leaning against my cot bed, I tore the page from the issued prayer book, sliding the paper into the front of my body armour where it joined maps, medical documents, and morphine auto-injectors. It was the Soldier's Prayer, and I liked it for its simplicity.

> Oh Lord, you know how busy I must be this day,
> If I forget you, do not forget me.

I wasn't the only member of the company who had suddenly embraced religion. Many of the books and Bibles the padre had delivered to us were missing pages, while other soldiers sported the plastic, army-issued crosses and prayer beads around their necks. During the vigils, I'd noticed how men had recited the Lord's Prayer with vigour, where usually there would only be muttering or silence.

'Covering my bases,' I told Danny as I sensed his sceptical look. He seemed to consider ridicule, but instead went back to his rant about how he had been issued a chain gun with a known fault for his Warrior armoured fighting vehicle. The gun had exploded during firing on the ranges that day, but luckily caused no injuries.

I added the final talisman to the inside of my body armour, a tiny, sparkling cross that had been sent to me by a friend. It would draw guardian angels towards me, she had told me in the letter, and I wanted to believe her. I would have sacrificed to Thor and Odin if I thought it would bring me safely through the coming months.

As if reading my thoughts and sending me an omen, the *whoomp-whoomp-whoomp* of a Chinook's blades passed over our tent.

'MERT,' Danny deduced from the heli's direction of travel.

'There's been two dead and a double amputee today,' Toby told us, the information overheard in the camp's dining facilities. This provoked Danny to thought.

'If you could choose which two limbs got blown off, what would you go for?' He threw the question to the group, our answers swift – we'd given a lot of consideration to such matters. The general consensus was that we'd choose legs, as prosthetic technology could make up for more in that area.

'But only if I still have my cock and balls,' Jay added.

'Obviously,' Danny replied. 'So what if you lose all four limbs? You want to live or die?'

'Fuck me,' Jake uttered, considering such a fate.

'Live,' Toby said, unblinking. 'As long as I can see my girls grow up, I don't give a fuck.'

'Not me,' I spoke up. 'If I'm in that much of a mess, just fuck up on the tourniquets. I don't wanna be a sandbag.'

'I'm gonna save you just to fuck you off then,' Danny said with a sadistic smile.

'Fuck's sake.' I shook my head as the gravity of the topic began to hang on me. 'I'm sure there's better conversations for lads in their twenties to be having.'

But if there were, we weren't having them.

'So, what would you rather lose?' Danny began anew. 'Your cock or your eyes?'

#veteranproblems

Palm Springs, California, 2014

I stood on the hotel balcony with Corey, or rather we propped ourselves against its wooden railings. It was dark, and we were drunk.
It was hot, but that's not why we stood out in the California night.
Our room was a party, and we wanted peace. We'd drank, we'd met
girls, we'd drank, we'd started a fight in the pool, we'd drank, we'd
been kicked out of the pool, we'd drank, and now we'd come to the
inevitable.

We talked.

We talked about war, what else? Corey, a Marine Corps officer,
was deploying to Yemen in a day's time, and I both envied and
pitied him. Earlier in the night, when we'd been happy drunks,
we'd swapped some light-hearted stories, and as infantrymen we'd
bonded over talking shit to the people who'd introduced us, our
combat engineer friends.

But now we were not happy drunks.

I was melancholy, he was angry. It was time for different stories. I
told him of Basra. Of Helmand. He told me of Fallujah. Of his Purple Heart. Of feeling ashamed to be proud. Different places, same
war. Different armies, same soldiers.

He arched back and I thought he was going to fall, but instead he
side-armed his empty bottle into the pool below.

'Fuck it,' he slurred, summarizing every emotion, every conflict.

I didn't like to have that talk, but I knew that it was unavoidable.
Like leaving the steel safety of your Warrior to check out a potential
IED, it was just something that you sucked up, and pushed through.

If you want to conduct a social experiment, give two veterans a case of beer and see how long it is until the topic is war, war, and more war.

For me and Corey, our tours were a blink in our thirty years of existence, and yet they consumed us, the default screensaver to our dysfunctional minds. The fun we'd had that night, the girls we'd caressed, we loved it all, but we didn't know where to place it. It was as if an overzealous editor had trimmed the rest away, leaving us just the war as the first, the second, and the final acts of our lives.

Now, like the sorority girl who fucks the football team, we began to feel shame after the deed was done, our minds naked, spread legged, and vulnerable. From experience, we knew that there was a simple fix to such a problem.

There was drink and drugs at the party, and so we went inside to find it, hoping that our ghosts would remain forever on the balcony, and knowing that they would not.

3

Lions, Donkeys, Dickheads

'The soldier, above all others, prays for peace.'
GENERAL DOUGLAS MACARTHUR

'Not the ones I met.'
LANCE CORPORAL GERAINT JONES

We were different.

We were different, because of a fact about the British infantry soldier that is conveniently forgotten.

We wanted to kill.

We could have taken a regular job and joined the local boxing gym, but they won't let you kill someone in the ring. We joined the infantry because we wanted to see destruction. To cause destruction. This is one of the reasons the Afghan mission was doomed from the beginning; they sent warfighters to be peacekeepers and builders. We were supposed to support the reconstruction of a country. Instead we flattened it.

If we could bomb a compound, then by fuck we were going to bomb a compound. We wanted to see shit blow up. We wanted to see bodies dropping in our sights. We wanted to shout about it. High five about it. Record it and photograph it so that we could relive it again and again and again.

This wasn't a conscript army, and we were all in Helmand by choice, or at least an extension of a choice. Yes, some had been seduced by the fabulous lies of recruiters. Yes, perhaps asking a

sixteen-year-old to commit to an organization dedicated to bringing death was unethical, but nonetheless we had all volunteered in
one way or another. The wars in Iraq and Afghanistan had been
waging since most below the rank of sergeant had enlisted, and so
those of us who wanted to be there had no sympathy for the troops
who developed cold feet. 'You joined the army, the army didn't join
you,' was the common refrain.

The infantry were the army's killers. 'Everyone else is just here to
support us,' we'd say. 'The infantry are the guys they make the movies about. Who'd watch *Hamburger Hill* if it was about some fat cunt
chef flipping burgers?'

Some men, mostly in their mid-twenties like me, had a love–hate
relationship with the army. We loved the way it allowed us to travel,
to shoot the fuck out of things, and put (some) money in our bank
accounts, but we hated the way that it cared about our appearance,
micromanaged our lives, and seemed incapable of meeting us halfway. It was the power struggle of a relationship between a teenager
and his parents all over again.

But the army was rigid for a reason. The bulk of infantry soldiers
are eighteen to twenty-three years old, and many simply lacked the
experience, or willingness, to think for themselves. This, of course,
is a great thing when you're trying to teach someone to kill without
compunction, but give a private soldier an inch and he'd either sell
it for alcohol or manage to kill himself with it.

Despite the loss of civil liberties, we loved the army for separating
us from society. Even a soldier like me, who strived to look as
unsoldier-like as possible, was proud to act and look the part when
it suited.

But most of the time, it didn't.

Our uniforms were issued to us, every man the same, except that
nobody was. The battlefield was a fashion parade.

Younger veterans wore the same combats they'd had in Iraq, pale
from the sun, the material of the knees shabby from Basra's streets.

Civilian boots were in vogue, the more scuffed and stained the better. Helmets were stripped of their elastic, then covered by scrim netting and banded with the rubber of an NBC boot. These would later be removed after an IED casualty had the rubber melt into his eyes, and so sniper tape took its place. Oakley gloves could not simply be worn as bought, they needed the finger tips cut off – how else do you feel out an IED? Like the boots, the more worn and stained they were, the better.

Types of camo should be mixed. In vogue that summer was a desert UBAC coupled with the traditional woodland temperate trousers. Or flip the outfit, putting desert combats with a temperate smock. I'd deployed with a pair of old-school lightweight jungle trousers, making myself the envy of many a battlefield fashion guru, but at the larger patrol bases wearing such garb was strictly verboten.

The sleeves of our UBACs had Velcro patches for unit and ISAF insignia – ISAF being the international force that we were a part of, though I'd be lying if I said we had any fucking idea what we were doing in Afghanistan, other than being there to kill Terry, of course. We soon supplemented these official patches with those that were 'ally'; soldier's slang for cool: Taliban Hillfighter, Major League Infidel, Taliban Hunting Club. Our wrists were adorned with bracelets, some for charities, others inscribed with the names of children or sweethearts. Our issued belts were discarded, replaced by thinner Velcro apparel. The army's webbing and chest rigs were shed in favour of civilian brands such as 5.11. No discerning veteran would allow himself to use the issued daysacks in the desert.

Just like school, we laughed at those who didn't follow the 'cool' way. In the classroom it had been the geeks, in Afghan it was the REMFs – the rear echelon motherfuckers. Wide-brimmed hats had been designed to protect from the sun, and yet if yours was not cut down, prepare for a piss-take or a sneering look, you fucking base-rat cunt.

There was no image less likely to instil confidence than that of a soldier clad entirely in issued gear, from his elasticated helmet cover to his unsullied boots. It meant that he had no backbone, no will of his own, for to follow dress regulations in the field was to deny yourself the identity of an individual. And when death could come for you at any moment, you want like fuck to be an individual.

When it came to rumour and gossip, the squaddie put the most bored housewife to shame. Even in the UK, hearsay spread like wildfire. In the boredom of a deployment, scandal transmitted through the soldiers with a speed that disgraced Ebola. Sometimes these rumours were born of fact before exaggeration and fantasy took its toll; a potential joint operation with the United States Marines turning into an imminent all-out assault on the Taliban's version of Castle Greyskull. At other times it was impossible to trace their origin. I was often accused by battalion soldiers, from outside my own company, of disintegrating an Iraqi grandmother with 30mm cannon fire, despite never having been a Warrior gunner in my life.

The soldier's name for rumour was 'gen', which could also be used to confirm or question such information.

'Gen up, now, we're doing a big assault on the Taliban's Castle Greyskull.'

'Gen?'

'Gen, mate.'

Rumour of dubious content would be labelled as 'scoff house gen'. More reliable sources were 'pukka gen'. To really drive home the trustworthiness of his intel, a squaddie could insist that it was 'pukka gen, no wah, forward assist'.

It wasn't only where rumour was concerned that squaddies had their own language within a language. A helmet was a lid; body armour was drama; food was scoff; rations were rats; a rifle was a gat; a GPMG was the General, gimpy, or pig; a Warrior was a wagon; camouflage fatigues were combats; a friend was a mucker; an idiot was a mong; a good soldier was a top bloke; a veteran was a sweat or salt; a new guy was a crow; a girl was a split-arse; a suck up was a bum snorkeller; the Taliban were Terry; the locals were cho-gis; extra was buckshee; unpleasant was gopping; good was gleam-ing; special was Gucci; sentry duty was stag; loading magazines was bombing up; Chinooks were whockas; British medical teams were MERT, the Americans' Pedro; the headquarters were the head shed; Jackals were free trips to the moon; a letter was a bluey; to tidy was to do areas; the artillery were drop shorts; camp soldiers were REMFs; to be cool was to be ally; to be selfish was to be jack; to sort out was to square; to go crazy was to go head gone; to lose something was to go diffy; to masturbate was to bang one out; to bring firepower to bear was to smash; to kill was to slot; to die was to die.

The words reaffirmed our position as a select group, a culture of youths who yearned to enjoy the same privileges as our civilian friends, and yet we eschewed their lifestyle in the same heartbeat. The irony was lost on us that the bulk of the words we changed would be redundant in that civilian world. When would they be asked to pick up their gats, lids and drama, and to clear a HLS for Pedro so that they could collect a mong who'd stamped on a snap peg, and gone diffy a leg?

I'm keenly aware that such terms as 'mong' and 'split-arse' are hardly PC, but neither is the business of killing people, or getting torn apart by shrapnel, or bleeding to death in a ditch. When you write a will at eighteen years old, you become a little desensitized. We were bred to kill or be killed, and decency of language is as much a casualty of war as anything else.

British soldiers in Afghanistan would die for each other – *did* die for each other – regaredless of race, regardless of colour, regardless of sexual orientation. The insults we flung at one another were often a sign of affection and taken as such.

These insults, like the war, came with rules of engagement. Mothers, even dead ones, were fair game. So were accusations of bestiality, necrophilia with family members, and racial slurs. Only a soldier's children were sacrosanct, and even the most venomous-tongued abided by that unspoken agreement.

Cursing was not cursing, but as ingrained in our speech as the sweat in our combats. Tone was all, cunt being used to describe a best friend or a hated adversary. To fuck something up was not necessarily bad, if that thing had been a Taliban fighter or a compound. 'Fuck' slid into our sentences as unconsciously as breathing, a thousand inflections for a thousand situations.

It was no surprise that our favourite comedians were those with the most twisted minds, men like Jimmy Carr and Frankie Boyle, and we'd read out their latest punchlines from *Nuts* and *Zoo*.

Such lads' mags were as close as many soldiers came to literature. Even without the distractions of life in the UK, few turned to books. Those who did inevitably read other soldier's stories, or fiction written by SAS heroes Andy McNab and Chris Ryan.

That the majority of the ranks were uneducated on paper counted for nothing. Many had simply not had the opportunities afforded to people like me, blessed with parents who put their children first, and others had been failed by the system. Almost all had left school at sixteen.

Danny, for all his insults about mothers and wives, was far more politically astute than the people who'd sat beside me during university lectures on that topic. Jay was intelligent, particularly when it came to the workings of our Warriors. He tried to explain these things to me, but he may as well have been describing dark matter and its relation to the universe.

Academic qualifications may have been rare, but the infantry taught the soldier his own mathematics; thirty rounds to a magazine; deliberate fire, one round every six seconds, one magazine every three minutes; rapid fire, one round every two seconds, one magazine a minute; one section of eight soldiers, eight magazines a piece, eight minutes of rapid fire, twenty-four deliberate rate. Breathing assessment of a casualty, listen for ten, multiply by six, breaths should be ten to thirty in a minute. No breathing? Thirty chest compressions, two rescue breaths, squared.

•

Among the troops, a man was often rechristened, or at least addressed in a way that had been unfamiliar to them in their civilian lives. Closest comrades might be known only by their surname, their first names a surprise if they were ever encountered. Where several soldiers shared the same family name, the last two digits of their army number were sometimes tagged on, often with the surname shortened; Williams becoming Will 18, and so on. Sometimes the letters were disposed of entirely, a man known simply by his last two, just like the Victorian defenders of Rorke's Drift. The alternative to numbers was to attach a distinguishing trait; Evs Worm and Evs Cry Baby both members of our company.

Some soldiers were known solely by nickname. This was usually a curse for them, as frequently the names derived from a physical characteristic. Men could be unfortunate enough to spend their entire army career being known as Chickenhead, Cow Face, or Monkfish. I was lucky to escape with Jonah 35 or Gez.

Perhaps among your closest friends you would be on first name terms, as I was with The Firm, but more than likely you just added a softening or a shortening to their surname; Jones to Jonesy, Bradley to Bradders, Tompkins to Tomo.

Senior NCOs could be addressed by name or nickname if it came from a long-serving junior rank.By the same token, an officer could be Boss, rather than sir. The OC and sergeant major were always Sir, and to them, you were your rank and surname.

An infantry company was a strange tribe, a soldier a rare breed in the nation, but to lump all troops together is like condemning the population of a town to a single personality.

Of course there were heroes and there were cowards. There were extroverts, introverts, and the grey shades in between. There were straight guys, bi guys, and gay guys. There was even an animal porn guy. There were the soft hearts, and the cold ones. There were the overcompensating, and the underrated. There were the workers, and the shirkers. The tour soldiers, the camp soldiers, the career soldiers, and the mistaken soldiers. They were the lions, the donkeys, and the dickheads.

I considered myself a tour soldier – I loved being on operations. That didn't mean that I ever stopped complaining – which is the soldier's prerogative – but deep down, I was where I felt fate wanted me. I'd volunteered for back-to-back deployments in Iraq, and I'd do the same in Afghanistan. I wanted to soldier, but I had a selective vision of what that entailed. Garrison duty was not for me. God spare me from irons, parades, and boot polish, and deliver me to unaccountable ammunition, sand in my arse crack, and adrenaline.

I was an anomaly in the ranks, because I possessed a university education. Whenever an officer learned of my qualifications, they'd ask me why I hadn't sought a commission. I found it telling that my friends in the company never asked me the same. After insisting that I meant no offence, I'd explain to the officer that I wanted to be the guy kicking in the door, not the one telling someone else to do it. Before university, there had been a time when I'd wanted the career of an officer, but that was during peace. Truly, to be a machine-gunner in a war zone was my wet dream come true. The boys would tease, calling me the most qualified gimpy gunner in NATO, but the weight of the ammunition on my shoulders and the feel of the gun in my hands was worth more than any other experience I could think of.

Yes, I was a tour soldier for sure.

I'm not sure what our OC was. He struck me as more of a worn-down teacher than a soldier. That didn't disqualify him from command, of course, but in my own mind I reckoned he had been put on earth to lead people through maths problems, not bayonet charges.

Danny's own assessment of the major was as brutal as usual. A conclusion drawn from genetics and evolution.

'You can't trust a soldier whose hips are wider than his shoulders.'

And The Firm did not trust him, but we were soldiers, he was our officer, and so what else would we do but obey him?

In the majority of civilian businesses, promotion is based on ability, but in the army, the most important factor in climbing the ladder was time served. Yes, there were courses that needed to be attended and passed, but Danny appropriately summarized the road to the higher ranks with his usual scorn:

'You're in the army for two years, and you do a course with battalion, run around a bit, and pick up your first stripe. Three years more, you go to Brecon, run around for a few months, and get your full screw. Four more, Brecon, sergeant. Five more, CQMS course, colour man. Three or four, you pick up sergeant major, and all you had to do to get it was be too scared to leave the army and run around like a dickhead.'

Of course, some men did climb faster than others, and the system produced many a sergeant major whose men would follow him into hell.

Sergeant Major Smith was not exactly of this kind.

Like the OC, we did not see Smith as a bad man, just not as a great leader. If he was in our lives as a neighbour, we would have enjoyed a beer with him, then remarked to our family that there seemed to be something a little bit off about him that was hard to pin down. Maybe it was the way he was always making his pecs dance, whether he was having a personal conversation or walking at the head of a parade. We couldn't decide if it was an involuntary spasm or if he was trying to distract us from the shit that he'd be spewing. He was an avid gym user, and the upside of Smith's hobby was that he'd turn a blind eye when we later pilfered gym equipment from the larger bases to equip our own home.

Our company was blessed with an abundance of good sergeants, and if command was based on ability, then any of them would have been perfect as a company sergeant major during operations, but the army's rank structure was as rigid and as unwanted as a teenager's classroom hard-on, and so we were stuck with our own throbbing member in the form of Smith.

At school we are taught that evolution is a result of natural selection, as the genes of those unfit to survive are wiped from existence. If Darwin had met a private named Nacho he would have torn up his theory.

Nacho was one of those people who possessed the rare gift of being able to look scruffy at all times. He could be swathed in a gaggle of NCOs tidying him up like a millionaire surrounded by Savile Row tailors, but after two minutes alone he'd once again look like he'd been mugged and gang-raped by a group of vicious gorillas.

Nacho was in the habit of leaving us gobsmacked, and we were once again speechless when the teenager had revealed his favourite pastime; he and his friends would go up into the local hills dressed as American wrestlers and fritter away the weekend in sweaty headlocks, giving speeches that promised vengeance against opponents either in the ring or in love. It was this alter ego that had led to us christening him Nacho, following the subject of the terrible Jack Black movie that had come out a few years earlier.

'I thought it was a good film,' Nacho had mumbled, surprising no one.

Even though his ineptitude could cause us to be torn apart in a bloody explosion, we could no more dislike him than we could a friendly puppy. Word of his actions quickly spread through the company, and he soon became a battalion legend by accident, much as we imagined he'd been conceived.

The veterans used the oldest tricks on Nacho. We sent him to retrieve camouflage paint from the quartermaster, and mortar blank firing attachments from the armourer. The jokes were lost on him even as he was turfed out by these stuffy men.

But there was nothing we could do to Nacho that would be as funny as letting him run his natural course. When we were ordered to write our ZAP Numbers in our boots – the first two letters of your name, and last four digits of your army number; to help with the identification of body parts – Nacho not only wrote in huge letters on the outside of the suede, but he somehow succeeded in writing them as a mirror image.

'He's Rain Man,' one of the troops had said.

Danny thought differently. 'Rain cunt, more like.'

But at least Nacho's hobbies were kept to such innocent pastimes as befriending flea-ridden hedgehogs in the patrol base. The same could not be said of Private Blake.

At Bastion, some of the more weary veterans flinched at the sound of a launching missile, or an explosion on the ranges. We knew that it was an ingrained instinct, but we could not understand why the eighteen-year-old Blake was flinging himself flat to the ground, rabbit eyes wide in his round face.

Blake was rumoured to have been the only known virgin in the company before the tour. A group of us had explained to him that sex was not something that he wanted to miss out on, and losing his virginity would be a lot more of an issue if he was a limbless veteran in a wheelchair, the image of Lieutenant Dan from *Forrest Gump* foremost in our minds. And so, in the spirit of comradeship, we had offered to pay for a prostitute.

'And not some fat stinker,' Toby had told him, enthused. 'We'll get you one of those stunners. An escort. The classy ones.'

But the youngster had declined, and so we pressed him on his sexuality.

'It's alright if you're gay, Blake,' he was told. 'We'll take the piss out of you a bit, but it's alright with us, honestly.' And it was. We had a soldier in the company who was known as Gay Sam, as camp as a *Carry On* movie. He was not openly gay, but he knew and we knew. It made no difference to us.

But Blake insisted that he was not gay. We pushed some of his friends for details about his sexual interests and they told us about Blake's large collection of porn – rumour mill had it on pukka gen that there were animals involved.

'If you'd have told us about that, we'd have bought you a sheep for the weekend,' we teased. It made no difference to us if the claims were true or not, and we ignored his protests.

Blake's alleged favourite pastime also left a lot to be desired – he was an avid bomb maker, downloading recipes from the internet, assembling the devices from readily bought components, and then blowing the shit out of stuff in the local woods.

'He likes to fuck goats and make bombs?' Danny laughed. 'He's a beard away from a drone strike.'

The domain of the infantry was an all-male affair, but the same did not apply to our supporting cast. We had a female company clerk, Baker, but she would remain in Bastion with the rear party, and so the solitary woman in our company to deploy was also our most competent medic. She was never a split-arse, or lizard. She was Emily, Em, or Corporal Ryan.

I could tell you that she was one of the boys, and that we treated her as we did each other, but that would be a lie. She was special. She was a connection to home. She was a reminder that this place was finite. She was a confidant in a way that your platoon mates could never be. She was these things because of her sex, and we were more protective of her than we were of each other.

For her part, she never tried to out-lad the lads. She knew who she was, and was comfortable in that skin. We respected her all the more for that. She took the pay, the rank, and wore the uniform, and so she faced the same risks, braved the same bullets and bombs. We didn't make a fuss of her because of it, and she didn't make a fuss either. It was duty done, nothing more. She had our respect because she did her given job well, and that was the end of it. She didn't pull a trigger, but that wasn't her occupation. If we were the army's killers, then she was our contradiction, an angel of mercy to the angels of death.

Yes, we were different, but it's not enough for you to know about the lions, donkeys, and dickheads. I know why you're here, what you're looking for, and why you're looking for it.

So let's get back to the war.

4

Steel Coffins

The company had it its first casualty, and it came at the point of a bayonet.

A soldier from Two Platoon, which was known as The Zoo, had struggled to remove his unsheathed bayonet from the end of his rifle. To gain more purchase, he had held the shooter between his knees, then pulled upwards.

Taking the point of the bayonet straight into his nose.

'Natural selection,' Danny had remarked, once we'd finally finished laughing.

After a couple of weeks and several false starts, it was finally time to leave Bastion. Our bergens were packed and made secure onto the outside of Warriors that were also stacked with spare road wheels, tracks, and water.

'I'm glad we're getting out of here,' Danny told me. 'I can't stand another man love Thursday.'

The day before, following the Afghan tradition, Toby had entered the showers with a hard-on, then requested that we soap his back, which we dutifully did.

'I didn't think I'd be mentally disturbed before we even got on the ground,' Danny added, then said his goodbyes; I was being loaned out to One Platoon.

A number of their dismounts had been flown ahead to begin the takeover of our patrol base, and so myself, Johan, and a new private would be making up the numbers in one of their IED-sweeping teams.

I was glad to have Johan along, the square-shouldered trooper a regular gym buddy of mine. South African born and twenty-two years old, he was a comrade of Iraq. On the inside of his forearm was a tattooed scroll that read; 'Lest we forget the fallen'. I hoped that we wouldn't be adding more names to those already remembered.

We crammed into the back of the Warrior with two of One Platoon's members, Evs 17 and Corporal Bailey, who would be commanding the team. We'd been in the same company in Iraq, and he seemed to like me. He was a rangy figure with an angry face, and covered in tattoos. I always pictured that he would have done well as a Napoleonic era NCO – callous, but with a deep love of the army, and pride in soldiers who did their jobs well.

The final dismount in the back of our wagon was the private who Jake had throttled following the vigil. I was glad to see him, purely because his slight frame took up little space.

The Warrior's interior stank of diesel, grease, sweat, and dust. There was no air conditioning in these Cold War relics, and even the upper hatches remained closed in a vain effort to protect our throats and bomb-jamming equipment from dust. And so, as we waited to leave Bastion, our rear door stood open in a pathetic attempt at ventilation. This left us vulnerable to the snooping sergeant major, who caught sight of my shirt; it was missing the unit insignia that should have been on my sleeves.

'Corporal Jones, where's your fucking flashes?'

'I didn't have time to sew them on, sir.'

'You've got the Velcro ones you cunt. Get them on. And shave your fucking sideburns too. Top of the ear.'

'Yes sir,' I said, fuming as he walked away. 'I'm glad they have their priorities straight here,' I vented to my crushed companions. 'We have one team medic pack between eight, when it should be a maximum of between four. Some of the wagons don't have a chain gun. I've got no spare barrel, sling, or cleaning kit for my gimpy, and most of the guys have only got one tourniquet. Last time I checked we had four fucking limbs. I suppose all of it gets made OK if my sideburns are a little higher?'

'Maybe?' Johan offered, smiling.

'Close the door!' Came the shout from the turret. 'We're off!'

The rear door moved slowly on its hydraulic ram, sealing us within our steel coffin. As the darkness and the heat consumed us, the young private, Evs 17, finally spoke up. 'We'll be in the patrol base in thirty-six hours,' he said to reassure himself.

He had no idea why the veterans started laughing.

We'd gone a kilometre outside of Bastion when the company had its first breakdown. We didn't know the details, only that we would wait for it to be fixed. More than fifteen Warriors were strung out in the darkness, but I saw none of it. Those of us in the back of vehicles sweated, swore, and snored. Three hours later, and the company was on the move again. It was now well into the night.

'We should just call it quits and go back to camp,' Corporal Bailey said. 'Leave at first light.'

I wasn't paying him much attention, more involved with the fidgeting lump of Evs 17 who squirmed beside me.

'Stop fucking moving,' I told him, again.

'I can't get comfortable,' he whined. He was a big guy, a rugby player, but as with many gifted athletes he had been pampered since childhood.

'I don't know how to make this any more clear,' I growled at him. 'If you keep moving, next time we stop I'm gonna drag you out of the back by your teeth and beat the shit out of you.'

Trying to control my anger was a difficult task in the sweltering heat, which rose in the enclosed space to above 60°C. Due to the IED threat, we were wearing helmet and body armour at all times, every inch of fabric soaked with sweat, our throats hoarse from thirst and dust.

There were more breakdowns during the night, more delays, but they became welcome, giving us a chance to disembark the vehicle. We stayed close for fear of IEDs that could have been missed during Three Platoon's clearance of the route at the head of the column, and I sat with Johan in the dust, both of us thankful to be able to remove our helmets. As night turned to day, and the breakdowns continued, we'd sleep in any shade thrown by the Warrior's armoured bulk.

'This isn't so bad,' I said to my South African friend, as we stared across the desert to where a range of harsh, barren mountains grew out of the sand.

'Eh, it's some view. Beer would be nice.'

'I'd take a cold water.' Our bottles had reached a temperature that was only suitable for brewing tea.

'Mount up!' came the order once again, and we wearily pulled on our helmets, and piled back inside of our steel coffin.

The first IED strike occurred in the afternoon.

The victim was an American truck and trailer that we were supposed to escort as far as Musa Qala DC. Although the route had been cleared by our leading platoon, the savvy Taliban had spotted a break in the convoy. Using motorbikes, they had rushed into the gap, deploying small IEDs onto the route that we wrongly thought safe. The devices were not large enough to cause considerable damage, but they did enough to bring the convoy to yet another halt.

'Pop and drops,' Bailey observed, referring to the IEDs. 'Fuck's sake. We should know better than that.' And he was right. This was a tactic we'd faced in Iraq.

'The OC wasn't in Iraq,' Johan pointed out.

'And neither was the sergeant major,' I added.

This first explosion was quickly followed by another.

A Warrior from One Platoon, callsign 1-1, was ordered to deploy its Barma team of five men so that they could sweep the area around the American truck with their metal detectors. Somehow, the commander of that Warrior, Victor, misunderstood his orders and instead rode to the rescue, ignoring the desperate pleas across the radio for him to stop.

He hit a second device, not large enough to penetrate the armour, but large enough to rip off a portion of the track and its running gear.

'Stupid cunt.' Bailey swore. 'It's going to be as dark as his arsehole soon. We're not going anywhere.'

The OC was of the same mind, and we were ordered to form a laager with the vehicles. We pulled off our helmets, the head shed instantly ordering them replaced, before an orders group was held on the turret of the OC's wagon, the officers and senior NCOs gathering on the exposed metal.

'Do as I say, not as I do,' Johan sniped, watching.

We spent the night in the open desert, sleeping on body armour folded out beside our trucks. Bailey asked the interpreter if it was a good area to stay in, and the Afghan replied that it was strongly Taliban. On his ICOM radio he had heard one commander ordering an attack on the convoy, but his subordinate had refused to take on the 'tanks'.

'Fairy Eyes reckons he saw an RPG team,' Johan said, referring to his best friend who had also come over to our platoon.

We were not looking forward to the next day. The company's route led through a large wadi. This particular dry river bed was between steep slopes, and had only one entrance and exit. As with most choke points, it was always heavily IED'd, in this case to intercept the regular supply convoys running from Bastion to Battle Group North West.

'So why don't we have a patrol base here to watch it?' Johan asked, but the answer wasn't ours to give.

It would now be One Platoon's turn at clearing the route, my first real work of the tour. I was nervous. Shitting myself, actually. If the Taliban had been able to infiltrate and drop IEDs among the convoy, then what would be waiting ahead now that we'd spent a night in the desert, our intended route obvious and channelled by terrain?

'Baptism by fucking fire, boys,' Bailey said, trying to hide his own anxiety. In Iraq, I'd heard that he'd run out from a briefing to vomit after being ordered to a similar task.

But our first clearance came before the wadi, after One Platoon's commander spotted an area of disturbed earth. We deployed to investigate, arseholes clenching whenever the Vallon metal detectors we carried gave off their shrill reading, but we found nothing.

We remounted, and five minutes later one of the wagons behind us hit another IED.

This wasn't a smaller charge like the pop and drops, but a 50kg killer. It was a miracle that the REME crew emerged unscathed, the vehicle itself a total wreck. A K-Kill.

It would have to be towed by another REME Warrior-variant that acted as a recovery vehicle, but first tracks that had been blasted apart needed to be replaced by new ones. Otherwise the company would be dragging a giant lump of metal through the sand, slowing us to a crawl. Already behind schedule, the OC sent One Platoon ahead to clear the wadi as the repairs were made.

Just standing in that heat and sunlight was effort enough. We patrolled along the track, myself and Johan leading the way. Whenever somebody found a metal reading, we slid onto our bellies, working away with fingers and a paint brush to uncover the cause, while the rest of the team lay flat, facing away, and hoping we would not obliterate them.

This continued for four hours, Warriors creeping behind us, the heat gripping us so badly that we chugged back the red-hot water that was stored behind the wagon's cage-like bar-armour.

The wadi itself was a wide, steep-sided valley full of poppy fields, where the flowers had already been harvested, leaving only dead husks behind. There wasn't much you wanted to step on in Afghanistan, but there was something deeply satisfying about the crunch of the dried poppies beneath my boot. This was the beginning of the world's heroin supply chain, and though I knew that much, I could never have reckoned on the irony that Helmand's crop would one day find its way into the veins of soldiers who had lost their own, invisible battles after fighting here. One of those victims walked beside me now, treading gently on the seeds of his self-destruction; crunch, crunch, crunch.

At the beginning of the track's rise out of the valley was a solitary compound, assumed to be the home of the valley's farmer, and it was at this point that our team was relieved. We chose to walk behind our Warrior rather than endure the heat within, and with the head shed distracted by the stricken REME vehicle, we were not ordered to get inside.

Inevitably, a large IED was found where the open neck of the wadi narrowed into a track. It was marked, and left for the bomb disposal team who had been seconded to us for this journey, while we cleared an alternate route through a field. The farmer and his son watched us go, the older man smiling as the child asked us for biscuits.

'The cheeky bastards,' I said to Johan. 'They would have watched us walk right onto that IED, and now they want biscuits.'

'You should give them to him. They'll probably kill the little fucker, or at least stop him shitting for a week.'

We neared the top of the wadi, the sound of retching making me turn. I saw Ginger Wally throwing up from heat sickness, but it was the panoramic scene that really caught my eye.

The sun was setting, catching the dust of the desert with an orange hue. Spread out through the wadi was the convoy, slowly winding its way through the now shaded valley. I had enough of a poetic view of military history to appreciate the vista, and wondered how many other armies had passed through this way on campaigns that were always doomed to failure.

I flinched, broken from my thoughts as the IED at the wadi's mouth was blown by the bomb disposal team. The sight and size of the explosion was enough to make me swallow, any romantic notions of war quickly dispelled as I pictured myself as a victim of such a hidden killer.

Very soon, I would not have to imagine anymore.

5

IED Strike

In the desert's oppressive darkness we arrived at FOB Edinburgh, an encampment that was home to the 105mm light guns of the Royal Artillery.

Our Warriors drew up in a Hesco-enclosed dust bowl, and I went in search of my friends and cold water. There was none of the latter, but I found The Firm easily enough. The artillery's chefs had prepared a meal, and by some magic Jay appeared with a cold can of Coke for us all.

'Where'd you get this?' I asked him, sighing as I ran the cold metal against my face.

'Sergeant major's wagon,' he said, his smile bright in the night. 'He's got a fucking fridge in there. I've been nicking stuff off him whenever we stop and he goes to the OC's truck for orders.'

We laughed, loving the thought of our friend getting one over on Smith and his army-installed fridge.

'It's jack as fuck, though.' Danny spoke up. 'Lads are nearly collapsing clearing the route. Where's their ice cold water?'

'What do you expect?' Jake asked him, and Danny had no reply.

'We're staying here tomorrow,' Jay told us, then explained the reason why.

The company that we were relieving had lost seven Warriors as K-Kills during their tour, and those broken hulks were now at this FOB. To make it back to Bastion, they'd need to be retracked so that they could be pulled onto the back of low-loaders.

'So we're track bashing tomorrow?' Danny demanded, angrily. 'Some fucking morale boost. "Hey, lads, come and work on these fucked-up trucks so you know what's waiting for you."'

Cheered by seeing my friends, I tried to be optimistic. 'On the other hand, nobody died in them.'

'Yeah, well, nobody died in them in Iraq at first,' Danny said, adamant, 'then look what happened.'

We knew very well what had happened. Among the victims were close friends of The Firm, some mutilated, others fallen.

The next day, it transpired that there was only enough track to equip one of the wagons, and the Fijians insisted on forming the team. They were big men, strong as bulls, and unless it was cold there'd always be a smile on their faces.

I sat in the shade of a large tent, watching as some of the private soldiers tried to run from one end of the rolled-out track to the other, while only using the spiked centres. The most successful was Sniper Hunt, who had been driving 1-1 when Victor had ordered it forward and struck the small IED.

He would now be my driver, as I was instructed that I would be taking over the Barma team in that vehicle. The OC had lost confidence in Victor, and so the Gambian would move to the gunner's position, while Breezy would command the vehicle, leaving them in need of a dismount commander. That would be me, and I didn't mind. I had done the job in Iraq, and little was expected of us for the remainder of the journey.

The company was to leave the FOB at 0500, following behind an American mine-sweeping unit to Musa Qala DC. I had no idea as to the distance, only that we were expected to be there by mid-morning at the latest – it was a running joke in the army that, like mushrooms, the infantry soldier is kept in the dark and fed on shit. Once the supplies had been loaded at DC, we would drive on to our new home at Patrol Base Minden, and be there before last light.

That was the plan, and like all plans in wartime, it would not survive contact with the enemy.

The drive to Musa Qala should have taken an hour, but the American engineer units leading the way discovered IEDs that then had to be cleared by the British bomb disposal team. I waited these moments out with the four men of my new team. We'd been told that the valley was heavily Taliban and were forbidden to step outside of our steel oven at any point, intelligence and experience in the area suggesting that we'd come under small arms fire if we did. Due to the oppressive heat of our armoured womb, we slipped in and out of blissful unconsciousness.

I was just coming out of such a state when we hit the IED.

The sound was beyond comprehension, the blast wave throwing my head back, my guts lifting within me as if they were being punched into my throat. The force picked up every grain of dust inside of the vehicle, forcing it into my eyes and mouth, choking me. The mortar hatches above were blown open, then slammed back down, the rear of the now unmoving Warrior filled with darkness, swirling dust, and shouting. We called to each other, purely out of instinct at first.

'One at a time, guys!' I tried to shout, instead coughing through mouthfuls of dust. 'Fuata? Will? Luke? Dicks?' All responded. All uninjured.

A miracle.

'Breezy!' I called up to the turret, getting nothing back. I tried my radio. It was dead. 'Breezy!' I called again.

'Gez!' He finally shouted down. 'I think I was knocked out! Victor's hurt!'

'Can you hear Hunt?' I yelled up to him, spitting to clear the dust from my mouth. The turret was in a closer position to the driver's hatch, Hunt unseen and unheard to us in the rear.

'No!'

I pushed open the mortar hatches above, telling the others to wait for my call. Adrenaline was dumping into my veins as I climbed into the sunlight, seeing compounds to our left, and a ridge to my right. We'd been told to expect gunfire if we were hit, but all was silent aside from the chugging of the Warrior's still-running engine.

I moved to the turret, seeing Breezy talking with Victor. He was groggy, slowly moving his head. No words.

'I'll check Hunt,' I told Breezy, stepping down to the driver's hatch at the vehicle's front.

I had worried about this moment for months; coming face-to-face with a casualty. Maybe it was the adrenaline, maybe it was the training, but as I peered inside, I felt nothing.

One look was enough to know that he was dead. He was slumped over, most of his face missing from the nose down. His jaw was hanging off, as if unhinged from one side. Clumps of flesh, teeth, and gum were stuck to his body armour, which like his trousers had been torn wide open by the strength of the blast-wave.

I stood, turning to the Warrior in front of me, where the One Platoon commander was craning in his turret.

'He's dead!' I called, then realized that he wouldn't be able to hear me, and so I made the chopping motion over my neck. It didn't feel callous. I was shaking slightly, but my mind felt more focused than I had ever known it to be.

It was a useless task, I knew, but we had been trained to operate in a certain way, and so I went on with my casualty drills as if there was hope. I put my hands inside the hatch, feeling around his body, searching for any huge bleeds. I found none, and went to the next stage. His airway.

I pushed back the twenty-one-year-old's head, his tongue lolling beneath his face. I couldn't think of anything else I could do, and in that moment, I cursed the people who had shorthanded us with our first aid equipment.

And then his tongue moved.

It moved up and down as Hunt began to breathe again. The

breaths came regularly, accompanied by an awful rasping sound. His brow felt cold against my thumbs, his hair wet and slick with sweat. When I tried to hold his hand, it was as limp as a baby's. Beneath me, the scorching heat of the metal armour seared through my uniform.

Dicks appeared by the turret, and as I saw him I noticed the red smoke grenade billowing behind the truck. In my haste to treat the casualty I had forgotten to order it done, the red signifying that we had casualties, but Will had the presence of mind to make up for my mistake. So much for my focus.

I told Dicks to prepare himself for a bad sight, then together we fully opened the driver's hatch, giving me a second chance to check for major bleeds that would kill Hunt within minutes. I looked again at his torn body armour, sure that the front-plate had done the grievous damage to his face.

I sent Dicks to retrieve a radio from the back and inform the company that we had a CAT A and CAT B casualty. CAT A was the highest priority for evacuation, and was only given to the most serious and grievous injuries; CAT B was a stretcher case. At this point, Jesus, the company signaller, arrived on the front of the Warrior, accompanied a few seconds later by Emily.

She came to me, inspected Hunt, and told me to keep holding his airway open. It was only then that I spotted an Apache helicopter patrolling along the valley's edge. There were three in position to cover us, which did a lot to explain why we weren't taking small arms fire.

I tried talking to Hunt, asking him to squeeze my finger, but there was nothing. I began to tell him about the pretty Danish nurses, and how he was making us proud by fighting on. It was the longest conversation I'd ever had with him, as clichéd as anything that you would hear in a bad Hollywood war movie. At intervals, his breathing stopped with a huge, harsh gasp that I worried was the death rattle; then an agonizing wait before his rasping breaths resumed.

The sergeant major arrived – I have no idea how quickly – and in a calm and gentle voice began telling Hunt the same kind of things that I had been saying. I noticed that he didn't have his rifle, and then realized that mine was still in the rear of the wagon. The years of training were not so ingrained after all.

'The MERT's on its way,' Smith told Emily.

I felt a hand on my shoulder. Bailey. 'Get in the truck and get your fucking weapon and radio,' he chastised me, his tone ugly.

'I'm holding his fucking airway open,' I spat back, in no mood to be talked down to.

'I'll take over,' he said. 'Go.'

I went, cursing Bailey beneath my breath as I climbed down into the troop compartment. It was now empty, and I had no idea where my team had gone. I looked around for my gear and found my rifle, but there was no sign of my radio.

'Fuck it.' Hearing the *whoomp-whoomp-whoomp* of the MERT approaching, I climbed back up into the sunlight.

Emily saw me. 'Help us cover him.'

We needed to protect Hunt from the dust storm that was about to be kicked up by the helicopter's landing, and so we huddled over our wounded comrade, the flying debris pattering on our backs and helmets. We couldn't stop it all, and sand clung to the wet flesh of his injuries. The look of it made me nauseous.

The MERT had landed fifty metres away, and was on the ground for mere seconds before lifting off, leaving four figures running through the churning sand that it kicked up in its wake.

Two of them were SAS troopers, and they looked the part; weapons and helmets spray-painted, faces stubbled. As soon as they arrived at the Warrior their body armour and helmets were stripped off, one turning to me and smiling.

'Don't tell my insurance,' he said before moving away. How many times had he used that one, knowing that the awed soldier would be momentarily distracted from the carnage around him?

We took a backseat as the true professionals went to work on Hunt. All we could really do for Victor was provide him shade in the turret with a poncho and give him sips of water. Breezy had gone, sent to sit in another vehicle and gather himself. To me, it hadn't seemed as though he was anywhere close to becoming undone.

I heard a voice behind me. 'Help me with this.' It was Jesus, holding a poncho that we then rigged up as a stretcher – Hunt would need to be lifted down from the Warrior and onto the more rigid spinal board below.

It was then that an explosion rang out in the valley, cries of 'Incoming!' passing up and down the convoy. We pressed ourselves flat against the Warrior's red-hot hull, expecting more of the crash and crump of mortars, but the next few seconds passed quietly – the short-lived attack was over, and now four of us gathered around the driver's hatch – it was time to move Hunt.

'Grab him where you can,' a member of the MERT spoke, and I took hold under a limp arm.

'Three, two, one, lift,' the SAS trooper ordered. Four of us grunted with effort, but there was no moving the young soldier – one of his legs was stuck fast, contorted and caught in the metal.

'We might have to take his leg off,' someone said, and my stomach lurched. Seeing injuries with adrenaline pumping through my veins was one thing. The thought of having to sit by and watch as my comrade's leg was cut off in front of me was another. My stomach was in my mouth as one of the MERT leaned into the hatch and began grunting with rough effort as he tried to free the trapped leg.

'Got it!' he shouted, and relief washed over me. 'Let's get him on the stretcher.'

As we did, it was obvious that Hunt's body was like a broken doll's, limbs at angles they should never assume. Blood was pooling internally above the knee, a thigh swollen to a grotesque size. The young soldier's face was swathed in bandages, with breathing tubes inserted. There was nothing else to be done as he was transferred onto the rigid stretcher with its attendant bearers, and so after a silent goodbye I made my way back onto the Warrior's turret.

One of the SAS troopers appeared beside me – he was looking for a way to get Victor free while doing minimum damage to his spine.

'It'll take me all day to cut through this,' he said, referring to the turret's thick armour. 'He can feel his toes. I'm just gonna lift him out. Come on, mate.'

The trooper leaned in, taking Victor beneath the armpits, dead-lifting him out before putting him up onto his shoulder. Even with everything that had happened that morning, I was still awed by the show of strength.

'Give me a hand mate,' the special forces man said to me, using his free hand to balance on my shoulder as we walked down the hot metal to the front of the Warrior, the IED's crater so deep that the vehicle's nose was only a foot out of the sand. To our right, the Chinook was touching down again. The trooper took off towards it, and I followed on with Jesus, carrying the gear that the SAS men had stripped when they arrived. We threw it on board, and in return Jesus caught a bag full of medical supplies to replace the equipment we'd used, a well-rehearsed play.

The Chinook lifted into the air, the downdraft from its rotors nearly bowling us over, and then they were gone.

I ran back to the stricken Warrior, asking the sergeant major where he wanted me, and finding myself surprised by his answer.

'Go and sit in my truck. There's a fridge in there. Have some water.'

Though my throat was parched, I poured half of the ice-cold water over my head before I chugged back the rest. I suppose that I was trying to cleanse myself. To break myself from what had just occurred. The cold water on my lips was bliss, but I had no intention of sitting alone while my comrades were still outside, so I went in search of my team.

I found them clearing an area so that the REME wagon could recover 1-1, and went man to man telling them about Hunt. I told them, and I believed it, that he would survive his injuries.

'He just might not be the prettiest,' I said to Will.

'He never was,' he joked in relief.

I took command of the team from him, and as we cleared I noticed a line of disturbed earth that ran from a nearby compound to the IED crater. At its far end was a gap in a compound wall, above which a black flag had been placed.

I caught the sergeant major's attention. 'Sir, that looks like a marker and command wire.'

'Maybe,' he conceded, though he didn't seem very sure. 'Go and have a look,' the man added, gesturing to the large hole in the compound wall.

'I don't know if that's a good idea, sir,' I said, thinking that we should be highlighting it to the bomb disposal experts who were attached to the company. 'It's a great spot for an anti-personnel IED.'

He laughed in a friendly way, and put a hand on my shoulder. 'OK, Corporal Jones. We don't want you any more traumatized than you already are.'

He left then, and I looked about me. We'd been told that this stretch of track was one of the most heavily IED'd in Afghanistan, and the ground sign was very likely from an older device. Still, I was irritated that my opinion was not taken more seriously.

Our clearance finished, I took the team to find shade alongside one of the other vehicles. Finally with a moment to reflect, we shook hands and talked through the experience. The boys had done well, we had survived intact, and we were confident that Hunt would make it.

There was no room for us in the Warriors, and so we were put into a Mastiff that had escorted the recovery team from DC. The Mastiff crew owned an impressive collection of porn mags, and we flicked through them as we were driven to Musa Qala. We made a stop en route at an observation post named Himmel, a scar on the hillside that I had noticed while I had been holding Hunt's airway open. I left my team with the Mastiff and went in search of water.

I saw a Warrior with an open back door, my platoon sergeant, Turkey, inside.

'Got any water?' I asked him.

'Go get your own water,' was his hostile reply, having no idea I'd been involved in the strike.

'Fuck off then, you prick,' I shot back, forgetting authority.

A few minutes later, Jay and Jake found me sitting alone in the shade of a shipping container.

'Got water?' I asked them. They did. I knocked it back as they asked me for details, having only heard fragments over the radio.

I told them enough.

We finally arrived at Musa Qala DC in the late afternoon, the base dominated by a block-shaped building decorated with the insignia of past units, and by a white house on a hill. Hesco bastions separated the tented areas, and the rank smell of the burn pit was strong in our nostrils as the OC gathered us in front of his Warrior so that he could address the company. He spoke for a couple of minutes about what had happened that day and the guys that the MERT had taken away. He was proud of us all, he said, and there was no mistaking the sincerity.

'Fair play, he hit the right notes there,' Danny said to me, before groaning as he saw Smith climbing up onto the armoured podium.

'Here we fucking go,' Jake added gloomily.

The sergeant major's talk seemed confused and unguided, trying to make us feel better but successfully undoing the OC's speech in a matter of seconds. As the gathering was dismissed, we still had trouble believing our ears.

'Did he really just say that?' Jake asked, before puffing out his chest and mimicking the man's voice. '"Don't worry if you weren't involved today. You'll all get a chance to practise your first aid on this tour." What the fuck, like?'

I had to return to 1-1 to collect my gear. My bergen had been hanging on the outside and was torn from shrapnel. I worried about my GPMG, which had been on the Warrior's deck plate, and would have received the full shock of the blast through vibrations. Our ankles had only been spared because we rested them on the opposite benches to avoid such injuries.

Hunt's bloodied and ripped body armour was in the rear of the truck, and we put it in a refuse bag to keep it from the sight of the younger soldiers, while Johan volunteered to clear out the blood, bone, and teeth from the driver's hatch.

Bailey found me there and took me aside.

'I didn't mean to be harsh earlier,' he explained, referring to when he'd ordered me to get my rifle and radio. 'I thought you would have wanted a break from the casualty.'

'It's OK. Thanks.'

'You're a good lad, Jonah. I wish you were staying on with our platoon.'

I nodded thanks, and told him I would be happy working with them anytime. Bailey fixed me with a look then. It was a sad look. Patient. 'He's not gonna make it. You know that, don't you?'

I didn't know what to say. I just knew that he was wrong. 'Yeah,' I said instead. 'I know that.' I just wanted to be free of the conversation, and after patting me on the shoulder, Bailey walked away.

I needed to clean up, knowing it was the last chance before we hit the patrol base, and I was heading for the ablutions tent when Toby caught up with me. He handed me a cold can of Fanta, which was heaven enough, and so I could have kissed him when he followed it with a letter from one of my brothers. I instantly forgot about washing, devouring the e-bluey, and then penning a reply that made no mention of what had happened that day, but perhaps highlighted my relief, fatigue, and confusion. Looking back at it, I suspect I was suffering from a concussion:

Yo, cheers for the e-bluey la. I got it today. Guess where I am?? Muuuuusaaaaaa Qalaaaaaaaaa!! The base where Ross Kemp was with the Scots. When we arrived here we had mail waiting coz it got flown (ooo gunshots) in. Let me tell you la I needed the morale boost after the last few days. We already have two Warriors written off. We will run out soon!!

So what's goin on at home then? Go on, tell me! This is the last fuckin tour I'm gonna do. If I ever try going on another please beat some sense into me with a sledgehammer.

Ross Kemp should come back out here. I've thought of plenty of Ultimate Force jokes for him. Has Afghan been in the news much? Do me a favour and when the rugby and NFL seasons start please send me any shit you see in the paper and stuff.

I saw some, god damn I'm so tired I can't even think what I was just writing. It's taken me about forty minutes to write this lol.

Say how do to Mum and Dad and all the rest of the crew. Now I'm out of Bastion and in the sticks mail will probably be slow but I'll drop a bluey in most weeks to let you know what's goin down.

Peace out broski!!

In the morning, we left Musa Qala for Patrol Base Minden. Being in the back of the trucks, I had no idea as to the distance, only that it passed without incident and within a short time. It was the final stage of our journey from Bastion that was supposed to have taken 36 hours. It ended up costing us two Warriors, two soldiers, and took 105.

Only 5,000 to go.

#veteranproblems

Hollywood, California, 2014

'So, have you, like, ever killed anyone?'

She was an aspiring comedian, and if I hadn't been asked the question a thousand times before, I'd probably have thought she was fooling around.

We were at dinner, our first date, not even a bottle of wine down. At least she'd waited until I had a drink inside me. Others hadn't.

'Yeah,' I told her, poker faced. 'But they were women and kids, so I can't really count them. More wine?' It was my standard answer, and I'd hope that she'd laugh, take the hint, and move on. She didn't. She was blonde, she was persistent, and I was trapped, so I gave her what she wanted.

'Yeah.' Time to change the subject. 'So how was yoga?'

She took it well. I was an anomaly to her. I'd seen women react in different ways to the answer that they'd dug for, some turned on, some a little afraid. Jesus, it's not like I was a released serial killer.

I cut into my steak, stuffing my mouth so that I could just nod politely to her follow-up questions. It bought me the time to wonder why she thought she had the right to ask such a personal question. It wasn't that she had caused me pain or bad memories – I couldn't give a fuck about dead Taliban. The more the merrier – but I'm pretty sure that if I'd ambushed her with 'How many times have you been fucked in the arse?' I'd have been finishing the wine alone.

But maybe it wasn't a personal question. The war belonged to America and its allies, so maybe she, as a citizen, had a right to ask what I'd done in her name. Iraq and Afghanistan had been beamed into her home since she was fifteen years old, and so maybe I was an actor, and she a hooked fan who wanted to learn more about my character.

I suppose I should have admired her honesty. I'd wanted to know the same thing of soldiers when I was a kid, only I'd been too shy to ask. Now, my life was thick with killers. What did my mum think when my childhood pal, Rhino, came to the house for a cup of tea? She'd seen us play soldiers since infancy, and now there we were, trying to laugh as he retold stories of the days he'd ended lives. He pretended to shrug it off, pretended he didn't give a fuck, and then dunked another biscuit into his tea.

I wondered about his kids. What they'd want to know as they grew up.

'Daddy, have you ever killed anyone?'

6

Zulu

Now that the journey from Bastion was done, my loan to One Platoon was over, and I was with Three Platoon again as we moved to our temporary new home at Checkpoint Zulu. A checkpoint was a small location that acted as a satellite to the larger patrol bases, which were in turn outposts for the battle groups' main toehold in the district centres. Zulu was a small building made up of a half dozen rooms, the mud walls that encompassed it also stretching around an orchard where we laid out camp beds beneath our ponchos. The engineers had visited, erecting sangars and a Hesco wall as a makeshift tank park for our three Warriors. There was no electric or water, the well having been contaminated with diesel. Essentials would have to be brought in from Patrol Base Minden, where the rest of the company would be settled, and water drawn from a local UNICEF-dug well. Welsh and Afghan flags were flown from the tallest radio antenna, but we were soon ordered to take down our own, lest we be seen as an occupying force.

Our new home sat on the edge of a wide wadi, the far side of which was firmly in the hands of the Taliban. ISAF forces had been pushed down the eastern side of this natural boundary, but not the west, and so the Taliban could come and go into the side of the ISAF 'controlled' area. Zulu had come into being to try and prevent these incursions, and that first night our Taliban neighbours across the wadi put on a show for us.

We watched from the rooftop as Terry attacked an Afghan National Army (ANA) base on the opposite side of the dry riverbed.

The base was further north than our own, putting us in line with the Taliban firing points. Two of our Warriors were with the Afghan army, and we cheered as they laid into the fight with their 30mm cannons. The ANA were firing huge bursts from their automatic weapons, streams of tracer arcing and bouncing across a sky that was turning pink with the dusk. The enemy replied with RPGs, most of which burst in the air, the explosions leaving sooty smudges against the horizon.

We watched, enraptured, as 105mm shells crashed in and erupted among the trees, feeling their concussions shaking the air even at a distance.

Our interpreter, Dewi, was listening in to the ICOM. We may not have understood the language, but we could make out the tears and anguish on the other end of the radio.

'What are they saying?' someone asked our Afghan. Dewi smiled his mischievous smile.

'His father is dying.'

And we laughed with him, enjoying our new home.

With drama like this, who needed television?

The Taliban were at it again, attacking the ANA base on the other side of the wadi. After a couple of days it was a show that had already grown old to us, and so I sat with The Firm in the orchard, finding shade where we could. When we were not conducting foot patrols to engage with the benign locals that lived in the nearby compounds, or manning Zulu's sangars, we spent most of our days here among the trees, passing the time with banter and naps, the dappled shade providing some relief from the heat.

Danny gestured to his bench, an empty Javelin missile container that had a plank of wood nailed to its top.

'I've been thinking, right. We use Javelin cases as chairs, the end caps as wash bowls, and empty ammo tins to store our kit and cook our food.'

'And?' Jay asked, expecting more.

'Well, that mong defence secretary John Reid said we were going to come to Helmand without a shot being fired, so if that had been true, then what the fuck would we sit on and wash out of?'

'Good point,' the corporal conceded, but he didn't have an answer for our friend.

'You're a full screw,' Danny chided him. 'You're supposed to know this stuff.'

'Hey.' I got the guys' attention. 'Look what I found when I went for my spare boxers this morning.'

None of them thought it strange that I hadn't changed my under-wear since Bastion, and there were no insults as I went to my new home, a construction of hessian and string that I had proudly named Chateaux Trente-Cinque (thirty five – the last two digits of my army number, monsieur). Maybe the name was a mistake, because Turkey realized it rhymed with ballsack, and called me that for a couple of weeks, but it was my castle, and I felt like a king living out of old ammo containers. Hanging on the branches of the tree that made one wall of my home was a chuff chart, a small piece of wood onto which I had drawn a calendar, each day struck off bringing the end of tour that little bit closer. Into the mud brick of the compound wall I had driven nails that acted as a rack for my rifle, my gimpy at home in the rear sangar. Right now, however, it was to my bergen that I went, retrieving a clump of army issue socks and boxers that were joined together by a lump of smooth metal.

'My bergen was hanging off the side of the wagon when we got blown up,' I told The Firm. 'All the straps have ripped off it, and shrapnel's melted my boxers together.'

'Tough shit,' was Danny's helpful reply. Then he groaned, because he saw Blake picking his way through the shrubs towards us.

'Fuck off,' Danny pre-empted him, but the youngster delivered his message.

'Boss wants everyone in the courtyard.'

The Firm exchanged looks, long enough in the army to know that this kind of summons was rarely a good thing.

The troops of Zulu assembled in front of the platoon commander, known to us as the Boss. He was in his late twenties, thin and pale, but by no means meek – there was an edge to the Boss that we all respected, but his default setting was to be cordial, competent, and sometimes devious. We knew that we were lucky to have him, an experienced officer, as he was the Recce Platoon leader. We wouldn't have to endure the mistakes of a Rupert fresh out of Sandhurst, and the Boss was comfortable enough in the presence of his NCOs that he could give and take in the banter as much as anybody.

At this moment, he did not mince his words.

'Private Hunt died today at 2 a.m., when his life support was turned off. His family were with him when he passed.'

I ground my jaw shut, willing my face to stay neutral. Some of the guys cursed, and one of the younger soldiers, Doyle, began to cry. I wanted to say something to him but I didn't dare – one word and my mask would break. Instead I tussled his hair as I went by into the orchard and the privacy of my poncho.

I fell face down onto my cot bed, and then my own tears came. They were few, more from frustration than sadness. I thought he was going to pull through. I'd already played out the reunion in my head. The drink we'd share as we laughed it off. I thought about Hunt's friends in the company – his close friends – and how they were denied the opportunity to say goodbye to their brother. They'd seen him in the morning, and then it was as if he had simply vanished. Helicopters came and took broken soldiers away – that was how it was in war, since Vietnam at least. Maybe their close friends were the ones to load them onto the birds, or maybe they watched the spinning blades from a distance, heart and stomach in mouth. Either way, they would never receive the closure of a funeral. They would never spill beer and tears at the wake. They would simply receive word that their friend was no more. No goodbyes. No closure. That was how it was for the soldier at war. How it had always been, and always would be. Pick up your weapon and fight on.

I heard footsteps approaching and blinked my eyes clear. It was Danny.

'You alright?'

'Yeah, I'm OK mate. It's just shit, isn't it?'

'Yeah, it's fucking shit.'

There was nothing else to say.

Across the wadi, the crackle of gunfire announced that the war went on.

The day after we received the news of Hunt's death, I raced in my flip-flops towards the rear sangar, Danny a half step behind me – rounds had cracked over our heads in the orchard.

We climbed up to the fighting position, finding the huge frame of Lump Head trying frantically to clear the gimpy. My gimpy. His words came heavy with saliva from between his two teeth, the only remarkable feature in his oval face.

'I saw muzzle fwash at the cowner of the tweeline, but the gimpy jammed after a few wounds.'

I went to work on the gun myself. 'Fucking dry. The sentries haven't been oiling it.'

A contact had broken out again on the far side of the wadi. It was a big one, but there wasn't much for us to see except for dust and tracer rising from the dead ground.

Danny wasn't to be deterred. 'Fuck it. That compound's close enough. Just fire on that.'

And so I did. The first shots of my tour, but the gun jammed after the first round. Swearing under my breath I cleared it, and fired again. Same result – stoppage. Then another. Then another. 'Fuck this! I fucking told them this needed test firing after we got blown up! Fuck this!'

My frustration grew as I saw armed figures darting between the compounds, dust puffing around them as bullets hit the earth – the Taliban were breaking from cover within range of my gun. It was a dream come true, if only it would fire. 'Fuck! Fuck! Fuck!' I tried the gun again and again, but it was a useless.

'They're too far for rifles,' Danny said, stating the obvious. 'They're bringing more in on bikes!'

And so they were, the Taliban taxi service shuttling men towards the fight. We watched, as much use as a limp cock.

I was shaking with frustration. Targets in the open, and nothing I could do about it. 'Why isn't the .50 cal firing?' I asked Danny, desperate for some distraction. He pulled a face, then moved off to investigate, quickly returning with a look of disgust.

'The .50 cal's fucked. Can't get a single round off. This place is a fucking joke.'

And so we were forced to watch the fight as helpless spectators. Artillery shells began to burst. A fast jet entered the fray. Our Warriors in the action reported at least two kills.

'I've had enough,' Danny finally stated. 'Let's go eat some shit.'

And so we climbed back down into the courtyard, shovelling ration pack pasta into our mouths, and leaving the fighting and dying to those whose weapons would function.

Life at Zulu was primitive. Conditions in Helmand's checkpoints and patrol bases ran from recently occupied compounds to large district centres equipped with cookhouses, internet, and British Forces television, and Zulu fell towards the lower end of the scale. The engineers had spent a few days there to reinforce the defences, but the home improvements had stopped at that.

And the toilets.

The shithouse was a wooden cubicle, the bare basics of an Alabama outhouse. The wooden seat had a hole in its centre, in which you'd place your shit bag, the plastic hot against your arse cheeks. The deed done, the bag was disposed of in a burn pit on the opposite side to the orchard's wall. There would be no burning shit in barrels, like in the Vietnam movies, and this left Toby deeply aggrieved. He'd been looking forward to handing out shit-burning duty to the usual subject of his ire, Evs 17. As it was, Blake usually volunteered for the task, the pyromaniac never happier than when setting something alight. At the rate he was using diesel, our Warriors would be immobile for the rest of the tour.

If you could somehow squeeze a piss from out of your dehydrated body, there was a plastic pipe dug into the ground at a forty-five degree angle. Some clever fucker, probably an officer at Bastion, had christened these 'desert roses', but as the heat baked the stale urine of the tube the only smell that came off them was the potent tang of bad shrimp. In the total darkness of the Afghan night, smell could guide you to the ablutions, but of course most of us pissed against the trees in the orchard. The argument that the tube, buzzing with flies, was a more sanitary solution was not a convincing one. The toilets were in Zulu's main courtyard, privacy an unheard of commodity in the field.

Zulu was not a large compound, and so only few metres away from the fetid piss tube was the 'gym', a collection of spare parts from the Warriors. Beside that was a wash area – an engineer-made wooden table, on which sat the end caps of a Javelin missile's container. Our water was limited and so the bowls were most often bone dry. Washing clothing was out of the question, and our combat bottoms were fast becoming bulletproof from a combination of sweat, dust, dribbles of piss, and sexual fluids. No, it was not too hot for that. A man has his needs, and it was one form of entertainment that did not rely on electricity.

The kitchen was a grill of Hesco mesh laid out over stones, but in that part of summer leaving a ration in direct sunlight was more than ample heat, with no need to use the fuel blocks from our ration packs. We built a fire pit from stones we gathered in the orchard, cutting down the shrubs to feed the flames in the night.

Men either thrived or despaired in these conditions. Many of us found it liberating to be away from phones and the internet. At night most of the platoon gathered around the flames, our sentries deployed in the sangars, and we'd tell tall tales, take the piss out of one another, and if someone was brave enough to begin, we'd even break into song.

One evening, we once again gathered together on empty ammunition containers as the darkness closed in. We lit a fire, for illumination and to keep the bugs away while we ate the chocolate of our

ration packs, an impossibility during the day's heat. This was the
time of night where we'd wet a sock, place a water bottle inside, and
put it in the high reaches of a tree, hoping that it would cool by the
time the sun came up.

Sergeant Davies, our Javelin expert, decided that it would be a
good opportunity for some of the younger, quieter guys to stand up
and talk about themselves in front of the group. The boys had already
seen a little of combat operations, but to stand alone, vulnerable and
open in front of your peers and superiors was a far more daunting
task, some visibly shaking with nerves.

Fathers were a popular topic, particularly the lack of them. Eventually, it wasn't only the young ones talking. We heard about how
one of our brothers had first met his father in a bar fight. Two of our
number had lost a parent to murder, and many others had come
from families of serial offenders, police raids on their homes some
of their earliest memories. For every man with a criminal father
there was another who simply did not know theirs. Those of us who
did sat quietly, counting our blessings and marvelling that these
kids had turned into the comrades we loved today.

Life at Zulu moved slowly. There were patrols, there were shoot and
scoot contacts against our sangars, but mostly we were spectators to
events across the wadi. One afternoon, our own artillery treated us
to a firepower display, 105mm rounds exploding just outside of our
perimeter. The drop shorts had mixed up their maps, and the
intended target was miles away. Had the rounds landed on our
heads, Zulu would have become a slaughterhouse. We breathed a
sigh of relief that it wasn't our lot to be on the end of such barrages –
at least, not intentional ones. For those of a nervous disposition, like
Blake, the incoming sent them scurrying into holes. Those of us
who'd been mortared and rocketed in Iraq knew that you couldn't
outrun them – if there was one for you, then so be it. A direct hit
would find you. As the locals say, *inshallah* – if God wills it.

At night, we feared the venomous insects that lived alongside us, but in the daylight we hunted them down for sport.

'What the fuck's going on there?' Danny asked me one afternoon in the orchard, his eyes on our interpreter, Dewi.

The Afghan was on his haunches, a stick in his hand that he was prodding into a recess in the compound wall. A small cluster of giggling soldiers stood about him.

We joined that group, an excited Blake only too happy to explain.

'He's found a black widow.'

'Shut up you cunt,' Danny blasted him. 'You don't get black widows in Afghan.'

'How do you know?'

'Because I'm a fucking lance corporal in the British Army.' But despite his scepticism, Danny leaned in for a closer look.

Jake came to stand next to me, less than impressed with the mischief.

'My fucking bedspace is just by there. He's gonna piss this thing off and it's gonna come chew my face off in the middle of the night.'

'Good,' Danny said, overhearing.

Our platoon sergeant made his way to join us. He was a rare sight in the orchard, the senior NCOs living within one of Zulu's rooms. His head bobbed on his shoulders as he weaved between the shrubs, and it was this gait that had given him his nickname.

Turkey had been a member of Recce for a long time, and epitomized its attitude. He had a sharp tongue, but held it back for when it was needed. He saw the tour for what it was, a hoop to step through and survive, and if there was any way of working around an idiotic order, he'd find it. He would never shy from danger or a fight, but getting his boys home alive trumped all else.

'Give us a minute,' he said to Danny, then turned to me. 'I need to trim you, Gez.'

I was instantly defensive.

'My hair's no longer than anyone else's.'

'No, you dickhead. Trauma Risk . . .' the remaining parts of the acronym escaped him, 'something Management? I don't know what it stands for. I need to talk to you about how you feel after Hunt, and all that.'

'I feel fine, mate,' I told him, and it wasn't far from the truth.

Once the adrenaline had worn off, seeing Hunt in a bad way had shaken me. Hearing that he'd passed had saddened me. I hadn't even allowed myself to think about the bigger picture, and his family.

But the truth was that I'd come to Afghanistan expecting that we'd lose guys. Infantry units did not come to Helmand and leave in one piece. In August it was Hunt. In July it had been my friend Jamie. In March it was H, a comrade of Iraq who had been a dear friend to the other members of The Firm. We were just six weeks into a tour of at least six months. I knew we'd lose more. Turkey knew we'd lose more. Maybe it would be one of us. Maybe he would be asking these questions again, and I'd be the subject.

But this was war in the twenty-first century, and it wasn't enough to just look out for one another. It had to be given an acronym, and logged in a record.

'I'm fine,' I told him again, and believed it.

It was night, and I was on stag with Toby. I looked at our surroundings through a night vision scope, the compounds and shrubs dark green against the paler tone of the gravel wadi.

'Want a look?' I asked Toby. I saw his silhouette shake its head.

'Mini-me talked to me today,' I then offered to the darkness.

Toby was suspicious of all the private soldiers, and particularly those like Mini-me, named for his minute stature, who had joined us from Two Platoon.

'Wanted to talk about Hunt,' I said, going on when there was no reply. 'They were mates. In training together, I think.'

'Maybe.' Toby softened now. 'They're about the same age.'

'Yeah. So he was talking to Hunt when we were at FOB Edi, the night before we got hit. Hunt was a little shook up after that first hit, and when he was told he had to drive again, it really snapped him. Bennett was supposed to be driving, see?'

'Well, why didn't he?' The scorn had returned.

'He was ill, or something. So Hunt had to drive again, and he told Mini-me that he was sure he'd get hit that day.'

'But he did it anyway,' Toby said, matter of fact. 'He did his job.'

'Yeah,' was all I had to say, and suddenly I wanted to change the subject. 'Bad week for the Fusiliers.'

The Royal Regiment of Fusiliers made up the rest of our battle group. We had little contact with them, but they were good to us at DC, and like all infantry units they were essentially a mirror image of ourselves. Within a few days they had lost four soldiers.

Conversation trailed away. We'd been living in each other's pockets for weeks, and longer than that for the pre-deployment training. Paired up night after night for sentry duty, we'd already exhausted the conversations of lovers past and present, rugby, and our dreams for the future. Like a married couple in their fifteenth year, we loved one another, but conversation had become stale, and we had no kids to distract us. It was time to spice things up.

I placed my hands on the GPMG in front of me, newly delivered to us from Minden to replace the one damaged in the IED strike.

'I want to know if this works,' I told Toby. 'Wanna see if we can kick something off?'

He did.

'Pass me one of those 1,000-metre shamoolies,' Toby told me, and I handed him the tube. There was a parachute flare within, an expensive firework. We could fire it towards the Taliban compounds under the guise that we were using illumination to check on movement we'd seen through the night vision aids.

'Get ready,' Toby told me, and a split second later the illum-round whooshed across the wadi, Toby and I giggling as it went.

'Boring fuckers,' I said a few minutes later, disappointed at the lack of a reaction. 'Do another.'

He fired two more, but the end result was the same. There'd be no shooting for us.

Toby was more upset than angry. 'What's the point in us being here if no one will shoot at us? I'm gonna go get us a brew.'

He placed his rifle down at the rear opening of the sangar, as he usually did before swinging himself onto the ladder, but the firing of the illumination rounds had robbed him of his night vision. He misjudged his position and pitched forwards out of the open back, crashing twelve feet to the floor.

He lay in the dirt, a groaning heap, helmet and body armour saving him from injury. I was helpless with laughter, and hastily unzipped my trousers so that I could relieve myself against the sangar wall before I pissed myself.

Toby tried to come up with a clever line, but could only groan between coughs of relieved laughter.

In the end, his words were a simple epitaph. 'I fucking hate this place.'

It had been decided by platoon HQ to make a new fighting position on the rooftop, and The Firm took it upon ourselves to build the sangar, seeing the chance to catch the sun's rays and get some exercise. Barely legal length shorts and sandals were the order of the day.

We formed a chain, Toby and Jay on the rooftop, Jake and Danny in the courtyard, with me on the rickety ladder to pass the bags upwards. We were soon in a rhythm, enjoying the labour, a break from the monotony of patrols and sentry duty.

But the work was not without its perils, Jay dangling his ballbag from his shorts so that I'd have to see it every time I turned to pass a bag up to him.

'You fucking love it,' he told me.

A split second later, an unwashed toe was shoved into my mouth as I turned my head back from the ground. Toby saw it and laughed, but our neighbours were not so amused.

A single round cracked by our heads, sending Jay and Toby sprawling to the floor, and me scurrying down the ladder.

I was running with Danny for the rear sangar when a second shot cracked by.

'This cunt again!' I shouted to my friend, the shooter a regular.

The sentry in the sangar was down below the parapet, no eyes on the ground. Danny gave him a kick to encourage proper observation. 'What the fuck are you going to see from down there, you cunt?'

We took over the task ourselves, and were rewarded as a shot was fired towards us, making us duck into cover. The crack and the thump were instantaneous; the crack being the sound of the bullet going by at supersonic speed, and the thump being the report of the rifle that fired it.

'He can't be more than a hundred metres,' Danny said, and I pointed out the likely compound, Danny lining up the gun.

'Come on you fucker, have another go.'

But he didn't, and so we turned our attention inwards, towards Zulu.

We needn't have bothered. After a short time on the ground, we already knew which of the troops would have rushed to a firing position and which would be lingering in the orchard, hoping not to be found by the NCOs.

Danny spotted three of them from our vantage point. The usual suspects. He'd thought long and hard about the best way to encourage them.

'Stick 'em against a tree and shoot 'em,' he said, and I had no doubt that he meant it.

It was evening, and we patrolled through the fields of the village as the skies turned amber. There was a terrific stillness to the air, every man feeling it, not wanting to break the magic through conversation.

We followed an alleyway between two compounds that were shaded by lush green trees, and emerged outside of the village mosque. There was a gathering of locals there and they smiled as they saw us. It was Ramadan, and they were laying out the evening feast.

The villagers were pleasant, and we spread out into a loose

formation, no fear of attack. Civilians who live in a warzone develop a sixth sense for trouble. If they were calm, we were calm, and now our commanders moved in to talk with the elders. Those of us on the outskirts sat back, taking the weight of our kit off of tired shoulders.

The locals asked if our interpreter was a Muslim, then invited him to join them in eating when he confirmed that he was.

By the time that we moved away, the amber of dusk had turned to the pink of sunset, the distant mountains to the west silhouetted like gnarled Titans rising from the desert.

I took my camera and climbed to the highest point of the patrol base, settling in beside the useless .50 cal, and watching as a perfect orange disc slid behind the mountains. Danny joined me. For once, he was silent.

Then, across the wadi, the first stream of tracer danced lazily across the pink canvas, followed a split second later by the sharp report of the shots.

'Here we go again.' Danny smiled.

I was livid.

A few days earlier I'd had the chance to use the satellite phone, and heard from home that my pay had come in £1,000 short. Through Baker, the company clerk in Bastion, I now had my reason why; the army had deducted an overpaid bonus, awarded in Iraq, that they'd since declared written off. I was given no reason for why they'd gone back on this decision – I just knew that I was worse off. They did this to me while I was in what was essentially a cut-off patrol base, with only a few minutes of phone time a week, at best.

'What if I had a family to pay for?' I complained to Danny.

'You don't,' he said, as sympathetic as ever. 'Nobody loves you.'

'You're a dick. I'd never hear the end of this if it happened to you.'

'But it didn't,' he grinned, and I went in search of a more sympathetic listener.

Instead, I found a patrol from Two Platoon entering the compound, a stranger in their midst. She was from the Royal Military Police, and she'd come to see me.

'Why me?' I asked her.

She was pretty. A little older than I was, and disarming. It would make her perfect for the job she'd been given.

'I need to take a statement from you about the incident with Private Hunt.'

I could guess at the reasons why. 'There's an inquest?'

She nodded. 'For all incidents like Private Hunt's. The statement is for the coroner.'

I thought it over.

'Because they don't class this as a war, do they? It's peacekeeping, or some shit.'

She smiled wryly. In her line of work, she'd seen the absurdity of that statement on a tragically regular basis.

'That's right. Now, I need you to tell me everything that happened from the moment you left Bastion.'

And I did, the words coming easy. I kept it to actions, not feelings, but still, I talked to her in the kind of detail that I hadn't done with any of my comrades. It was a long process, and when it was over I felt that I'd been more intimate and vulnerable with her than if we'd made love.

But the pretty red-cap left, and Danny appeared in her place.

'Get your shit. It's election day,' he informed me, which meant patrols for us, and expected enemy attacks on all polling stations. 'Let's go get ourselves killed, so some goat-fucker can vote the Taliban back in.'

Danny's prophecy about election day proved wrong, and so did the threat warnings suggesting of numerous Taliban attacks. For us, that faltering step towards a doomed democracy passed quietly, but within days the far side of the wadi was a battleground again.

Today was different. Afghan troops, with some support from our infantry brothers in the Fusiliers, were making a push south.

I was with Danny in our usual position of the rear sangar. It was not our turn for sentry duty, but we waited there like gentry, desert combats in place of tweed, hopeful that the beaters would flush some of the Taliban towards us.

Black smoke was billowing from a fire in a compound. There was the occasional burst of automatic fire. For the most part, however, it had been quiet.

But then, a cluster of figures were spotted bursting suddenly from the treeline, throwing themselves into a depression in the wadi, their backs exposed to us.

'Shit!' I tugged at Danny's sleeve, adrenaline beginning to dump into my veins. 'Can we fire on them?'

I was asking because the far side of the wadi was shrouded in trees. Somewhere among that green zone – the area of dense vegetation and irrigated farmland – were the friendly units, and we couldn't be sure where. Danny went to the Boss for permission, but came back empty-handed.

'They're in line with us. We'll hit them if we overshoot.'

We couldn't believe it. The enemy were lined up in front of us like ducks in a fairground shooting gallery, and we couldn't pull the trigger.

Instead, we watched as the ANA advanced on the trapped Taliban. A firefight broke out between the two sides.

'If they run south, we can hit them,' Danny said, hopefully.

But they didn't run. Their ammunition dwindled quickly, and the ANA advanced on the enemy en masse, firing heavy bursts, no thoughts to fire and manoeuvre, or taking cover.

'Probably all off their faces.' The ANA were well known for their love of marijuana and opiates.

High or not, the wave of Afghan soldiers overran the ditch, pouring in fire from close range. Hands were thrown up in the final seconds, but no prisoners would be emerging.

'Well, that's that then.' The Afghans began to pick over the bodies of their foe. They weren't the only ones to die, other sites of fallen enemy identifiable when the soldiers of the Fusiliers paused to point and talk, gathering in small groups as they snapped mental photographs of their stricken foe.

'Lucky cunts,' I grumbled.

That night, the combined operation withdrew, leaving ten Taliban corpses behind, seven of which lay in the ditch.

'The locals loaded them into wheelbarrows,' Danny told me later. 'You could just see these stiff legs poking into the air.' He smiled at the memory.

In the course of the operation, caches of weapons had been found in the compounds opposite to us. Stocks of mortar rounds, 500kg of ammonium nitrate for making IEDs, and small arms. It was a nice haul, but the ground was ceded back to the enemy the very next day – there simply wasn't the manpower to hold it. One Afghan policeman had died during the fighting, when the RPG on his shoulder had blown prematurely.

'I'm ready to get out of here,' Danny told me, referring to Zulu. 'It's like watching porn. You either want to get stuck in yourself, or you need something dirtier to get you off.'

I couldn't disagree with him, but we needn't have worried. The next day our platoon was relieved, and we joined the bulk of the company at Patrol Base Minden.

It was our turn to get fucked.

7

Stay Low, Move Fast

'Contact!'

If you're lucky, this is the moment where you engage the enemy. Usually, it's the moment where they engage you. A moment where the air is split, your heart pounds out of your chest, and your lungs hang out of your arse. Contacts are dirt and sweat in your eyes, shouts in your ear, and hot brass on your skin. They are seconds, minutes, hours of wide eyes, choked laughter, and snatched triggers. A time to remember your training, forget your sanity, and to pray to strangers in the clouds. They are, if you survive them, the most memorable moments of your life.

'Contact. Wait, out.'

It was time to take our first patrol to the forward line enemy troops (FLET), a couple of kilometres south from Patrol Base Minden, which sat on the southern edge of what was now the benign village of Yatimchay – benign after our sister company had fought to take it in the summer, several of its compounds now appearing like broken smiles where bombs had smashed into the Afghan land. Due to this carnage, the village was sparsely populated, and part of our mission as a company was to set conditions so that the locals could return, conveniently forgetting that our war was the reason that they'd had to leave in the first place.

The site of Minden did little to dominate the ground in the local area, and patrols needed to be sent out into the environs. At two corners of the PB these were narrow and dusty alleyways, and at others open ground of deserted fields. Behind them, either rising hills that overlooked our position, or green zone that allowed the enemy excellent concealment. Every armchair general knows that in guerrilla warfare an attack can occur anywhere, but, even so, you could draw lines on a map where what lay on the other side was clearly 'enemy territory'.

'So they won't acknowledge this is a war, but they will acknowledge a front line held by the enemy?' Danny had asked the Boss, with his usual scorn for politicians and officers, the Boss and the other platoon commanders of our company excluded.

Everything we'd been told in the patrol briefing had us expecting trouble. The front line in question was a deep wadi known as the M4, passable by vehicle in only a handful of heavily IED'd places. The compounds and villages to the south of the M4 were firmly in Taliban hands, as was the opposite side of the main MSQ wadi that would mark the western boundary of our patrolling. The higher elevation of these places made it the perfect position for an ambush.

It wasn't a good place to be walking into.

Our platoon was on its own, twenty-four soldiers split down into two groups, known as multiples. I was in the second half, under the command of Turkey. As gimpy gunner, I was bringing up the rear, Toby there to watch my back. My trust in him was absolute, but not even a sweat like him could have predicted the first attack of that day.

It came just moments after leaving the patrol base – a huge Afghan hound harassed the platoon, which was strung out in single file along the dirt track. Since Bastion we had known that Blake jumped at his own shadow. With the dog baring its fangs, the youngster had nearly run to Sangin before Turkey could corral him back in.

As we came to within a few hundred metres of the M4, we began to notice fleeting movements in the compounds ahead of us, either Taliban planning for an attack or just civilians with the sense to get out of the way. Whatever the cause, our balls began to retract into our bodies.

The Boss's half of the platoon reached the M4 untouched, an eventuality that we hadn't planned on. Including the company that held the area before us, no prior patrol from Minden had made it this far without contact. After a moment to consult with company HQ, the Boss began to follow that deep wadi at a parallel to the right, within thirty metres of the nearest compound, and out into the open of a barren field. Our multiple snaked along behind them, the whole platoon in movement at once.

Not a good thing to do in front of the enemy.

The front half of our snake now turned north, heading across the open field, fully exposed to the Taliban side of the MSQ wadi. Toby and I were bringing up the rear, the last pair to come parallel to the M4 wadi, when the inevitable happened.

Without warning, the crack, buzz, and clatter of rounds stung by our ears with angry venom, followed a split second later by the hammering of automatic fire. Within the blink of a sweat-filled eye, the field around us was suddenly spewing geysers of mud as rounds chewed the dirt.

'Contact!'

We knew the steel rain had been due, but even so the fire took a few seconds to register. Your brain doesn't like to admit that somebody is actively trying to put holes in you. You almost have to push it into acceptance.

And that's when the fun can begin.

Instinctively, from the crack of the bullets, we could tell that the fire was coming from across the larger wadi, and so that's where I ran with the gimpy, remembering the old maxim of the infantry soldier as I sweated and stumbled: Stay low. Move fast.

I stayed low, bent double, but moving fast was out of the question under the weight of my kit. I hustled as best as I could, shouting, 'Moving up!' as I went.

One of my comrades went down. He jumped straight back up to his feet, and continued his vain quest to find cover in the bare-ass field.

Now in line with the Boss's multiple I threw myself onto the ground. Rounds continued to split the air overhead, but our own guys were firing now, the rattle of LMGs joined by the crack of rifles and the pop of grenade launchers.

I pulled the butt of the gun into my shoulder. This moment had been drilled into me in countless lessons and exercises. Identify the firing points. Only fire at confirmed targets.

Fuck that.

I pulled back on the cocking lever, chambering the first 7.62mm round. The bolt pushed forward with a satisfying clunk. I know it did, because that's what the GPMG does. Was I aware of it at the time? Not a fucking chance. I had only one thing on my mind.

Pulling the trigger.

I fired that gun like I was in a Vietnam movie. Treelines; brass 'em up. Compounds; get some! Something moved? Kill it!

It was the most exhilarating moment of my life.

In no time I'd gone through the first belt of ammunition. Jay appeared beside me, handing me another from my daysack. Formed into an L-shape, the platoon brought its firepower to bear on the wadi's bank. It was a fucking riot, and in no time we'd won the fire-fight through sheer volume. Rounds were still coming our way, but a torrent had calmed to no more than a trickle.

The Boss now had his chance to extract the platoon. He'd not been idle, and 81mm mortar rounds from Minden began to burst across the wadi, high explosives and smoke, the dull concussions vibrating through the air. *CRUMP-CRUMP-CRUMP!* We threw our own smoke grenades, and as Turkey's multiple laid down a screen of fire, the Boss's ran with heaving, scorched lungs to a small building a hundred metres away. There, they returned the courtesy for us.

It was as we pulled back that the Taliban on the other side of the M4 finally decided to join the party. Some of them were in the compound that had been a mere thirty metres from us. I can't explain why they hadn't opened up when we stood there like hard dicks in front of them. I can only think that it was down to the presence of mind of veterans like Toby, who didn't get sucked into trying to fight a one-directional battle and kept their weapons trained across the M4 – the Taliban had enough experience of British infantry by now to know that it wasn't a good idea to open an attack when we were looking down our sights.

Buzzing with excitement, I dropped behind a small embankment outside of a compound. My gun peered hungrily over the lip, and Jay fed it more ammunition. I'd brought 600 rounds with me, and it was going fast. It was at this point, the fire slackening, that I first realized we had a casualty. He was being treated behind the compound, but from the demeanour of the people around him it didn't look too serious. I asked Jay who it was.

'Jake. He's been shot in the neck.'

One of my best friends, shot in the neck.

Fuck.

Maybe he hadn't stayed low. Maybe he hadn't moved fast. Jay saw my look.

'It's not serious.'

'How the fuck can you be shot in the neck and it not be serious?' But there was no time for answers, as the Taliban picked up their fire from both directions.

Contacts are funny that way. You can gain the upper hand from weight of fire, but as soon as you slacken off you can pretty much guarantee that the other side will pick up the pace.

I was still firing across the larger wadi, which meant my rounds were travelling a few metres from the compound's walls at my two o'clock. I nearly got my first kill when Danny ran in front of me to position one of the LMG gunners. Luckily, I was taking a second to look over my sights, and so he escaped a burst of 7.62. It scared the shit out of me.

'What the fuck are you doing, Danny? Get the fuck out of my arcs!'

'Fuck you, you prick!' he shot back, and for a second all thoughts of the firefight going on around us were lost. We were just two jacked-up young guys, wanting to beat the living shit out of each other.

'I nearly fucking shot you, you cunt! Clear my fucking arcs! Now!'

'Fuck you. I'll fucking slot you myself!'

'Fuck you!'

'Fuck you!'

Jay stepped in, overruling the pair of us with rank and presence. He'd seen the whole thing and knew that Danny'd been in the wrong. He also knew that if he didn't act, we'd still be arguing in the same spot that night.

'Danny, get the fuck out of the way! It's basic fucking safety drills.'

It didn't hit me as ironic at the time that Jay was quoting range safety drills while enemy fire cracked above our heads.

A sullen Danny moved the gunner out of the way, and I resumed my fire across the wadi. Seconds later I heard the same gunner shout out, claiming that he'd dropped a Taliban fighter on the rooftop of the nearest compound on the M4. No one else saw it, but it was hard to see anything with sweat, dirt, and smoke in your eyes.

The fire on both sides died down now. We'd pulled back far enough that the rifles were better off saving their ammunition, and now it was a tit for tat skirmish of machine gun fire. Jay had pulled his binoculars and was kneeling beside me, searching for targets. I was amusing myself, trying to take down the motorbikes that ferried Terry back and forth to the front line. They were out of my range, but my desire to topple them was strong. Maybe I could will the bullets that extra hundred metres.

Or maybe not. I cursed as another burst fell short of my target.

'If we had the tripods like I asked, we'd be hammering these cunts.'

The larger, stable firing platforms were easily man portable, and would almost double the accurate range of the gun. Having served in a specialist machine gun platoon, I'd petitioned the OC that we should deploy them, but my advice had been unwanted.

I went back to my fantasy shoot, but Jay soon snapped me out of it.

'Look, look! Moving down to the treeline from that compound! You see them?'

I did. Two figures, moving at speed towards the cover of the green zone.

'Yeah, yeah! I see them!'

I looked down the iron sights. Led them. Pulled the trigger. A five-round burst, then another.

They ran straight into it.

I couldn't believe it.

'Fucking hell, did I hit them?'

Jay had the binoculars to his eyes. 'Yeah! One of them's down! He's not moving! Boss! Jonah got one!'

The Boss looked up from his map. 'Good job.'

I'd seen it, and yet . . .

'I definitely got him, yeah?'

'Yeah! He ran straight into it.'

A moment of detached disbelief, then pure joy. I high-fived my brother.

'That one was for Hunt, you cunts.'

Yes, I said that. They say it in the movies, and when they do you think it's a cliché. But I said it. And I felt it.

Now I just wanted to get more of the fuckers.

The roar of diesel engines and squealing tracks announced the arrival of the quick reaction force (QRF), a corporal sticking his head out of the turret of his Warrior as the beast rocked forwards on its breaks. 'I can't shoot anything from here!'

'Well move your fucking wagon then!' Turkey shouted.

The sergeant major's wagon arrived next and backed in to collect our wounded. Miraculously, Jake was the only one hit. With him on board, and belching smoke, the two Warriors moved away up the track. The rest of us would be walking home.

Except, of course, that the Taliban are not inclined to let you walk away from a contact. And so we ran, or rather we shuffled. With that much gear, and with the level of fatigue you feel on patrol in forty-five degree heat – let alone after the dash and sprint of a contact – it doesn't matter how much the adrenaline is pumping, your body can only do so much.

But it wasn't the retreat from Stalingrad – this was why we'd trained hard – and we made our way back in an orderly single file, except where NCOs had to move alongside struggling soldiers, pulling them along by the straps of their kit. I was at the back with Jay, and I felt like I was walking on air. That was partly due to my excitement at dropping one of the enemy, but also down to the fact that I'd gone through almost all of my 600 rounds and the 200 that Jay had carried as reserve. It made for a light pack.

The mortar rounds continued to pound the treeline, but rules of engagement forbade them from targeting the compounds. These the Warriors engaged, 30mm cannons pumping rounds into the thick walls, 7.62mm coaxial machine guns spraying in bursts.

At one point, the Warrior commanders found themselves blind-sided by compounds on the track's side, unable to fire due to the restriction in their arcs. The enemy took this last chance to up the rate of fire, just as our platoon crossed an open area between cover. I dropped down, desperate to fire the last of my ammunition and return to base 'guns empty', but a Warrior roared into my field of fire.

And so, we had only one more attack to face.

The hound.

It was waiting where it had ambushed us only an hour before. It had probably masterminded the whole thing, but we gave it amnesty. Maybe we should have even given it a commendation, as its slathering jaws did the job of harrying our fatigued soldiers through the base's gate.

I was panting hard, sweating from every pore, but fatigue didn't enter my mind. I had always been one of the fittest of the group, but there was more to it than that – I was smiling. As I turned to give Jay another high five, I saw that he was smiling, too. We were the last into the base, a team coming off the sports field. Some guys slumped, exhausted, but the majority of us traded high fives, whoops, and insults.

I saw Jason, a good friend from Iraq, in his mortar pit. They were still hurling rounds.

'Go on Jas, fuckin' give it 'em!' I shouted, and he gave me his big old stupid grin in reply.

As we stripped out of our gear we asked after Jake. We got the story from Wayne – Pinkmist had been hit in the initial wave of fire, a round going in and out through the back of his neck. Jake had no idea he'd been hit and began returning fire. Alongside him, Wayne had noticed the blood gushing from the wound, and jammed his thumb in to stop it. Then, for Jake, came the most horrific part of the experience.

Gormley, a medic who resembled a fat Ewok, came running to the sound of Wayne's calls. As he squatted over his patient, the crotch of his trousers split, and there was no underwear beneath. Jake had to endure the man's sweaty, hairy balls in his face as he was dragged to cover.

We went to say our goodbyes to our friend before he was taken to Bastion, but he was high on morphine and in the care of the medical staff. After pats on the shoulder and insults that went unheard, we let him be. He was evacuated by helicopter soon after, and in the hospital at Bastion the surgeon would tell him that had the bullet passed millimetres one way it would have left him paralysed, and millimetres the other would have left him dead.

I found Danny, who was still sulking after our argument.

I offered my hand. 'Cheer up, you grumpy cunt.'

'I would have shot you, but I didn't want your mum to look like a fat crying mess at the funeral.' That was as good an apology as I could ever expect from him.

Jason appeared. I told him about my kill, and Danny snorted.

'He just tripped over his flip-flops.'

'Fucking ask Jay then you cunt!'

He laughed. I simmered. It was a pivotal moment in my life, and almost the end of Jake's, but The Firm was still The Firm.

8

Actions and Reactions

Afghanistan was a story of shortages. Water, helicopters, manpower, fresh food, mail, common sense. The list went on.

'Got plenty of fucking IEDs, though,' Danny remarked, and he was not exaggerating.

So far into the tour, barely a day had gone by without an IED strike or find. The most spectacular discovery to date, barring a detonation, occurred when One Platoon was driving along Route Pink, a dust track that served as the main road between our patrol base and the district centre. The first two wagons drove over a container of home-made explosive (HME) buried in the dirt, the second vehicle's tracks hurling it into the air, the third truck being able to stop just in time before colliding with it. Miraculously, the pressure pad had not been touched. This was at a choke point known to us as Hole in the Wall. The engineers had blown an adjoining section of compound wall here earlier in the summer, during the fight to take Yatimchay, but what had once been a way of flanking the enemy was now just a funnel into which A Company poured its Warriors, and Terry his IEDs. It was not a fun place to pass through.

The day after our contact at the FLET, our platoon was sent back down to the M4. I was in a good mood, intelligence sources confirming that four Taliban had been killed in our skirmish. I'd packed extra ammunition that morning in the hope that there would be a second round.

Between the bells, Terry had not been idle, our point man soon finding an area of disturbed earth on the main track. The alternative route was a narrow alleyway between compounds which had IED City written all over it. Turning back to the trail, a second device was soon found. It was clear that there would be no more strolls to the front line.

The Taliban were watching us playing their treasure hunt, the ICOM chatter heavy with threats. Myself and Johan, that day's machine-gunners, were pushed outwards to cover across the wadi. As we moved along the narrow track, Turkey asked Johan if he was happy with where we were going.

'Yup,' Johan answered over his shoulder, before losing his footing as his eyes left the trail. He finished in the splits position at the bottom of a ditch and had to be pulled out by Turkey – once he'd stopped laughing, of course.

Now that we gunners were in position, the ICOM sparked up again, the terp – short for interpreter – translating that, 'We can see two machine-gunners in the field. Shall we attack?' It is an eerie feeling to know that unseen eyes are planning your death, but we laughed it off, giving the treeline the finger and hoping that somebody would pull a trigger. Nobody did, and we left without incident.

One Platoon headed back into the area the next day. They found our IEDs had been moved and discovered three more. The resourceful Taliban had relocated the explosives as soon as we had sniffed them out.

Time to reset the treasure hunt.

After discovering the cluster of devices that were waiting to kill us, the war decided it was time to concentrate on shortages again. The Boss gathered the platoon together.

'What I am about to tell you does not get back to the UK. Not on the phones. Not on emails. Not in mail.'

'Like we get any mail anyway,' somebody muttered, and was ignored by the Boss.

'A Chinook's landed in a ditch and rolled over. It had to be denied. That means they dropped a bomb on it. Another's been shot down near Kajaki, so that means two things. Because it was shot down in daylight, the RAF will now only fly them at night. And, there are now only four Chinooks to cover all of Helmand. That includes the MERT, too.'

'So basically, Boss, don't expect any mail?' Danny asked.

'I'm glad the fuckers crashed, anyway,' I put in. 'Every time I mark out a HLS the cunts come in the wrong way. Downdraft from the last one put me on my arse. Grit nearly took my eyes out.'

Danny smirked 'That's why you get issued goggles, you cunt.'

'Fuck off. You know what I mean.'

The Boss cleared his throat to get our attention back.

'We're doing overwatch for the IEDD team tomorrow. Should be a long one.'

And it was, ten hours spent on a baking, bare hillside, overlooking the IED disposal team clearing bombs from a crossing point on a wadi. We prayed for an attack, anything to kill the boredom, and instead we had to settle for throwing stones at one another, the hillside becoming a schoolyard as the first of the explosions rang out.

'Fucking hell, that was a bit big, wasn't it?' I tried to say in a flat, matter-of-fact tone. I was filming the detonations on my digital camera. Danny came to join me, and we began parodying Ross Kemp with our commentary of the operation, our accents varying from cockney to Aussie.

'Here we are with Three Platoon, A Company. Nacho is just moving forward to confirm a suspected IED. Let's see what happens to him,' we narrated, as the engineers prepared to explode another device. As the smoke of the huge eruption cleared, we tried to suppress our giggles and complete our report.

'That dust you're seeing there is all that's left after Private Nacho conducted his five and twenty metre checks,' I commentated.

Danny sniggered. 'Or didn't.'

'He died as he lived,' I tried to finish, 'screaming in agony.' And we both burst into laughter.

Six IEDs were destroyed in all, their explosions sending birds to the air and leaving our ears ringing. Their detonators were the snap peg type, sensitive enough to be triggered by a man on foot. A snap peg used a very thin stick, or a sliver of metal, from stopping a plunger from being depressed into the device. When a foot – or an arse – was unlucky enough to find it, the peg would snap, the plunger would depress, and somebody would be torn to pieces.

Watching one explosion after another, we laughed it off as we realized what little would be left of the soldier unlucky enough to find one with his feet. We laughed, and pretended that we didn't know those bombs had been planted there for us.

Patrol Base Minden had been occupied prior to our tour, and its selection had been made on the basis of comfort rather than tactical advantage. It offered terrible views of our surrounding area of operations, and so we were obliged to push out a fire support group (FSG) of two Warriors whenever a patrol went onto the ground, rather than being able to support them from the base. Such mutual support was an essential concept of war, vital for deterring enemy attack, and covering the mobile callsigns on the ground if things did kick off.

As far as Afghan compounds went, Minden was prime real estate, with smooth concrete walls in the rooms that were set back from the dirt courtyard interior. These rooms were highly prized, and The Firm claimed one as its own, Jay christening it the 'Viper's Nest'. Any man entering, regardless of rank, was in a free-fire zone of abuse.

Most of the junior ranks at Minden slept in the courtyard, beneath ponchos and mosquito nets, the base taking on the look of a heavily armed refugee camp. Outside of the building there were the Hesco walls that formed the tank park, and the prefabricated sangars installed by the engineers. Two more sandbagged emplacements were mounted at either end of the compound's rooftop, home to fifty calibre and grenade machine guns.

Also in the tank park was Cortez, a highly powered thermal camera system that sat atop a fifteen metre pole. The camera fed into a small, purpose-built Portakabin which housed the camera's screens, recorders, and its two squinty eyed operators, both of whom had been trained for the job from the Territorial Army.

Cortez was a brilliant asset in countering an insurgency, but due to the poor location of the patrol base, much of its vision was blocked by ridges and hills. A feed was linked from the camera into the company's operations room, and this screen quickly became known as 'Kill TV'. It gave the hierarchy the excuse they were looking for to not have to venture onto the ground, and also allowed them to watch the patrolling soldiers, berating them on their return for such transgressions as not having both hands on their weapons, or for removing helmets during a halt in the baking sun.

Although we came to hate Cortez for these reasons, it did come with its perks. If a contact had occurred in an area that the cameras could see, then we had access to an action movie starring ourselves. The bookish operators were easily persuaded to play back the footage for us, their protests dying quickly as we used our own digital cameras to record directly from the screens.

The wooden outhouses and piss tubes at the base were the same as those at Zulu, and every other patrol base in Afghanistan, but at Minden the wooden shacks had become the canvas of many a budding artist and poet. The machismo of American actor Chuck Norris was a popular theme, with slogans like, 'Chuck Norris doesn't do press-ups. He does world-downs'. This appeared to be a constant across Helmand, though nobody could explain why.

After a clean-up operation led by the sergeant major, the deep well of Minden was declared fit for use, and this meant water for washing one's self and one's combats. It was a shock to the system for us as we tried to scrub out sweat and grime by hand, marvelling at how our great-grandmothers had done the same with the coal-stained clothing of our ancestors.

We bathed from the end caps of the Javelin missile containers, or if we were lucky we got our hands on one of the few solar showers in the company. Some men, such as Nacho, were averse to soap, and had to be prodded into the wash area like sheep into the dip.

Minden afforded us some communication with the outside world. There was a satellite phone that you could book for a twenty-minute time slot, using the credits that we were issued by the army on a monthly basis. The phones were battered, and signal often scant, but provided you could make your slot, you could hope to get between five and ten minutes of conversation between the patchy signal and dropped calls.

Minden also had a text link device; a heavy-duty laptop that used satellite to send texts or email from our personal accounts. Its use was also dependent on our credit, and I preferred it over the phones due to its reliability. Received emails and texts could be stored, and to read them again and again was priceless for morale. Unless, that is, the message was to let a guy know he had been given the push by his girlfriend – a lot of frustrated 'Fuck!'s could be heard shouted from the direction of the device.

The most personal touch to Minden came in the courtyard. It was a large wooden cross, cut out and decorated by the Two Platoon youngsters, and dedicated to their fallen friend, Sniper Hunt.

'You hear about Jay?' I asked Johan.

We were alone in the back of a Warrior, our feet up, and helmets off, chilling as our truck provided overwatch for a patrol.

'His mum and dad got a letter from the brigade saying that they were sorry for the loss of their son.'

'What the fuck?'

'He's got the same surname as Hunt.' I shook my head. 'They fucked up. Scared the shit out of his family.'

Before Johan could respond, a burst of gunfire split the evening. The truck's rear doors were open, and the shots came by close enough for me to lift my head before dismissing them. I turned my attention back to the Bernard Cornwell book in my lap. Sharpe's war against Napoleon seemed a lot more interesting than my own against Terry.

'What's that smell?' Johan asked me, and I took a deep whiff of the air, finally recognizing decomposition. A dead bird had fallen into one of the hotter parts of the turret and was now cooking. Johan flung it out of the hatch, but some of the carcass had melded to the floor. In the distance, there was more gunfire.

'Let's get some air.'

We stepped out of the back of the truck. One Platoon's patrol were in dead ground to us. The same dead ground where the gunfire was increasing. Danny called down from the turret and confirmed it. 'One Platoon are in contact.'

I took hold of the headset that hung from the Warrior's intercom system, pressing it to my ear.

'Fuck! Fucking contact! Fuck!' The panting voice came across the radio, accompanied by the snap and crackle of rifle fire.

It was followed instantly by a large explosion in the distance, Johan turning with a look of dread.

'Fuck. IED.'

Our worry faded as we finally saw a pillar of smoke from the south-east.

'Too far to be our guys,' I said, relieved.

We watched the distant contact for five minutes, enjoying the tracer that bounced into the darkening skies, but the fight was beyond us and soon grew stale.

'I'm gonna finish my book,' I said, climbing back into the vehicle. Johan joined me, picking up a novel of his own, but his head was soon back out of the door.

'Smith's driving up here,' he said wearily, and sure enough, here came the sergeant major's Warrior, the man himself sticking out of the turret like Rommel.

I turned to Johan. 'Why the fuck's he bothered? Contact's in dead ground.'

But Smith addressed me before Johan got the chance. 'I saw you two out of the vehicle! Get back in there and keep the doors shut down!'

His Warrior lurched away, Johan spitting.

'I know when to get my fucking head down.' With an angry jab of the finger, he hit the button to close the rear door. Senses now cut off from the fight, I shouted up to Danny.

'What's happening?'

'OC wants us to push onto the reverse slope. He's fucking nuts!'

Pushing onto the reverse slope would mean driving into territory that couldn't be watched from Minden. If it couldn't be watched, there were IEDs.

'The contact's still in dead ground to us even if we do move forwards. Boss told him we're not moving.'

Johan and I smiled, sinking back into our seats and books, and thanking the heavens for our platoon commander.

A rare delivery of mail had arrived, but this day it was bittersweet. With the letters and parcels came newspapers, and they carried the stories of Hunt's death. His mother was on the offensive against the defence minister, demanding answers about our equipment and vehicles. Images of his torn body armour and ruined face flashed into my mind. I tried to quickly push them away.

Breezy was alongside me as I read the stories, and I tried to steal sideways looks to see how he was taking it. His face was impassive; I hoped mine was too. We both knew we were bullshitting with our indifference.

I put down the paper. Pointed out the story.

'Hard, seeing his mum.'

Breezy nodded.

'How you feeling about it?'

'Bit better after Friday night's contact. Got some aggression out. I don't know though. I can handle the shooting, but if I get blown up again . . .'

There wasn't much I could say to that. Breezy had already had his wagons hit twice on this tour, and he'd been smashed in Iraq on several occasions. The little things, like having a vehicle blown out from underneath your feet, are liable to get to you after a while.

'Well, I've got good news,' I said, trying to lighten the mood.

'Since the temperature's dropped, I've finally stopped having straw-coloured piss.'

'I'm proud of you, mate.'

'You hear Ricky's claiming two kills from Zoo's contact?'

We both laughed at that. Two Platoon had hit a contact the previous night, when Sniper Fullback had fired a warning shot at a dicker, a Taliban lookout, and had been answered by fire from an estimated eight to ten Taliban fighters.

'They had a fucking PKM, mate,' Fullback had told me. 'Good gunner, too. Bursts were controlled and accurate.'

'Couldn't have been that accurate if he missed you, you fat cunt. You get any kills?'

He laughed, a little embarrassed.

'Boys brassed up a few goats and a cow. How's Jake?'

I relayed the news I'd received from our company clerk, who had just visited the patrol base to take care of pay issues.

'Shook up. Baker says he speaks about it all the time. He wants to go home, but he doesn't want to let the boys down. Me and Danny told her to tell him to get home, and not to worry about us.'

'Fucking right, mate.' Fullback nodded in agreement. 'He got shot in the neck for fuck's sake. What more can they want?'

Another explosion ripped through the afternoon.

'That was bigger than the last one,' Toby said from our position at the back of the Warrior.

I looked at the dirty cloud blooming against a bright blue sky. 'They're all fucking big'.

'Well that one was bigger.'

I wasn't in the mood to argue. We were escorting the engineers, their task to blow the bombs our recent patrols had found, and to make sure that we hadn't missed any others.

'The IEDD team said that last one had an anti-lift device on it,' I told Toby, who wasn't too interested.

'I'm not trying to pick up any IEDs.'

'Yeah, well the ANA do.'

'Good. Let the cunts get blown up, then we wouldn't have to sit here all day.'

I couldn't argue with his logic, and so I looked down into the area where the engineers were working. The smoke was clearing now, revealing a narrow track that led to a concrete bridge over a steep-sided wadi. It was known as 'Greg's Bridge', named after one of our predecessors who had hit a large IED here, the explosion tearing the turret from the hull of his Warrior. Greg had died on the MERT, only to be brought back by the skill of the medical teams. He'd lost his spleen, but he'd live. The site of his strike was a series of overlapping craters now, impassable to anything but our tracked vehicles. The Taliban knew it was the only crossing point of that wadi east of the patrol base, and so it was constantly sown with armour-killing bombs.

Today, the engineers had blown four in an area the length of a tennis court, and half as wide. That was after clearing an anti-personnel IED on Route Pink – a 25kg charge on a snap peg trigger. Enough to wipe out a team of dismounts and send them home in a soup tin.

One of the engineers came to join me, rivers of sweat cascading down his face.

'There's water in the truck if you want some,' I offered. 'Think you got 'em all?'

'I reckon. You guys keeping overwatch on the place tonight?'

I shook my head.

'Just clearing for the sake of clearing I think, mate.'

'Bit daft then really, isn't it?' he asked, knowing I had about as much control over my life as he did over his. 'I mean, once we leave, they're just gonna plant them back up.'

I nodded. It seemed like every soldier in Afghanistan could figure this out, except those in command.

'They only replant because we got rid of the last ones.'

He shrugged.

'Vicious circle,' I offered, but decided that wasn't enough. 'It's shit.' What else could I say? And the engineer nodded, because there was no more to say.

'Hey, Gez,' Toby called from the Warrior, wearing a smile for the first time that day. I knew what that would mean before he said it. 'Mount up. We're going back in.'

And so, after a day of infantiers and engineers risking it all to find and clear the explosives, we left the choke point and its craters to the enemy. The next morning, the IEDs were back.

'They want to send us on a fucking night patrol?' Danny growled, as we sat in the Viper's Nest. 'He knows I fucking sleep at night, yeah?'

But the OC wanted a night patrol, and so we went.

The theory was sound. We had excellent night vision optics, after all, but the practicalities were different. Four men, operating in stripped-down equipment, could perhaps make an attempt at stealth. Sixteen men, weighed down with 30 to 50kg, were not going to be a graceful act on the rocky and uneven surfaces of Afghanistan.

They could probably hear us across the border as men stumbled and swore. As the patrol went on, and frustration grew, the volume and intensity of the curses grew with it. The Afghan night is a silent place, and we realized the futility of our endeavour within the first hundred metres. It would be impossible for us to look for IEDs at night, and so we had been sent across the fields. Fields dissected by ditches, and more ditches.

A young soldier known as Ming was the first to take a spectacular fall. We'd come to a wide ditch, and the leading men had jumped across. Ming was carrying the largest piece of ECM equipment, as cumbersome as it was heavy. He hesitated at the lip of the bank.

'Just jump,' prompted Danny. 'You'll be fine.'

And the stupid bastard believed him, leaving the ground like a bag of cement, and crashing face first into the bottom of the ditch. His groans were drowned out by the laughter of those of us who had been close enough to see the silhouette of his Icarus-like descent.

'Shut the fuck up,' Turkey hissed, between coughs of laughter.

Off to our right, the other half of the patrol was making similarly good progress. Ginger Williams was lead man, Toby behind him. When Ginger stepped over a narrow ditch, he neglected to tell Toby of its existence, and the ground took his leg like a snare.

'You fucking ginger bastard!' echoed across the countryside, and the laughter on our own side of the patrol began anew.

'I think maybe the patrol's been compromised,' Danny put in, affecting the air of an aggrieved professional.

'Fuck it,' Turkey agreed. 'Let's go to bed.'

9

The Treasure Hunt

'Watch your feet,' we'd say to each other, but this was no warning to avoid getting dog shit on your boots.

When civilian friends asked what I was doing in Afghanistan, they were surprised to learn that most of our time was spent looking for IEDs.

'Don't the *Hurt Locker* guys do that?'

They'd be referring to the bomb disposal teams, who did indeed perform a courageous job and found countless IEDs, but the numbers of these specialists were small, and so it was down to the infantry to clear their own routes on a daily basis. From what I saw with my own eyes, nine out of every ten IEDs discovered were by the young private soldiers and lance corporals of the rifle platoons.

We lived by a simple rule: if you couldn't constantly watch an area, then it hid IEDs. The Taliban knew where we lived, knew what tracks we'd be forced to take, and this gave them the ability to concentrate their most effective weapon in areas that we could not avoid. The greatest asset of an armoured infantry company is in its manoeuvrability, and the firepower that can come along with that, but by placing us in a ground-holding role in fixed positions, the higher ups had taken our greatest strength and turned it into our biggest weakness. Limited to a few tracks, we were hemmed in by IEDs, and any effort to use our wagons meant first having to orchestrate a break out from our own base.

There is a symptom of the human condition where we feel that we *must* use what we have, and so our armoured beasts would be rolled out onto tracks where the enemy had prepared for us. The strength of a Warrior's armour is from the tracks up, not below, and the flat hull meant that there was no dispersion of a blast, unlike newer machines like the Mastiff with their V-shaped hulls. The entirety of an explosion would transmit through a Warrior, lifting those within and slamming them against the metal of their steel coffin. More often than not, worst hit was the driver, like Sniper Hunt, who sat almost above the track on the front left-hand side, and who would therefore take the full blast wave of an enemy IED.

'Hearts and minds' was the second factor that truly doomed us to become governed by the Taliban and their bombs. On our tour we were forbidden from making new tracks through fields, or through compound walls, and this provided the enemy with a number of choke points that were guaranteed to yield explosive devices. The risk to our Warriors could be negated by sending troops ahead on foot to clear the vulnerable points, but if the Taliban were as savvy as the militias in Iraq, then they'd soon start deploying anti-personnel IEDs in these areas – and they did. IEDs that could wipe out a team. We knew this from experience, paid for in lives, and yet we were time and again ordered into such choke points, knowing that if the enemy were on their game, there could only be one winner. But for those balancing the books, maybe it was better to lose a team of dismounts than a Warrior, and better to lose a Warrior than upset the locals by creating new tracks through cornfields, for which they'd be compensated, regardless.

There was a set protocol for clearing tracks along which the vehicles would follow. Two troops, known as the hedgerow men, used their Vallon metal detectors to scan the outer edges of the tracks and looked for signs of command wires that could be used to detonate a device. While they were observing and sweeping the earth they also had to scan ahead of the patrol for danger, as the hedgerow men would be the first to walk into any ambush.

Behind them came the track men, two soldiers who swept directly ahead of the vehicle. They were followed by the team commander, whose job it was to ensure that the arc of each of the four individual metal detectors overlapped, leaving no part of the ground uncovered. The commander – a role I filled when we were using the Warriors and my GPMG was overshadowed by the truck's 30mm cannon – also watched the nearby fields and compounds for markers, or any other trace of an impending attack. Often, he was called forwards to confirm metal readings that the Vallon men had found.

During foot patrols, two men swept the track ahead and nobody strayed from the cleared path. That was the theory, but the practice was very different, and soldiers trusted their own instincts about where to place their feet or slump down during a rest. A veteran learned that Terry targeted areas where there was a high probability of a device being stepped on, such as a narrow alleyway between compounds, and did not usually waste time on the chance that somebody would hit a centimetre-wide snap peg trigger in a thousand-metre-square field.

Once a metal reading was found, the patrol stopped, the Vallon man sliding onto his belly, gently working away at the soil or sand to uncover the source. If a device was identified, command wanted as much of it exposed as possible. Photographs needed to be taken to brief the IEDD team, who would eventually arrive to destroy or recover the device. Eighteen-year-old infantrymen were touching bombs a foot from their faces, their only protection a pair of ballistic sunglasses. It was scant comfort to know that if they fucked up the uncovering of the device, they'd never know about it.

In summer, the churned up tracks were a fine sand, perfect for burying an IED in a matter of moments. In winter, the sand would turn to a muddy porridge, where it was harder for the Taliban to quickly emplace a device without leaving footprints, but the sometimes thigh-deep mud made our task of finding them all the harder, and more exhausting.

'Tiredness kills,' we are told by information boards on the British motorways, but taking a break was not an option often offered to soldiers, and fatigue was a powerful factor in the route clearances. When a man was fresh, he examined every reading from his metal detector with painstaking precision. After a few hours in the heat, or wading through mud, he was too tired to care. The motions of exposing a potential IED became faster, eventually disappearing altogether when the soldier, beyond exhaustion, simply began stamping on any metal readings he encountered. His teammates would not discourage him, because they too were at the same level of fatalistic fatigue, nothing on their minds except reaching their destination and collapsing into sleep.

Often, men reached this state of fatalism with the aid of their commanders. It was hard to remain calm knowing that you were fingertips away from a device that was put there to obliterate you, but the squawking of a radio in your ear, constantly telling you to hurry up, could be enough to push you over the edge and into a red rage, where you would simply get to your feet and tap dance on whatever was buried ahead of you. I lost count of the number of times I jumped onto what could have been the end of me, cursing my stupidity when the anger or fatigue faded. And yet, as often as not, I'd do the same thing the next day, and the next.

I fancied myself a student of military history, and I'd asked my platoon commander why our Warriors couldn't be equipped with flails, like those employed to clear minefields during the Second World War. These could detonate the IEDs, but a Warrior can withstand a blast in front of it. His best guess was that they'd tear up the tracks so much they'd become unusable to the locals. In the illogical war that we were fighting, the Boss's reason sounded like the most logical answer. I'm sure my own plan had a lot of flaws – not to mention that Terry was always quick to adapt – but it seemed better than driving on top of the fuckers, or hoping to find them with a metal detector we had barely touched in training.

Tracks were not the only place where IEDs were to be feared. Compound walls were nothing but stacked dirt themselves, perfect for concealing devices with the aim of taking out foot patrols. Trees, too, had to be watched in the green zone, as claymore-like devices could be hidden among the fruit. The only limits to the placement of IEDs were the enemy's imagination. It is easy for Westerners to be disdainful of an Afghan's intelligence because of the conditions of their country, but proof of their ingenuity lay beneath our feet.

There were many ways to detonate such an IED. Electronic commands could be sent via radio frequencies, for which we carried jamming devices both on our backs and in the vehicles. Command wires negated this defence of ours, but were rare in our area of operations. We speculated that this was because they could not be as hastily laid without the operator remaining in close proximity, and the Taliban we were facing did not want to take such a risk.

And neither did they have to, because their most successful kind of IEDs were victim operated. These could come in a variety of shapes and sizes, but the principle was the same. The device exploded when the 'victim', either a man on foot or a vehicle, triggered the device. This could be via tripwire – and the Taliban did enjoy placing these above head height to be snagged by radio antennas – but the most common form of victim-operated IEDs used pressure pads.

The IED would be buried, and the trigger mechanism with it, the depth varying on the kind of pressure pad. Common for vehicles were two saw-blades, separated by small blocks of wood and wrapped in plastic. When the weight of a vehicle depressed the uppermost blade, a circuit was completed and the device would blow. For the Taliban, the downside of such mechanisms was that they gave off a high metal reading for our Vallons. Needless to say, they soon found ways to compensate with lower metal content devices, such as snap peg triggers.

The content of the devices, and their size, differed according to their purpose. For taking out a vehicle, the aim was to use as much explosive as possible, the size of the blast accounting for the damage. For dismounted soldiers, the device could be as small as a glass jar or paint can, filled with nails, metal filings, stones, or any other form or shrapnel that could tear through flesh, sever arteries, and otherwise maim.

The enemy watched us as we hunted for these buried killers. They watched, they studied, and they adapted. When they realized that the Afghan army were digging up the bombs that they found, they placed anti-lift devices that triggered when the weight was removed from above them. When they later saw British soldiers exposing bombs with fingertips and paint brushes, they equipped the devices with small solar panels that initiated the explosion when exposed to sunlight. Their skills were constantly evolving.

The treasure hunt was a deadly game, and one that we could never win. At best, we could hope to break even; find the treasure, destroy it, but know it would be replaced the next day. For the enemy, any result was a victory. They wanted to maim soldiers and smash vehicles, but even if the IED was found and disposed of, they had tied up the assets of an infantry company, a rare bomb disposal team, and the equally rare helicopters that were required to ferry them. Sometimes, an infantry platoon would have to keep overwatch on IEDs for days before the engineers could arrive, so in demand were they across Helmand, and these were days when soldiers could not be employed in taking the war to the enemy. All it cost the Taliban was a home-made bomb, using explosives and components that were in inexhaustible supply.

For all of the shooting, artillery fire missions, and air strikes, Helmand was an IED war. Every part of our lives, from the way that we patrolled to the time it took our mail to reach us, was a result of this simple, war-winning tactic.

It was Terry's treasure hunt, and we were doomed by our leaders to play to its bloody conclusion. Politics bound us to live by its rules, and we knew that winning was not an option – it was only the degree of the loss that mattered. We hated it, we questioned it, and yet we did it anyway.

Because that's what soldiers do.

10

Theirs Not to Reason Why

Our platoon was mounted in the Warriors, moving down the green zone track and into the wide wadi below. The intention of the patrol was to locate crossing points on the wadi's far bank. The dismounts would be left behind in the green zone after the Warriors returned to base, in an attempt to surprise anyone who planned on leaving us an IED for our next jaunt.

But Terry had already beat us to it, and it wasn't long before Lump Head discovered a large IED buried in the dirt – the Taliban were one step ahead, as usual. We congratulated the grinning brute on his find, Lump Head admitting with a giggle that he was 'shitting himself' at being so close to bloody ruin. I don't know if there was a more solid soldier in the company.

The trail was too narrow to avoid the device, and so we mounted up, the Boss making the decision to break track and cut across a cornfield in order to reach the gravel of the wadi.

We remained in the Warriors as we reached its far side, coming beneath the shadows of the crag, a well-known haunt of the Taliban. They seemed unwilling to take on the three armoured vehicles, perhaps expecting a trap, and it was easy enough for the Boss to reconnoitre his crossing points from the relative safety of the turret. He then decided that enough was enough, and we returned to the green zone, where the Warriors disgorged me and the other dismounts under the command of Turkey.

The Boss had come up with an idea, which was usually a bad thing for an officer to have, but we had full faith in our own leader.

We knew the location of an IED, and we knew that the Taliban would likely move it now that it had been discovered and marked for avoidance. And so, instead of watching the track for new bombs, we looked for a vantage point to watch the old, hoping to meet the owner of the device with a belt of 7.62mm greetings.

As we made our way through the greenery, I saw that the man ahead of me was struggling to keep up. It was Nacho, suffering under the weight of his pack. A pack that had an antenna protruding from it.

'Nacho, what's in your daysack?'

'ECM Blue,' he told me, referring to our heaviest and most cumbersome piece of electronic countermeasures equipment.

I looked down the line at the rest of the patrol, failing to spot the other sets of ECM that would cover the whole spectrum of radio frequencies and devices.

'Who told you to bring it?' I prodded.

'Well, I had it on the last patrol.' And so he had taken it upon himself to bring it again. Maybe he was being overly cautious for good reason – at the end of one patrol I discovered that he'd left his ECM turned off for the entire time that we'd been on the ground, and I'd gripped him by the throat to try and drive home the point that I didn't want us to die. Today, I didn't know whether to commend him for his initiative, or chastise him for not paying attention in the patrol briefing. In the end I settled for laughter.

We set up shop in the ruins of a compound. It didn't give us a great view onto the IED site, but it was the green zone, and visibility would always be blocked by the densely packed trees and shrubs unless you wanted to sit on top of your target.

I found myself a nice spot for the gimpy; a little shade from a crumbling wall, and a view out onto the wadi. I removed my helmet, as did the rest of the patrol. Turkey was good like that. He understood that our biggest threat at that moment was from the heat. We settled in to wait.

We didn't have to linger long for action, but it wasn't in the form that we'd expected.

A group of Taliban fighters had been spotted in the trees on the far side of the wadi, and we watched as twenty high explosive mortar rounds exploded on their heads. The detonations made a crumping sound, the flashes of their explosions a few metres above the ground; the shells had been rigged to trigger that way, to cause a steel rain of shrapnel.

I enjoyed the show, zooming in as far as possible with the digital camera that was always in the pocket of my daysack.

Ginger Pubes joined me at my vantage, an eager smile on his pale face. Whereas most of the platoon had bronzed from the sun, Ginger's only colour came in the form of red blotches of heat rash, the white-skinned goblin accused of moonbathing by his friends.

'Good this, innit?' he beamed, and we watched until the final shells had landed, their smoke and dust scattered by the wind.

'Missing Sad Act?' I asked, referring to his closest friend. It was Turkey who had named the pair after the Harry Enfield characters, and they were usually inseparable, but Sad Act had not been chosen as part of the standing patrol.

The pair were on their first tour and had come to us from Two Platoon while we were in Bastion. They'd gotten off to a bad start in Three. Sad Act's rifle had been inspected by an NCO who found that thick layers of dust and grime rendered it useless, but since that moment they had been mending their ways, and their mischievous nature made them impossible to dislike. They were coming on well, and we now considered them our own.

In the baking heat and boredom of the patrol base, it was the little things that made your day, and the exploits of Sad Act and Ginger Pubes made for good entertainment for the men who weren't their victims. These were usually the OC and the company 2 I/C, who often found that the seat of their trousers had been cut out when hung up to dry, or that prized possessions such as their mugs or berets ended at the top of the base's flagpole.

I moved to join Danny and others beneath the shade of a shrub. As we pushed the scoff into our mouths, I made sure that they were all aware of Nacho's ECM workout.

'That's nothing,' Danny began. 'The other day he was telling us about this really shit carnival he'd been to, with no rides. Sergeant Davies is from the same area as him, and asked where it was. Turns out, it wasn't a carnival at all. It was a fucking car boot sale!'

I laughed, turning to look at Nacho over my shoulder.

'You daft cunt,' I said, then noticed he wasn't eating. I asked what was wrong.

'Didn't bring any rations,' he shrugged.

'Water?'

Another shrug.

'You daft cunt,' Danny spoke, echoing my own words. 'You bring what you're not told to, and don't bring what you're supposed to. You fucking mong.' He added the final statement as he tossed a packet from his own rations at Nacho's head, followed by a water bottle that bounced off the younger man's body armour.

'Fucking mong,' Danny repeated, to offset the kind gesture.

Very little escaped the locals, and soon we were joined by two men around my own age. Their presence was a sure sign that the Taliban were not in the area, as to be seen talking to us was a one-way ticket to a beheading. Turkey led the conversation through our interpreter, Mohammed.

We talked about women, family, and the war. One of the men showed us where the Taliban had whipped his feet for clearing the dense greenery. Turkey asked why, and Mohammed provided the answer.

'They want it for cover. For attacks. But it's no good for these men. They need to clear, for farm. And if no clear, there is too much snakes.'

The mention of snakes put us more on edge than when we thought the enemy had been lurking.

The other local man began to talk, and Mohammed kept up his commentary.

'He said that if you shave, the Taliban will cut off your head.'

The patrol was obviously a dud, but at least Turkey gained some local gossip; there were Taliban in the villages south and west of us.

This was not news, but every small piece of information went towards building the bigger picture. After a couple of hours in the greenery we returned to Minden, where I sought out Jason at the mortar line.

'Come and watch this,' he told me, and I followed him to the Cortez Portakabin. They had footage of the mortar strike, and I was amazed at the powerful zoom of the cameras. We watched, smiling, as we saw the four Taliban fighters get the good news. One had made a crawling bid for freedom, taking refuge in a bush, an airburst shell shredding the ground a few seconds later.

Later that evening, The Firm were in the Viper's Nest when the Boss came to join us.

'What's up, Big Nose?' Danny greeted him cheerfully.

The Boss ignored the jibe, helping himself to a seat on Danny's cot bed. He was pissed off, and he knew that we were the people to vent to.

'I just got a bollocking for driving through that cornfield.'

'What?' we asked, perplexed.

'Well, not a bollocking, but I was told that I should have cut the patrol short at that point, rather than flattening the guy's crops.'

'Don't they get compensated for that?' I asked.

'Yeah, but they're trying to limit it as much as possible. They say it's not an issue of money, but they just don't want to aggravate the locals.'

I couldn't believe what I was hearing. 'Well if the locals told us where the fucking IEDs were, then we wouldn't need to go through their fucking fields.'

The Boss shrugged. Danny picked up the baton.

'So basically, all they need to do is plant one IED on each track, and we're totally contained at the patrol base?'

'Yep,' the Boss replied, having come to the same conclusion, and with the same disgust.

'Well, we may as well go home then,' Danny finished. 'You know, as long as we don't damage any crops on our way out.'

The next day the Boss led a vehicle-mounted patrol. His Warrior hit an IED, the destroyed engine block mercifully absorbing the blast, Danny and the others inside escaping without injury.

Someone had forgotten to tell the Taliban that we were all friends.

Morale arrived in the form of a resupply convoy, and a shipping container half filled with mail. Sergeant Davies topped the parcel count with twenty-two, and these he handed out among the platoon. They'd been sent by primary school children in his wife's class, each packet of biscuits and toothpaste accompanied by a note to their heroes.

'Little fuckers,' Danny said, clearly touched, and unhappy to be outside of his bitter comfort zone, 'their spelling is shit.'

We were happy to receive the gifts, but it truly was the thought that meant more to us. The Afghan heat did wonders to limit an appetite and, coupled with the packages that our own families had sent, we had an abundance of confectionary that would only fall prey to the mice if we held on to it. Danny and I stuffed the pockets of our combat trousers, and headed to the burn pit.

There, every day without fail, would be a gaggle of children hoping to be given the scraps of food that would otherwise be burned with our shit. They saw us coming, and so began the familiar chorus.

'Chocolate! Biscuit!' they shouted, pronouncing it chock-oh-late and bis-queet.

We threw some treats across the wire, withholding the remainder until the bigger kids shared what they had with the smaller, some barely older than toddlers. Our pockets finally empty, the kids with their hands full looked disappointed that there wasn't more.

'No bloody pleasing some people,' Danny grumbled as he walked back inside, but I knew that he'd enjoyed the brief moment as much as I had. There was a reason that the children were there every day, and that was because soldiers would come out like we had, every day.

•

The next morning our platoon set out to patrol the local village to the north. This kind of outing was known as a reassurance patrol, but I failed to see what was reassuring about a group of heavily armed strangers appearing with no warning in your garden.

As usual, we expected no trouble there, a feeling that was further confirmed by the troop of children who followed in our wake, as if the Pied Piper had exchanged his flute for a rifle.

After an hour of aimless wandering in the sun, we stopped to rest in the shade of a compound wall. I was at the rear of the patrol, Sergeant Davies and Toby with me. One of the NCOs had an abundance of candy from his wife's pupils, and he handed out a lollipop to a young girl, grinning as she licked it.

'Yeah, you like that, don't you? You like how that tastes. Oh yeah.'

Toby and I laughed at the sick words, but the girl had her own sense of dark humour. A naked child, no older than three, was with her, and now she held the kid's penis, making pissing noises as she aimed it towards us.

'Fucking hell,' Toby muttered. 'The fuck's wrong with these people?'

I had a bayonet on the front of my body armour, and could see a teenager taking a keen interest in it. The teen was a boy, of course, all girls of that age locked away by their families. Eventually he made a grab for the weapon, purely out of mischief, but I was ready for the move, and chased him along the alleyway with the blade in my hand. We stopped, laughing, and I tried to get him to pronounce the word.

'Bayonet,' he finally managed, and so I tried a sentence on him.

'You're a shithead,' I told him, the boy repeating the words several times, and to my satisfaction. I pointed him in the direction of Sergeant Davies, the kid understanding my intention.

'You're a shithead,' he told the big man, who laughed.

We prepared to move on, but the boy now wanted to rap his knuckles with Davies, who obliged him, then gestured that the kid should do the same with me. He took a huge swing, bringing his knuckles hard down onto my own, not realizing that they were protected by the Kevlar in my gloves. He tried to hide the pain, but rapidly disappeared holding onto what would soon be a bruised hand. Davies' laughter began anew.

Halfway through the patrol, six of us detached ourselves from the platoon and made our way along a narrow footpath to the high ground of the green zone. We were to lurk there, paying particular attention to a known Taliban haunt named the Block House, which sat alongside an entrance to the west side of the wadi.

Sergeant Davies commanded the group, with Jay and Lump Head providing the Javelin team. I had the gimpy, Ginger Pubes the LMG. Mohammed the terp was the final member. It was a happy little troupe.

We found our vantage at the edge of a cornfield, taking up positions in a dirt ditch that was shaded by a large tree. We could see the Block House clearly, and hoped that we could identify something that would justify us calling in a fire mission (artillery or mortars) or an air strike.

We hadn't been in position long when the echo of exploding mortar rounds came to us, distorted by the greenery. Davies listened in to the radio, then explained that the MFC at Zulu had spotted some armed fighters in the open and had called in the high explosives.

'They're fucking idiots,' Jay began, meaning the fighters who by now were probably dead, or dying. 'You'd think they'd figure out that we can't mortar the compounds. Standing around the green zone with a gat is just asking for it.'

Mohammed was listening to his ICOM scanner, which was buzzing with chatter about the mortars, but the talk was limited to giving orders to keep a low profile and gave no details on casualties.

'If they're not reporting they're under attack, then maybe they're dead?' I suggested.

'Or they're not high enough up the ranks to have a radio,' Davies replied.

The Block House appeared quiet, as was the green zone in which we'd gone to ground, and so we took turns to nap in the pleasant shade, enjoying the cool breeze that blew up from the wadi.

We whiled away the afternoon in that fashion, the only interruption coming when Mohammed translated a joyous message picked up by the ICOM scanner.

'This Taliban, he says he find a man who . . .' He lacked the words, and so he mimed cutting hair.

Several voices supplied the answer. 'Barber.'

'Yes,' Mo went on, as if he'd been testing us. 'A barber. He working for ISAF, and so this man tell his friend that he cut off his head.'

'Fucking animals,' Jay spat, offended by the actions of his unseen enemy. I saw it in a different light.

'So they cut your head off if you shave, and they cut the head off the guy who cuts your hair?' I asked, thinking of how I loathed the bullshit of the British Army. 'I'm changing sides.'

Jay overcame his revulsion of the Taliban to say that he'd join me.

We were given another hour of peace beneath the swaying branches before the inevitable call from company headquarters ordered us home.

'I'd almost forgotten about them,' Jay said, speaking for us all.

As I got to my feet, groaning at the weight of my pack, I took in the view of the grey gravel wadi, the fertile ground on its banks, and the mountains that grew out of the desert beyond. Sometimes, I thought to myself, it really was a lovely war.

I forgot about the headless barber, who doubtless would have disagreed.

Another hot day. More IEDs, six of them, in an eighty metre stretch of track. Half of our platoon pulled security as the experts denied devices that had waited maliciously beneath the dirt.

The last explosion crashed out across the countryside. 'Thank fuck,' someone said, desperate to get out from beneath the beating sun.

It wasn't to be.

'New orders,' Sergeant Davies informed us. He was our leader for the day. 'The OC and One Platoon are on their way back from DC.'

They'd gone there for our company commander to attend a patrols conference with the battle group head shed. Sergeant Davies let us know that they would be returning via the wide, gravelly wadi, and we were instructed to clear a route down to them from Minden, in order to facilitate a speedy return.

'And how the fuck are we supposed to do that with one team of dismounts and two Warriors?' Jay asked, of no one in particular.

He had a point. The track from the patrol base to the wadi was winding, surrounded by thick greenery on both sides. In other words, it was perfect for IEDs and ambushes. Lump Head and other soldiers had already found devices there. As we had learnt from bitter experience, a cleared route only stayed that way if you could sit atop of it, and observe every inch. With the track's twists and turns, and the dense vegetation, that would be impossible, and so Sergeant Davies made the best plan he could under the circumstances. He left Jay's Warrior, with myself included, halfway along the track, then took his own vehicle and Barma team to clear the remainder of the route – without eyes on it, the top section would need to be recleared once One Platoon and the OC arrived.

'Dai's going to bring his team back up and start clearing the top as soon as One Platoon have got good eyes on the wadi entrance,' Jay told me from the turret. It seemed as though Sergeant Davies was doing everything he could to help hasten the OC back to Minden.

To our relief in the static Warrior, the clearance by our comrades was completed without incident. There was always the chance that Terry might try and sneak up on us to hit our Warrior with an RPG, but it was the IEDs that we feared – give us small arms and RPGs all day, everyday. It's the unseen enemy that haunts you.

'Any news?' I asked up to the turret. The steel womb of the wagon was not a comfortable place to be in the heat, and I was looking forward to the moment where I could strip off my gear back in the Viper's Nest.

'One Platoon have eyes on the wadi entrance. Dai's moving up now to re-clear the track.'

I hoped that the boys would be careful. That it had been clear the first time meant nothing.

Sitting in the back of the Warrior, I didn't see what happened next. It was relayed to me first by Jay, and later by dozens of others. There seemed to be no doubt.

One Platoon's Warriors reached the track's entrance in the wadi. As it had been cleared by Sergeant Davies, whose group was now Barma'ing further up the track, One Platoon's wagons were able to head straight into the green zone, and out of the open wadi. They disappeared into the lush vegetation one after the other, until only the last Warrior remained on the gravel of the wadi.

This was the OC, following in the tracks of One Platoon's wagons.

The Taliban on the opposite side of the wadi must have been disappointed that the Warriors avoided the IEDs they'd planted in the gravel, but they didn't give up easily. Now that the mutual support of the platoon had been lost, and only a single armoured beast remained in the wadi, they let loose with an RPG.

Thanks to thick armour from the tracks up, an RPG against a Warrior is not a big deal. In this instance the RPG missed anyway, but that didn't mean that it didn't do damage. The OC's truck drove off the track and into the vegetation – the twisted bar-armour told the tale of how it had smashed into a large tree.

Clearly embarrassed, the OC came on the company radio net and publically chastised Sergeant Davies for 'leaving him in the lurch'. He went on to say that Davies should have been waiting in the wadi, to follow on as the final vehicle. I could not help thinking that RPGs seemed to be fine for Dai, who had been tasked with clearing and holding the green zone track. Something that we could not accomplish by sitting in the wadi, as the entire stretch would have needed clearing from scratch, during which time a backlog of wagons would have been queing up beneath the Taliban's favourite haunt of the crag. Not a clever idea.

Sergeant Davies was a good soldier. He didn't say much about his broadcasted reprimand. I don't suppose that he needed to, when we did it angrily on his behalf, the story spreading like wildfire through the company. If there was one person we felt was leaving us in the lurch, it certainly wasn't him.

Later that week we left the briefing room, heading for our kit. The patrol would leave in a half hour, yet another stumble around in the darkness, but that wasn't why we were sour faced.

At the conclusion of the brief, Turkey had reluctantly passed on a message from the head shed that we were to get a grip on our drills. This was following the negligent discharges (NDs) of weapons by two soldiers from the other platoons. As our own platoon was blame-free, we felt that the message affronted our pride.

I took my UBAC from its nail hanger on the wall, shouting out in pain as I pushed my hand into the sleeve, feeling a sting between the index and middle fingers of my right hand. I dropped the shirt to the floor, expecting to see a hornet buzz out, but instead it was a scorpion that revealed itself to be my assassin. Despite the effort we put into catching them, I was the first person in the company to fall victim to their venom, and so I immediately pictured the worst-case scenarios – perhaps an amputation or death. I rushed past Toby, trying to stop the toxin spreading by applying pressure to my wrist.

'Tell Turkey a scorpion's stung me!' I told him as I went by. 'I'm going to the medic!'

And so I did, and was horrified to find out that Emily's treatment began by consulting a book.

'You don't *know*?'

'Oh shut up, you baby. How big was it?'

'Huge,' I told her. In reality, it may have pushed three inches, and that with its tail stretched.

'That's good then,' she smiled. 'The smaller ones can't control their release, so they give off more venom.'

'I lied. It was tiny,' I admitted, watching her impatiently as she continued to study the pages. 'So what do we do?'

'Nothing,' was her final answer. 'Just try not to do anything that will increase your heart rate.'

At that moment, Turkey pushed his head inside of the med centre's door.

'Come on, you skiving fucker. We've got a patrol to go on.'

'I can't feel my arm, mate,' I told my platoon sergeant. 'And I can't close my hand. How am I supposed to shoot?'

'You'll figure it out. Come on, we need the numbers.'

'He's supposed to stay under a medic's supervision for twenty-four hours,' Emily told him.

'My heart bleeds purple piss.' Turkey smirked. 'There'll be a medic on the patrol. Let's go.'

So much for not raising my heart rate. I returned to gather my kit, where a laughing Toby was waiting for me.

'Toby! Toby!' he shouted in his best thespian. 'The scorpion got me! I can't go on patrol!'

'Fuck off.' I laughed. 'Did you at least avenge me?'

Toby pointed to the dirt, where the tiny scorpion had been flattened into the floor.

'Thanks, mate,' I said to my hero. 'Now can you help me get dressed?'

After an hour of stumbling and groping our way through the darkness, we stopped on a bare hillside. My arm was still numb, and I had to ask Toby for help once again as we settled into position on the hard stone.

We'd been ordered there to overlook a village to the south, hoping to surprise the Taliban at dawn. For one thing, it would be us who would be exposed by the rising sun, lying there in the open while the enemy was among the compounds. For another, we knew via the ICOM that the Taliban's dicking screen had spotted and reported us the moment we'd left the patrol base. Aside from the usual special forces raids, the twenty men of our platoon were the only ones on the ground in Helmand Province that night.

'Which means we're either on the same level as the SAS, or we're the only cunts stupid enough to do this shit,' Danny whispered angrily in the darkness. 'Have a guess which one.'

I simply grunted in acknowledgement. I didn't know who had planned the mission, or why we didn't turn back when it was clear we had been spotted, but I had my suspicions.

Turkey made his way down the line, informing us that there were locals sleeping in a small hut at the end of the slope.

'Do they know we're here?' Toby asked.

'Well they came to talk to us, so I'm guessing, yeah,' he answered before leaving.

A few minutes later, a hushed message came down the line of men. Nacho was close to us, where we could keep an eye on him, and he relayed the Chinese whisper.

'Convoy tractor.'

Danny's face was hidden in the darkness, and so I could only imagine that it was as confused-looking as my own.

'What?' he asked, an edge of scorn to the tone.

'Convoy tractor,' Nacho repeated, matter-of-factly.

'What the fuck is a . . .' Danny let the question trail away, and instead got to his feet, heading in search of Turkey. He was back quickly.

'Convoy tractor is it, you fucking mong?' he spat at Nacho under his breath, then turned to Toby and me. 'ICOM chatter!' he explained, and we laughed, aiming our own insults towards Nacho.

'How's your arm?' Toby asked me as our giggles died away.

'Still numb.'

'Wanna wank me off then? It wouldn't be gay if you can't feel it.'

I tried to stifle my laugh, then shifted the weight on my backside. The stones made for a harsh seat.

'Only six hours to go,' Danny said with sadistic satisfaction.

But Turkey would be our salvation. He sent up a few illumination rounds – apparently we'd seen someone approaching our position. We were lit up brilliantly. Unfortunately, as Turkey then explained over the radio to the OC, the patrol had now been compromised and we'd have to return to base.

The next morning, One Platoon took the OC to a shura – a meeting with the local tribal elders. When they returned, a shot rang out from inside of the base.

'Someone else having an ND,' Toby snorted, shaking his head at the lack of professionalism. 'Wonder who it was this time?'

It was the OC.

I was laughing as I leaned back against Jay's Warrior in the tank park. He was telling me a story from his time at Bastion, where he'd been recently sent with suspected appendicitis. It had turned out to be kidney stones, and Jay had fainted while taking a piss in the hospital, his urine-soaked body having to be dragged back to the ward by the nurses.

'So what do you think happens with the OC?' I then asked the man who was more familiar with the army's machinations than me. 'The whole patrol saw him ND.'

But Jay was just as stumped. 'I'm not sure. I've never heard of it happening before. Frodo and Evans got fined a month's pay, so it's only fair he gets the same. More really, 'cos he's an officer.'

Jay climbed up into the turret of his Warrior, joined there by Owens. Twelve of us, the Boss included, were taking two Warriors and a recovery vehicle to Musa Qala DC, where we would act as the battle group's quick reaction force. As we would be operating exclusively from the trucks, I had exchanged my GPMG for a rifle, and would be commanding the Barma team from out of the back of the Boss's wagon.

We were looking forward to the change of scenery, but first we had an obstacle to overcome. Route Pink, the dusty and winding track that connected Minden to DC, would need to be cleared by me and my team.

And my team included Nacho.

From my position at the centre of the track, trying to observe the

Above The Firm (minus Toby, who was on R&R) standing in a crater on OP Hill.
From left: me, Jay, Danny and Jake, aka Pinkmist.
Below The Boss – our platoon commander – in a Warrior. We were lucky to have him.
An experienced officer, and a great man with a biting sense of humour.

Left Checkpoint Zulu – a satellite for the larger patrol bases like Minden.

Below Like Zulu, Checkpoint Khabir was made up of half a dozen rooms. There was no electricity and the water from the well was undrinkable. We relied on Patrol Base Minden to supply both places.

Below My humble abode at Zulu. A construction of hessian and string I proudly named Chateaux Trente-Cinque (thirty-five – the last two digits of my army number, monsieur).

OPPOSITE PAGE
Top Me and Danny (rear) patrolling along the M4, a deep wadi passable by vehicle in only a handful of heavily IED'd places.

Bottom Me in a shit state after a summer patrol. Behind me is the orchard in which we lived at Zulu.

Top Me and my team looking for IEDs – I'm the one knee-deep in the track.
If we fucked this up it was game over and, even if we did find them, Terry would
just move or replace the bombs the next day.

Above left A partially uncovered IED with a snap peg trigger.

Above right Danny was the oldest of our group. When I first met him in
pre-deployment training I wanted to punch his face in, and the feeling was mutual,
but by the time we got to Afghan, we'd die for each other.

Right Jay and Jake, looking like members of a Mexican cartel. Pinkmist's shit tattoos put me off ink for life.

Below Toby and Jay on patrol. Toby was a career army man, on his fourth tour by the age of twenty-six. He was also responsible for naming The Firm.

Me and Danny in The Firm's room at Minden, which Jay christened the Viper's Nest. Anyone who entered, regardless of rank, would be in for some merciless piss-taking.

OPPOSITE PAGE

Top Between Zulu's fetid piss tube and the wash area was our beloved gym, made of spare parts from the Warriors.

Right The rear sangar at Zulu. I spent many, many hours here, a lot of them with Danny. I fired the first shots of my tour from this vantage point, before getting a fucking stoppage. Seeing Terry escape still haunts me.

Below The Warrior. Not invulnerable to Terry, but God help the enemy if our gunners smashed him with the 30mm cannon.

Every day, a gaggle of children would gather outside the wire of Minden, chanting their familiar chorus: 'Chock-oh-late! Bis-queet!' Even a grumpy fucker like Danny had a soft spot for these kids.

I'm about to give this kid an extra-strong mint. He's in for a shock. You can see here how heavy my patrol kit is, roughly the weight of a small man.

Swapping headgear with one of my 'Smoke and a pancake' fan-club kids. I think of them a lot. They probably fucking hate us now, and who can blame them? Their childhood was spent begging for food, escaping death, and carrying away the enemy dead.

sweep of four Vallons and scanning ahead for danger, my eye was constantly drawn back to the dishevelled youth. He was the left hedgerow man, the position where he could do the least damage, and was swinging his metal detector as if it were a cow's tail brushing away flies.

'Nacho! *Nacho!* Keep that fucking Vallon head flat and lower,' I shouted again. The position of the Vallon's handle and the pattern of its movement placed a strain on the user's forearm and wrist, and Nacho was getting tired. We hadn't even left sight of Minden.

He stopped.

'Well?' I barked.

'I've got a reading,' he replied in his monotone.

'So fucking tell us and clear it,' I growled, lowering myself to the dirt, but seeing Nacho unmoving.

'For fuck's sake,' I chewed out the words as I picked myself up and joined the consummate professional. 'What the fuck are you doing?'

Nacho looked back at me blankly from beneath his bushy eyebrows, his left hand groping blindly about his body armour. 'I can't find my brush,' he finally mumbled.

'You mean you fucking left it in Minden,' I hissed, barely keeping a lid on my temper. For a Barma team, a paintbrush was as important as a soldier's rifle.

'Get out of my fucking way.'

I pushed him backwards, taking a knee, and quickly confirmed the metal reading myself; scrap. Time to move on. I pushed my brush into the loops of his body armour.

'Don't lose it, you cunt.'

I took up my position at the rear of the team.

We'd barely covered another twenty metres when Nacho stopped again. This time, he did go onto his belly.

I looked around the area, assessing. It was an unlikely spot for an IED, too exposed for the man who would have to lay it, but you could never be too careful. After five minutes of waiting, I called forwards to Nacho to report. He said nothing back, and with a stream of curses, I once again left my position in the formation.

Nacho was trying to brush away baked dirt with the brush. At the rate he was clearing, we would see out the rest of our army careers in that spot.

'Get up,' I told him, planning on finishing the drill myself. 'You need to use your bayonet when it's hard like this.'

His silence told me all I needed to know.

'You don't have your bayonet, do you?'

I didn't give him time to reply, pulling my punch just enough to limit the blow to the side of his helmet.

'Get in the fucking truck, you cunt!' I screamed into his face, grabbing the Vallon from his limp hand and shoving him back towards the vehicle.

The Boss was watching from his turret, and didn't need to have it explained. He gave me the thumbs up, and I stamped on the area that had caused the metal reading, too enraged to care about what was under my feet.

We made quick progress after that. I had enough faith in the other team members to trust them to overlap their sweep, and so I remained in Nacho's vacated position. Finally, we came to an Afghan army patrol base and remounted our Warriors. We'd be driven the rest of the way.

As I climbed on board, I looked at the trash-strewn compound of the ANA, and remembered a story told to us by the men whom we had relieved at the beginning of the tour. A dead Taliban commander had been brought here, before being hitched to the back of a pick-up truck and dragged the rest of the way to Musa Qala. By the time he had arrived there, and was posed for the obligatory 'corpse smoking cigarette' photos, half of the man had been spread in the dirt and gravel of the town's tracks. Like the enemy, it seemed as though our allies were also free to wage a war without rules.

After gulping back water, my eyes came to rest on the sulking Nacho and I immediately felt regret for being violent towards him. He was a gormless idiot, but he was a nice kid. Fate had been cruel in making him a soldier. If only he'd landed someplace he could do no harm.

'Oi, Nacho. Look at me.'

He did, with the same blank face as always.

'I'm only getting angry with you because I don't want you to die, or go home to your family with your fucking arms and legs missing, OK? You're a good lad, but you need to switch the fuck on.'

He nodded acceptance, but I knew that my words were only to ease my own conscience. Nacho was no more capable of becoming a good soldier than Danny was capable of becoming the next Mother Teresa.

We arrived in DC, and were accommodated in two green canvas tents. It was a welcome change of pace after our time in the patrol base. Our meals came on paper plates from a cookhouse, our water from fridges, and we were able to make calls home from hardwired lines. Toby even found a TV that was showing rugby on the British Forces network.

We were a reaction force, but there didn't seem to be anything for us to react to, and so we enjoyed the chance to lounge about. It was on our second night that we came under assault – this time from the skies. It was no mortar attack, but a Chinook helicopter.

We were sitting on our cot beds, shooting the shit, when we heard the sound of the whocka's blades in the distance. DC's HLS was on top of a hill, and the helis often made their approach from the direction above our tents, coming in low, and so at first we were not surprised at how loud the sound of blades was becoming.

Then, in an instant, a rush of sparks blew through our tent from the burn pit on the opposite side of the Hesco wall. We hardly had a chance to curse before the downdraft snapped the two-inch diameter poles of our tent and the canvas collapsed on top of us.

We lay smothered in the darkness, helpless with surprise and laughter. My head throbbed from where a pole had hit me.

After crawling our way out into the night we surveyed the

damage. One of our tents had pancaked flat. The other had been squashed vertically, and was now the width of a man.

'The fucking mongs must have thought the burn pit was the HLS,' Jay deduced, and we didn't argue with him. Perhaps, through the night vision of the pilot's goggles, they had misinterpreted the glow of the fire for the infrared strobe that should guide them in. If they hadn't blown off the landing at the final moments, some of us wouldn't be around to laugh.

The Boss left to report the incident to the base's commander, while we rescued our belongings and went in search of a new home.

The next day, the Boss was called to the operations room. When he returned, he told us that the Joint Helicopter Squadron had denied any involvement in the incident.

'Must be a rogue Chinook on the loose,' he said with scathing sarcasm.

Later that day, the Boss was called away again. This time he was not smiling when he returned.

Two Platoon had hit an IED.

The only details we had at this point was that there was a CAT B and a CAT A casualty. The CAT A label worried us.

'Who are the casualties?' We asked, but there was no way to know. We all thought of our friends in that platoon and secretly wished that it wasn't them who had been fucked up.

We got our answer the next morning. As soon as we saw that it was the colonel and regimental sergeant major of the battle group approaching, we knew that the news would be worse than we'd expected.

'I'm sorry to tell you that Private Prosser died in the hospital this morning,' the CO told us with genuine grief.

Nacho and Ming paled as they absorbed the news. They had both come to us from Two Platoon and were good friends with Prosser. *Had been* good friends with Prosser.

'You want to talk, lads?' I asked them. Neither did, at least not to me.

In the cookhouse that evening, I was given the first clue that the tour was affecting me more than I realized.

I was at the fold-out wooden table with Jay, Danny, and Toby, enjoying the food and talking about the day's events. Jay said something about Hunt and Prosser – the actual words instantly lost to me in the flash of anger that gripped my body – and all I wanted to do was to be away from that table.

'You fucking prick,' I snarled at him as I surged to my feet, pushing back on the flimsy table, which shot towards Jay opposite, spilling juice into his lap. Toby, thinking I was about to assault our friend, threw himself across the bench and between us.

For a second the busy cookhouse was silent except for the pounding of blood in my ears, and then the other soldiers resumed their meals. In a battle group of tired nerves and grated patience, this wasn't anything they hadn't seen before.

'Just sit down, Gez,' Danny implored me, tugging at my sleeve, and I eventually did.

We sat in silence, Jay dabbing tissues onto his soaked lap. Nobody wanted to be the next to speak.

Toby saved us, bursting into laughter and spitting a mouthful of chicken onto his plate.

'You looked like Hacksaw Jim Duggan!' he blurted, and mimed the stomping gait of the professional wrestler from our childhoods. It was the intervention we needed, and I joined Toby in laughing. Apologies passed around the table. All was forgiven.

That night, the discussion in our tent turned to politics, Afghanistan, and its future. The critique of UK and NATO policy was long and hotly debated, but the conclusion was simple.

'This place is a fucking shithole,' Jay summarized, 'and it's not worth one of our boys dying for.'

A memorial service was held for our comrade. The troops of the base were gathered in their cleanest combats, with berets and regimental belts, the red and white hackles of the Fusiliers standing tall. We had deployed from Minden with the very minimum, and so we were bare headed, our combats worn and oil stained.

There were the usual prayers, and then the Fusilier's CO gave a reading. Again, I noticed how he was clearly moved by the loss of a young soldier under his command. A soldier he had never met. The Boss spoke briefly about Prosser's life – how much of a life can you have when it's cut short at twenty-one? – and then it was the turn of Ming and Nacho to read their eulogies.

They spoke well, Nacho surprising us all. We had spent all day trying to make him presentable, but he still looked as though he'd washed in a ditch, an irrepressible darkness to his skin. The strangers in the ranks listened patiently, as we had done during the vigils at Bastion.

The Lord's Prayer was recited, followed by The Exhortation. 'We will remember them,' we echoed. How could we not?

The bugler struck up the last post. Perhaps his throat was dry from the heat, or worn out by one vigil too many. The weakness of his notes was a mirror to our own failing mission.

I fixed my eyes on a stark mountainside in the distance, its sheer flanks now peach in the dying sunlight. It was known as Mount Doom, its summit visible from across the battle group's area of operations. If Sauron's eye was open there, then surely the evil entity would be enjoying the futile struggles that were being played out beneath its gaze.

The parade was dismissed. Toby and I sought out Nacho.

'You did well, mate,' we told him.

There were no tears in his eyes, only confusion. Two friends of his gone on this tour, their broken bodies bundled onto Chinooks, never to be seen again. A vigil was to be their comrades' closure.

'You did him proud,' we said on Prosser's behalf. 'Come on. We'll help you with your kit.'

We had been recalled to Minden.

•

Back at the company home, we were told how Prosser had come to lose his life.

He had been driving a Warrior along the green zone track to the wadi. The same track where Lump Head had found an IED, and the Boss had been berated for making his own way through the fields. For whatever reason, the Barma team had missed the device during their clearance and the large charge had detonated directly beneath the young driver.

Led by the gunner, Evans, his comrades had stabilized his external injuries of protruding breaks and deep lacerations, but like Sniper Hunt it was the internal damage to his brain that killed him.

The second casualty was a member of the Barma team, hit square in the back by a road wheel thrown outwards by the blast. His pack and body armour had saved him from paralysis.

I'd not known Prosser well, but I'd liked the friendly young man who was always smiling. In the last four months, four good men that I knew were dead, in a cause that was by the day showing itself to be unworthy of their sacrifice. This is not the clarity of hindsight; I wrote in my journal that night that I hated seeing these boys dying for a lost cause. But at least I lived to see my regret for the mission I had once thought laudable. Prosser did not.

The company had waited for our small contingent to return from DC before holding its own service for the fallen soldier, a touch that I thought reflected well on the nature of our hierarchy. They may not have been suited to be leaders in war, but they were good men.

The service was held in the courtyard of Minden, its order now well established. We were without a bugler, the notes replaced instead by muted sobbing from among the ranks. Our Fijians sang a hymn, friends confiding to each other later that the dams of their grief had almost burst at that point.

As the sergeant major walked to the front of the parade to speak, I caught Danny's eye. We remembered his talk following Sniper Hunt's CASEVAC. What drivel would the man speak this time?

But he kept his words simple, if repeated, going over the same sentiments a half dozen times. We had to remain professional; there would be a chance for payback on an operation tomorrow. The parade was dismissed, and the ranks seeped back to their nooks and crannies throughout the patrol base.

In the courtyard, a few young soldiers placed a second cross beside Hunt's.

11

Omelette

We had been recalled from DC to join the remainder of the company in a clearance operation, and this would be carried out with the Afghan army elements that were based in our area of operations (AO). Embedded with these indigenous troops were the British members of the operational mentoring and liaison team, better known as the OMLT, which we pronounced 'Omelette.' This small section of troops came from the Yorkshire Regiment, and among their number was a petite female medic.

Danny turned to me with a predatory grin. 'I'd like to embed myself in her.'

We were sitting at the back of our Warrior, still in the tank park of Minden. H-hour had come and gone, but an oversight had meant that the secure radios of the OMLT did not have the same fill – encrypted frequencies – as our own company's, and now we waited as our signallers rushed about with their gadgets.

'This is wank,' Danny grumbled, observing the mass of Afghan and British troops who were milling in the dust, waiting for the order to depart. 'Terry's dickers are gonna be seeing this and know there's an op on. We're not gonna find a fucking thing.'

'Except IEDs,' I added, stating the obvious.

'Well, yeah.'

When the order to leave eventually came, one of our platoon's Warriors promptly broke down as soon as it had pulled out of the gate. This was Jay's truck, and we cursed him as a lucky bastard to be left out of the operation.

For the day's activities, I would be a Vallon man in the Boss's wagon, under the command of a corporal named Rabbit, a well-liked career soldier who we ribbed mercilessly over his habit of borrowing items that he would 'forget' to give back. Rolling out of Minden, our Warriors then passed through Greg's Bridge, the area made safe by the engineers, and out into the desert beyond. We soon came to a track between compounds, the Boss wanting the area cleared, and the order coming down from Rabbit that we needed to secure the vulnerable point.

'Isolate the VP,' he told Nacho, to be met by the perennial blank stare. Good start. I took over for him and completed the drill myself, which involved boxing around the vulnerable point to search for command wires. Once this was done, the track itself could be cleared.

Our next task was to clear an emergency helicopter landing site, which could be used in the event of any casualties being sustained. This required every inch of the designated area to be cleared, as an IED strike on a helicopter would be devastating. Once again, Nacho was less than helpful, wandering aimlessly about the desert. I lost patience, launching a rock that he managed to duck – surprisingly, he did possess reactions after all.

We finally came to our assigned position, forming part of a cordon around a scattering of compounds and trees that sat below a long, bare ridge, on which we could now see the Warriors of another platoon. Beneath them, the troops of the Afghan army began to enter into what looked like a deserted parish.

Sniper Palin climbed up onto the back decks of our truck and used his daysack as a rest for his rifle.

'See anything?' I asked him.

'Just the ANA sitting around,' he told me, our allies seemingly uninterested in taking the war to the enemy.

I sat on the step of the Warrior's back door where I was joined by our interpreter for the day, Mohammed.

'So what do you think, Mo?' I asked him, waving a hand in the direction of the village, which was not a place we'd visited often.

'Waste of time. There are no Taliban. Everyone know we are

coming,' he told me, referring also to the locals, their absence from view confirming they had cleared out prior to our deliberately staged operation – good sense, as the Afghan army had itchy trigger fingers.

And there was little surprise that they did know what was coming. Having seen the Soviet occupation, a civil war, and then our own operations, the locals knew war inside out. They had seen our patrols sent out to recce routes. They had seen our engineers clearing paths through the IEDs. They had seen through the plan, and likely sneered at its amateurism.

'We need more helicopters,' I told him, thinking that was the only way we could overcome the obstacles of the IEDs and surprise the enemy.

'Yes,' he agreed simply.

'How's it going, Boss?' I shouted up to the turret.

'Fucking ANA are trying to bluff their way out,' he told me, listening to the messages over his headset. 'They told the Omelette that they'd been recalled to their patrol base, but the Omelette checked with DC, and they've had no orders at all, the bluffing fuckers.'

We could only shake our heads at that. If the Afghan army couldn't be fucked to fight for its own country, then what were we doing there on that ridge?

I settled in to discuss this, and other things, with Mo. We talked about family. He couldn't understand why British couples divorced so often. He was himself engaged to a cousin in Kabul.

'Have you ever met her?' I asked him.

'A few times, when we were children.'

A couple of weeks earlier, an Afghan man had visited our patrol base, wanting medicine for his wife's painful headaches. When Emily had quizzed him on when she suffered such attacks, the man's reply could have been describing the colour of the sky: 'When I hit her,' he'd said.

I asked Mo if he would do the same. He considered it, but shook his head, as if trusting it would not be necessary. 'No. I hope to love her.'

Changing the subject, I told him about the countries I'd visited. Mo had never left Afghanistan. There was a high chance that the people in the village before us had never ventured further than the nearest town of Musa Qala. The idea of a government in Kabul was as alien to them as if their president had been based on the moon.

The ANA's 'search' of the village finished a couple of hours later with no tangible results, and our cordon collapsed, heading back for Minden. On the way, Turkey's wagon broke down, and I stood outside my own truck, watching, as the new REME crew began the recovery.

Gunfire echoed from the opposite side of the ridge, separating the unflinching veterans from the fresh faces, the green soldiers scuttling for cover behind the armour of the Warrior. They coloured as the old hands laughed at their skittishness.

The rifle fire was soon followed by the sound of an RPG's detonation. Word quickly came over the radio that it was an ND by an Afghan soldier and had caused a CAT B casualty.

'So it's one nil to the Taliban today,' Danny snorted when we returned to base. 'And they didn't even have to turn up.'

12

Kill TV

Following the OC's ND, the toilet graffiti had reached a fever pitch. Most highly commended was a well-drawn caricature, with a loud 'BANG!' emanating from the rifle and a simple 'Oops' in a speech bubble. There was much discussion as to the identity of the artist.

'It was me,' giggled our Boss, confessing to The Firm. No one could resist.

'Now tell me who did the one of me,' he pressed, referring to a caricature with a huge beaked nose that dominated one of the toilet's walls.

'Sad Act and Ginger Pubes,' Danny said, shifting the blame for his own work onto the two most believable culprits.

The Boss slammed his hand down, 'I fucking knew it!', then left to find and punish the scapegoats.

Whether under orders from the OC or not, Smith decided that it was time to remove the graffiti, and decreed that the interior of the toilets would be painted.

In white.

Either there was an epidemic of dysentery in camp when the paint had dried, or men could simply not resist the carte blanche.

That wasn't Smith's only home improvement of the week. There was ample paint left over following the provision of the fresh toilet canvases, and Smith ordered the mud walls of the gym painted to 'brighten the place up'. This put the gym off limits until the decorating was completed. Within a few days the white was a depressing shade of dirty brown dust.

The courtyard of Minden had been a popular place for the troops to lounge and sunbathe, but now Smith decided that it would be covered with a huge parachute.

We weren't happy about losing our suntrap, but during its erection Blake put a smile on our face when the wobbly ladder disappeared from beneath his feet and he was left wriggling from the parachute's top. We were too helpless with laughter to effect a rescue and he finally sprawled in the dirt.

Even a broken clock tells the correct time twice a day, and Smith sometimes came up with a good idea. He'd discovered that there was a big water bladder in storage at the base, and this he filled with water from the well to make a paddling pool. He even took it well when the Fijians picked him up and threw him in fully clothed. I took a dip with Toby and Ryder – a respected private with several tours under his belt – spending a relaxing hour in the muddy brown waters.

Smith had his hobbies, and we had ours. Like everything in the army, a soldier's pastimes were given operation names, the three most popular being Op Head Down, Op Bronze, and Op Massive. These were sleeping, sunbathing, and lifting weights respectively.

Minden's gym was growing throughout the tour, as each trip to DC gave us the chance to liberate more equipment. Smith was also the perfect combination of bored and gym obsessed, and oversaw the construction of benches and pulleys. On the occasions that I found myself alone with him 'in the gym' I enjoyed our conversations regarding our mutual hobby. Not for the first time, I wished that he was not our sergeant major, as I liked the man who was behind the rank.

Now that Smith had covered the courtyard, those seeking sun were forced onto the rooftops. At times these resembled a seal colony; if seals were stripped to their boxer shorts and caked in baby oil, a prized commodity that must be brought back by all soldiers returning from R&R.

It was these hobbies that kept a soldier sane during the tour, and when downtime was taken away from a man on operations, it always lead to resentment and sometimes fireworks. We were in need of some relief, and thankfully we were provided this during a patrol one afternoon.

The air was hot and stiff as we moved in silent formation along a narrow dyke, the ditches either side of us ankle deep with water. I was bringing up the rear of the patrol with Toby, covering our backs for possible attack, when in front the big-man medic Edwards lost his footing and fell face first into the water. The chubby soldier struggled to lift himself and thrashed about like a salmon, his face submerged. He probably would have drowned if Sergeant Davies hadn't rescued him, Toby and I having to lie down because we were so heavily racked with laughter.

About half an hour later, and with the justifiably vengeful eyes of the medic upon us, I sat with Toby in a ditch as the patrol halted for a water break.

Movement caught my eye, and I saw a kid emerge from behind a compound, pushing a motorbike out onto the track that we had just patrolled in on. He left the bike in position and shot off, throwing nervous looks over his shoulder. At that same moment, all the other civilians began to slip away into compounds, and that 'here we go' feeling began to rise from my stomach.

I asked Toby for his rifle, wanting to use its scope, and saw that there were bags strapped to the bike. I passed the information up to the Boss, and we used another track to leave the area – no enemy contact harried us on our way. A few days later, we received intelligence that a number of motorbikes had been rigged with IEDs, and I felt smug knowing that we had not fallen for that ruse. After a couple of months in Afghanistan, we were getting wise to Terry's tricks.

We had an hour before going on patrol, so I picked up my book and was about to leave the Viper's Nest to go and read in the sunshine.

'You're always doing that,' Danny sneered, and I stopped at the threshold.

'What?'

'Reading books, or sending emails.'

'So what do you want me to do?' I shot back, irritated by my friend.

An evil grin crept over his face. 'Sit on your bed and cry.'

I was still laughing when we left the patrol base's gate, but it didn't stay on my face for long. The heat had crept back in to the low forties, and we did the first half hour of the patrol without stopping. When we did finally halt, I had to ask Toby to lift the gimpy's sling over my head, my arms having gone numb from the weight of the equipment pulling down.

At that rest, we were missing four men. They'd been dropped onto a lurk to watch Greg's Bridge in an attempt to catch the IED layers that seemed so busy there, but like the other lurks we had conducted we didn't hold out much hope for their success. The team were lying up in a cornfield, but rather than allowing the patrol to cut across it and lose the men inside and out of view, we had been ordered to leave the crops untouched, and the four men had detached themselves and moved into the greenery as we patrolled nearby – we felt sure the action would have been seen and noted by our enemy.

'No fucking way they don't get seen,' Toby agreed with me, knowing how well we were dicked upon leaving the base.

The small group was made up of Danny, Fullback, Ratty, and Owens, whose tiny spectacles and beaked nose reminded us of the Nazi caricatures we had seen in history books, and so had earned him the nickname of The Jew. He was a fellow machine-gunner and a top bloke, and I was happy enough for him to be the one taking a gimpy into the cornfield. Among the crops the temperature would be a punishing 50°C.

The rest of the patrol eventually returned to base, and I found a copy of the *Sun* newspaper that had been delivered to us, now a couple of weeks out of date. Inside, they covered the story of the downed Chinook helicopter from last month, and how a dozen Taliban fighters – more likely local scavengers – had been killed when the Chinook was denied via a 1,000lb bomb. This was dressed up as a victory, but I was sure that the Taliban would see twelve deaths in return for us losing one of our few helicopters as the bargain of the century. In other wars this kind of article would have been known as propaganda. Now it was just an innocent media spin.

I was called into a small room that functioned as an annex to company headquarters, and asked to write up an account of lessons learned from the day 1-1 had been blown up. Other than avoiding the same tracks and using helicopters to ferry troops, there was little I could think to add, but the duty got me out of other mundane tasks such as doing areas and filling jerry cans, and so I was playing solitaire on the laptop when I heard excited chatter emanating from the ops room.

I peered through the hole in the wall and saw the headquarter staff looking up at the screens of Kill TV. I recognized the area as Greg's Bridge, and saw that there were three men involved in burying an IED.

Danny and his team were in the perfect position to make the kills.

Word quickly spread throughout the base, troops hovering quietly at the ops room door, but this was quickly closed in their faces.

'This isn't for your eyes,' a head shed officer told the friends of the men on the ground.

Two of the Afghans moved out of the screen behind the cover of FSG Hill, not half a kilometre from our position. The third, wearing a white man-dress, suddenly threw back his arms and dropped to the floor, the report of the shot coming to us across the fields a split second later.

It was like watching a cup final penalty, the operations room bursting into cheers. Tracer began to dance across the picture on Kill TV, the GPMG's reports following. I cursed Owens' luck beneath my breath.

The quick reaction force should have been moving as soon as the shots were fired. I don't know why they didn't. Expecting a counter-attack, Danny and the team were left with hearts in their throats for a full twenty minutes before the sergeant major led the QRF to the bridge. There they found the dead man with his feet on the device he'd been planting. We noted how he was wearing sandals, not shoes, the implication being that he had been paid to plant the device rather than being a hardcore Taliban fighter. One of the sergeants wanted to pump a few rounds into the man to make sure that he was dead, but the ops room wouldn't allow it. Like many men of dirt poor countries, the insurgent's age was impossible to guess. His face was like rubber, and we debated as to whether or not this was a result of his death. Even with his white clothing the scene appeared bloodless.

The man who'd pulled the trigger posed for photos beside his kill, a proud hunter, and Smith joined him, an arm over his shoulder, an equally proud father.

Fullback was applauded, Owens lambasted.

I was furious with jealousy. 'How the fuck did you miss with the gimpy, you four-eyed cunt?' For days – years – I would picture myself in his place and cutting down the fleeing enemy.

The body of that day's loser was left at the scene, and Kill TV filmed its recovery by a gang of children who struggled with the stiffening limbs.

Soon after, we were all called onto parade, the OC addressing us. 'Any of you who have taken pictures of the body, or with the body, need to delete them at once. We don't do that kind of thing.'

Beside him, Smith maintained the straight face of a career soldier. 'Totally unacceptable, sir,' he agreed.

The OC was just relaying the army's orders, and how could you fault their logic? It was one thing to take a man's life and to cheer the action in the ops room, but to photograph the body? Despicable.

I sat with The Firm, and we wondered once again just who it was who drew up these twisted rules of war.

#veteranproblems

Malibu, California, 2014

The morning was almost over, and I was in bed, the open curtains bringing in the sound of waves along with the sunlight. I looked at the girl beside me, naked as I was, but asleep. I thought about waking her to fuck, but decided I didn't have the time. We'd fucked plenty the night before. The balcony, the beach, the bed.

She was a Swedish au pair, and I liked her. I liked her because we'd fuck on the balcony, the beach, the bed, and that was as far as our commitment went, one night at a time. She'd never asked me to take her to a bar or restaurant. Perhaps she had a local boyfriend. Perhaps she didn't want to be seen with me. Either way, it worked for us both.

I rolled out of bed, waking her, and pretended I hadn't noticed. I went out onto the balcony and watched as the waves of the Pacific rolled across the beach.

I should never have been staying in a place like this, and from today I wouldn't be. It was far beyond my means, but then so were the bar tabs, the restaurant bills, the cars, the clothes. Money came and went. Debt came and . . . I'd figure out the rest later.

I was hardly the only thirty-year-old in debt and with a frivolous spending mentality – YOLO – but I had memory enough to know when the trigger had been pulled. Before Iraq, I had plans to buy and flip houses. After my back-to-back tours, I had enough to put down deposits on two. Instead, I blew through that money in three months of accumulated leave. Gym, drink, womanize, repeat. And then there were the cars. One write-off after another, but to feel that familiar tingle of adrenaline made every roll of the car and the dice worth it.

I looked along the row of beach houses. Thought of the people who lived here – celebrities, entrepreneurs, sports stars. Life's winners. I looked and I smiled. I'd been a chameleon in this place. If I did die today . . .

Yeah. As much as I wanted to, I just couldn't shake the romanticism from war, because don't all the best romances revolve around tragedy? Here I was, my debt about to crash down on me like the white horses on the sand, but it had been worth it. Every loan. Every credit card. I was scared of life. Terrified of its finality, and that had driven me to come here, to live for that moment, because there would never be another.

I owed the war for that.

13

The Great Deception

I was sitting in the back of 3-1, trying to sleep in the midday heat. I had the troop compartment to myself, and so I was sprawled out when Wayne called down to me from the turret.

'One Platoon are seeing bikes bringing guys into the compounds below OP Hill. Looks like the civvies are bugging out, too.'

I sat up, pulling my body armour over my head. We were on immediate notice to move to support One Platoon's patrol south, and if they hit a contact we'd be on our way. My pulse picked up a little at the thought.

'They want us to move down there in case it kicks off,' Wayne called to me again, and seconds later we heard the first bursts of gunfire in the distance. 'It's kicked off!' he shouted down, the truck's engine revving harder, the Warrior roaring and shaking as the driver opened up the throttle.

Within moments we were bouncing across the empty fields, our gunner, Ratty, opening up with the coaxial machine gun. I watched as empty cases and broken link fell into the base of the turret. It was all I could see, but I could hear the sound of the fight growing around us.

The truck lurched to a stop, and instantly Wayne ordered Ratty to switch to the 30mm cannon. *BANG-BANG-BANG!* The concussion from the rounds felt like a hammer hitting my helmet. I called up to the turret.

'Wayne! Where's One Platoon? Wayne! Drop me off!' I had the

GPMG at my feet and was desperate to get into the fight. 'Wayne! Oi! Wayne!'

But I got no reply, and so I hit the button to open the rear door, and it pushed back on its hydraulic jack with agonizing slowness.

I stuck my head out, the sound of the gunfire instantly sharper. Smith's truck was over to our left, the cannon belching shells towards the compounds. The view to my right was blocked, but I was certain that was where the bulk of our own firing was coming from. I put one foot on the ground, then imagined myself being left alone in the centre of the field.

'Fuck!' I screamed with frustration, and moved back inside, closing the door, and looking up into the turret. 'Wayne!' I shouted, but I was ignored as the cannon continued to spew out rounds. I sat there for minutes, furious and frustrated, until I saw the Warrior's door opening behind me.

It was the One Platoon guys, half a dozen of them, and they piled into the troop compartment with whoops and smiles.

I noticed one of them had his safety catch off, and made the others check theirs. Hard work when their veins were full of adrenaline and combat.

'Where were you?' I asked one of the NCOs.

He shouted back with wide eyes. 'In a ditch! About thirty metres to the right!'

I cursed Wayne, who shouted down from the turret that they had at least two kills. The Taliban had been knocked into silence by the 30mm shells, and now children were collecting the bodies.

'Smith will be claiming those next,' said the NCO, and he was right.

Orders came over the net, the NCO relaying them to his team.

'We're going back to Compound 14 to look for IEDs.'

'Fuck it. I'm coming with you.' And I followed them out into the field, seeing Compound 14 close by to our right.

I looked towards OP Hill, puffs of dust still drifting lazily in the air where cannon shells had hit dirt walls. I saw movement, a black shape popping up and down behind the highest wall.

'You see that?' I asked the NCO. 'Looks like they want to hit us again.'

'Fucking hope so,' he replied with hunger.

But they didn't, and the search turned up empty. We gazed above us, where a pair of A-10s circled in the blue.

'They've got eyes on ten guys,' I was told by someone with a radio. 'But they can't engage unless we're engaged first.'

And so the orders came.

'We're moving north. Gonna try and get them to hit us on the extraction.'

We moved off, slowly, and in the open. Nobody complained. We all wanted to see the A-10s swoop in like angels of death, obliterating the village in a salvo of high explosive carnage. If we had to expose ourselves to witness that, then so be it.

But the Taliban wouldn't oblige us, and so we went miserably to ground before we cleared out of the enemy's range. We strung out along a deep ditch, and out came cigarettes and water bottles as we waited.

I was reclined next to One Platoon's sergeant.

'What's the next great plan?' I asked him.

'They should just push us south. Now. Either Terry has to open up on us and they get smashed by the fast air, or they'll have to pull back. Sitting here's the last thing we should be doing.' He chugged back his water, then shook his head. 'Fuck me.'

'Sarge!' came the call from down the line. 'Boss wants you for an o-group.' And so the man got to his feet and picked his way over the prone soldiers in the ditch.

When he returned, it was hard to tell if he was more amused or furious.

'I've just . . .' His words failed him. 'I've just never heard anything like this.'

Someone had come up with a plan. A plan so cunning it would put the Horse of Troy to shame.

'I wonder who fucking dreamed this up?' A junior NCO spat, with a look back towards Minden.

Men muttered. Heads were shaken.

Smith's wagon would fake an IED strike.

'How the fuck do you fake an IED strike?' I asked.

'He's gonna drop a grenade close to the wagon.'

We laughed at this, but the sergeant pressed on. 'Then he's gonna pop a red smoke, and we're gonna simulate a casualty extraction.'

'I'm lost,' one of the boys piped up. 'Are we actually on the ground or back in pre-deployment training?'

'It's not a bad plan,' the sergeant shrugged, trying to take the company line.

'It's a fucking joke.'

'Yeah, I know. Fuck it.'

And so we watched as the wagon moved off, every man's eyes glued to the spectacle.

'The thing is,' I said to no one in particular, 'the Taliban know where the IEDs are. *They* put them there. And a grenade passing off as a twenty kilo charge?'

Nobody had an answer.

We saw Smith's frame appear out of the turret, our jaws tightening in anticipation.

'Grenade!' he screamed, broadcasting it over the radio net, causing the sergeant to flinch at the shout in his headset. Smith then hurled the frag like a major league pitcher. As the small explosion detonated twenty yards from the vehicle, a much bigger one erupted from our ditch.

It was an explosion of laughter. Helpless laughter. Can't breathe laughter. Piss your pants laughter. We had high hopes for failure, but the execution of the great plan exceeded everyone's expectations.

In a further bid to kill us all from asphyxiation, Smith then threw the smoke grenade within a second of the frag grenade's detonation. The dense red smoke was like a matador's cloak, taunting. Goading. Willing us to verbally assault our leaders.

If any act could sum up what we thought of our head shed, this was it, and we cried out in shame when we discovered that no one had thought to video the inevitable cluster-fuck.

Barely two minutes later, we received the order to return to base. As we entered the gates, men raced for their marker pens and the awaiting canvas of the wooden toilet walls.

14

The New Sheriff

The OC was returning from DC with our new battle group CO. The Fusiliers were gone, replaced by the Household Cavalry Regiment (HCR), and so there was a new sheriff in town. With him came a group of British civilians, who we assumed were government types.

'Probably the same wankers that would rather we drove onto IEDs than through the fields,' Toby spat, and we watched the civilians with hate-filled eyes.

'Wonder what this new cunt's got in mind?' Danny asked, referring to the fresh CO. 'Maybe he'll get his guys to take over Zulu or the QRF,' he added hopefully.

Due to having troops away on R&R, and providing a battle group QRF at DC, we were too shorthanded to send fighting patrols south and so we were spending as much time in the more benign northern villages as the locals. At this time, some American patrol bases were coming under huge Taliban attacks, with large numbers killed on both sides, the enemy determined to overrun a garrison. This did little to fill the men at Zulu with confidence. When patrols were sent out from that checkpoint, the garrison was reduced to four men. By concentrating their attacks on one of the three separated sangars, a small band of Taliban could have run riot. The company was becoming overstretched, and we assumed that the new CO would do something to remedy this.

But assumption, NCOs will tell you, is the mother of all fuck-ups.

The CO's visit lasted for sixteen hours, rumour in the company saying that he was asleep for most of it in the annex to the head shed. Whether that was true or not, it was fact that he didn't address the company, nor move about the base to engage with soldiers on an individual level. Maybe this CO had a good reason not to which we were unaware of, but that didn't matter to us. As the infantrymen under his command, this made us feel abandoned by our new leader. That we were his pawns, nothing more. We would be expected to carry out his orders, and maybe die doing so, and yet he seemingly hadn't been able to ask a single one of us our names. No enquiry about our families, our towns, our pasts, or our hoped-for futures. This seemed to me to be a basic failure to understand the way an infantryman thinks and what he needs from his officers.

We fucking hated him for this.

We hated him so much, that we hoped that he would die.

I was bored.

Civilians and soldiers alike have a tendency to think that war will be a blur of excitement, but the truth is that for every minute spent in a contact, or hurtling across the country in a helicopter, there are days of mind-numbingly boring sentry duty – sangar bashing, to the troops – the lonely time where a soldier is left with nothing but his thoughts for company. Inevitably, these thoughts are concerned with how shit his job is, and how soon he can sign off from the army.

It should not be a rational emotion to want to be shot at, but during his watch a sentry prayed that Terry would come out to play and allow him to pass the time by putting rounds down range. Shots could often be heard echoing from the sangars, but these were not always directed towards an enemy. Instead, they were the result of a bored soldier playing with a weapon system, and pulling the trigger when a round had been chambered. The result of this action would be a fine of a month's pay. The best way to avoid punishment would be to shout 'Contact!' and continue firing – nobody could disprove your claim you'd seen an RPG gunner at the end of an alleyway – but usually the young soldier was too shocked by his action, and still stupefied when a raging NCO arrived on the scene.

Mini-flares also offered a form of escapism, and were used to deter children or adults who were getting too close to the sangars. Jason nearly choked on his laughter as he told me about one sentry on his guard rotation who had fired a flare, only to have it hit the camouflage netting and bounce back inside the sangar, landing in a tin of gimpy ammo. Rounds cooked off, whizzing and banging as the sentry dived clear of his post.

There was one sure way to pass the time in the sangars, and that was to masturbate. This was usually mechanical and automatic, rather than from any sexual deviancy, but it gave the sentry some-thing to concentrate on rather than what poor decisions in his life had led to him being in that place. So thick were the sangar's walls with semen that they could withstand a nuclear blast, and any rag present had likely been used to wipe the cocks of every junior sol-dier in the company. A typical guard duty rotation at Minden con-sisted of four sangars, an hour on each, and the sentry would do his best to blow a load in every one. Acts of nature also needed to be taken care of in situ, and bottles of bright yellow piss hung in the camouflage netting where the laziest had tossed them. Shitting in situ was frowned upon, but forgiven in an emergency so long as it wasn't on the sangar's floor. Conditions on the front line often left soldiers with runny arses and vomiting sickness.

At night, sentries should have been doubled, but the company's overstretch made this an impossibility. Even full corporals would be drafted in to stand guard, whereas their usual position would be that of guard commander, coordinating the rotation and listening in to the company's radio.

The task of providing the base's guards fell to a different platoon about every eight to ten days, and now it was Three's turn to supply it. I was alone on the rooftop sangar, which sat above company HQ and as such was not a good spot for masturbating, and so I was thinking about that day's company gossip – Private Thomas had recently returned from R&R and was now overjoyed at the news he received via the satellite phone; his girlfriend was pregnant.

'So she happened to fall pregnant the first day he's home, and happens to take a test twelve days later. Why?' Jay had posed mischievously.

My own knowledge of biology was a lot more limited.

'So what's it mean?' I pushed him.

'Means his girlfriend probably got knocked up before he was home – or he lasted two seconds after arriving.'

Other troops had come to the same conclusion, and told Thomas as much, but he wouldn't believe it.

I looked across the compounds, and at an empty alleyway. The previous night two men had been spotted there carrying a package, but they had fled the scene by climbing over a wall when the guard had fired an illumination round.

My eyes were drawn back to my front as I heard the *pop-pop-pop* of rifle fire. After these few single shots, all went quiet, and it was my turn to rotate to the burn pit sangar.

When I arrived there, I found Emily behind the Hesco.

'Someone just shot at me when I went to throw my stuff in the burn pit,' she told me matter-of-factly.

I went up into the sangar, and during my hour there a further ten single shots were fired towards the south side of the patrol base, but nobody could determine from where.

'They're firing from Middle Hill,' I was told over the radio by Biscuits, the ageing mortar man who was in sangar one.

'No chance,' I argued. 'They're not gonna try single shots from that distance. Probably in one of the compounds, firing through a murder hole.'

My relief appeared, and to try and confirm my theory I paced up and down in front of the exposed burn pit. The boredom of guard duty made you do stupid things, and offering yourself up as a live target was one of them.

No rounds came my way, but the next morning the elusive shooter was at it again.

'He's fucking shit,' Danny remarked. 'Fifteen shots and he's not hit a thing.'

But the firing point remained a mystery, and Toby came up with a solution.

'The Boss is gonna charge Evs Cry Baby because he keeps fucking up. I say we put him outside until he identifies the position or gets shot, and then we wipe the slate clean.'

The Boss gave our proposal some thought, but regretted to inform us that, following an in-depth risk assessment, he'd have to turn it down.

Wayne entered the Viper's Nest, a parcel in hand.

'What's in the box,' Jay asked the orphan, 'your mum?'

The rest of The Firm burst into laughter, the downtrodden Wayne turning on his heel quickly to escape further insults to his murdered mother.

'I didn't know BFPO delivered urns!' Danny shouted after him, and we tried hard not to piss ourselves.

Soon after, I was called away to mark the HLS for an incoming heli. I popped the coloured smoke when ordered, but for some unknown reason the Lynx pilot disgorged his cargo 200 metres away, beside a compound. These were two engineers, ironically there to recce a permanent HLS. The two confused figures finally spotted the patrol base and stumbled their way to its walls.

Guard rotation began well that night, as I was joined in the roof-top sangar by a JTAC (Joint Terminal Attack Controller) from the despised RAF Regiment. After managing not to puke all over myself, we got talking and he revealed himself to be a good bloke. He was in comms with a couple of American F-18 pilots in the skies above us, watching the footage they relayed to his portable screen. The pilot's callsign was Uproar 2-3, and I wished aloud that our own units could enjoy such cool names. The JTAC told me how these aircraft flew from a carrier in the Indian Ocean, refuelled over Helmand, performed their mission, then returned to their home at sea. It was an impressive feat of logistics, and a projection of power that only the Americans could accomplish.

Back in the burn pit sangar later that night, I heard over the radio that Cortez had spotted a group of men digging on the summit of Tabletop, one of the ridges that overlooked the patrol base. ICOM also confirmed that the men were 'preparing a weapon'. Looking through my night-sight I could see the suspects, a tingle of excitement running through my body – I thought that they were in range of the gimpy. A Javelin team and the mortars were stood to, and I contacted the guard commander, Rabbit, informing him out of courtesy that I would be opening fire as soon as the mortars put up their illumination rounds.

Then, to my horror, I was told to hold my fire. The Javelin would be taking a shot, and I asked why I could not follow their fire with my own. I was given no reason, only an order to keep my finger away from the trigger. The inaction ate at me. In range or not, I just wanted to get in on the fun. I wanted something to break the mind-numbing-fucking-banality of my days. I hadn't put my life on the line and come halfway around the world just to wank in fucking sangars.

With a *whoosh*, the Javelin announced its launch. I followed its flight through the thermal sight and it looked like a good hit, the flare of the explosion white against the grey of the hillside. A couple of minutes later, a second Javelin impacted into the same spot.

Troops rushed to the Cortez cabin and Kill TV, anxious to see results of the Javelin's strike, which I now learned had been fired by Jay. Unfortunately, it became clear from the footage that, on hearing the telltale whoosh of the launch, the men had fled the scene. The anti-armour warhead was designed to punch through tanks, not spread shrapnel, and we had seen the enemy survive impacts from as little as a metre away.

'They wouldn't have heard the gimpy and GMG rounds until they were landing among them,' I told Jay. He was disappointed to have seen his quarry escape, but could still smile at the thought of blowing through ordinance worth as much as his home.

The next morning, a patrol was sent to Tabletop to conduct a battle damage assessment.

They found no blood.

'Get your kit on. We're going out.'

Turkey was gathering up half of the platoon, slapping sleeping heads and putting a soft boot into upturned backsides.

'Come on. Get up. We're going out.'

'What's the fucking head shed got planned this time?' Danny asked.

'They want us to do an assesment on the IED that went off earlier,' Turkey replied, trying to leave.

'Well, it didn't hit our boys, did it?' Danny protested, at the same time as pulling on his boots.

'Some of the locals apparently. Call it hearts and minds. Front gate in five minutes.'

The patrol pushed south along Route Pink, coming to a culvert that lay alongside a compound. It was in dead ground to the patrol base. A beautiful place for an IED.

An IED that had been made to take out an armoured vehicle, but had instead been triggered by two men on a motorcycle. We'd seen the explosion replayed on Kill TV. One minute they were scooting along, the next . . .

There was little sign of them, or the bike.

'Hopefully it landed on some cunt in Bastion,' Danny said, smiling at the image.

Turkey pushed the patrol out into a defensive formation while he took the terp to question the locals. There was a couple of dozen of them, some crying softly, others wailing.

'Oh shut the fuck up,' Danny moaned under his breath, before turning to Wayne. 'They go on and on about Allah and his fucking paradise all the time, then when someone dies they won't shut the fuck up. You can't have it both ways.'

Wayne ignored him, watching a man who approached the cordon with a heavy bag in each hand. Turkey spotted it too.

'Wayne. Search that bloke.'

Wayne did as he was bid, gesturing for the man to place the bags down so that he could peer inside.

'It's OK,' he told our platoon sergeant. 'They're just bags of meat.'

Turkey did his best to hide his smile from the grieving villagers. 'That's the guys from the bike, you dickhead.'

Wayne looked more embarrassed than appalled.

'Hey,' Danny nudged Turkey with an elbow, unable to help himself, 'you wanted hearts and minds.'

#veteranproblems

Somewhere Over the Middle East, 2014

I was in the window seat, CK alongside me. He was an ex-para, a career soldier, and we had just completed a security job together, escorting a merchant vessel through the Gulf of Aden, until recently a pirate-infested stretch of sea.

I was reading the memoir of a German soldier, then a youngster who had fought on the Eastern front. It was as harrowing as I had imagined it would be, and I was entranced by his experiences. I read on, until his friend was hit by the cannons of an attacking aircraft.

He explained the injuries in detail. The mangled face. The flapping tongue. I was instantly nauseous, my skin goosebumped, ice in every muscle and sinew of my body. As the image of Hunt pushed its way to the front of my mind, I began to get lightheaded.

I pressed my skull against the glass of the window, screwing my eyes tight, but that only made the images more vivid. I opened them, looking around the aircraft for distraction. Anything. I took the airline magazine from the seat pocket, trying to drink in every detail of the photos within, terrified that CK would notice my panic and, worse, that he would ask me about it.

Eventually the ice melted, the dizziness passed, and the images faded. I climbed over my friend and asked the stewardess at the rear of the aircraft for a water. I went to the toilets, seeing the bronze had been taken out of my cheeks. I thought of the Eastern front, what those men must have endured, and I looked at myself in the mirror, disgusted by my own weakness.

'Man the fuck up.'

I went back to my chair, and held the book in my hands. After consideration, I gave a silent apology to the author. I wasn't made of the same stuff. His stories would have to wait for another day, until I could control my own.

15

Aids-Gate: Part One

Danny was into one of his rants. Today's subject was the army, in which he'd served for twelve years. I was on my bed, looking for distraction in my journal.

'I can't fit all of this in, mate. You're gonna have to summarize.'

The reply was instantaneous.

'Unimportant people who think they're important, stitching other people up.' He thought about that for a second, then went on. 'I've got a new motto for A Company. "I'm OK, blow the bridge." What's that in Latin?'

I told him I had no idea. I had other things on my mind. Burning things.

'Why the fuck do you keep rubbing your cock?' Danny pressed me, more in puzzlement than disgust.

'Must have got something on my hands on the patrol. Fucking balls are on fire.'

'Good,' he said, with his sadistic smile.

Then, with my hands stuffed down the front of my trousers, I joined the rest of the platoon for a briefing.

'There's been an IED at Bastion,' the Boss told us, raising eyebrows. 'Pressure-pad IED on the ranges. One killed and a few injured.'

'Slack,' Toby put in. 'Fucking RAF Regiment cunts not doing their job.'

I thought back to our time at Bastion, using the ranges outside of the wire. Our checks had been lax at best, undertaken with an air of complacency because we seemed to be in the middle of an endless desert. But the ranges don't move, and the Taliban don't miss a trick. They do their homework, take their chances, and that was why there could only be one winner in this war.

We left the briefing, heading back to the Viper's Nest. Wayne was sullen. He'd received a message from his wife that morning, but it had been sent to a 'Wade'. There was a picture file attached that couldn't be opened.

'Probably of her taking a massive cock,' Danny said helpfully. None of us pointed out the likelihood that 'Wade' was just a typo – his rambling worry was just too enjoyable.

Toby put his arm around Wayne's shoulders, offering his own comfort. 'She looks like a fucking yeti anyway, mate. You'll be better off without her.'

We were settling back into the Viper's Nest when Ginger Pubes stuck his head through the open door.

Danny greeted him. 'What the fuck do you want you fox piss cunt?' Ginge said nothing at first, but he had that sly smile that always preceded mischief, and so we invited him inside. 'You been cutting the arse out of the OC's trousers again?'

The likeable private shook his head. 'Have you heard what happened when Doyle and Waddle got back from R&R?' he said, referring to two men in the company.

This introduction did little to enthuse Toby.

'So fucking what? Useless cunt and an ugly useless cunt.'

'They got Aids,' Ginge smirked, dropping his hook.

'Stop talking bollocks you ginger fucker.'

'No. Seriously. When they got to Brize they were told their flight had been delayed twenty-four hours, so they went into Oxford. They were in their uniforms, and they met this girl who took them back to hers.'

'Bollocks!' came from several voices.

'No! Seriously! They both fucked her!'

'What?' asked Toby. 'At the same time?'

'I don't know,' admitted Ginge.

'I think I'm gonna puke,' Danny added, but told Ginge to go on.

'So when they were leaving, the girl said, "I fucking hate squaddies, welcome to the Aids club." '

'Bollocks!' was again the group consensus.

But apparently we were wrong, because the Boss had heard the same story and came into the Viper's Nest specifically to talk to our clique.

'They're both shitting themselves,' he said, trying not to smile.

'Isn't the fucker Doyle married?' Toby asked, the Boss nodding.

'And that fatarse Waddle is engaged.'

'Fuck 'em, Boss,' Toby spat. He was a rogue in many ways, but to him, marriage was sacrosanct. 'They did the crime, they do the fucking time.'

But the war had other ideas.

16

Us and Them

The day before my R&R was due to begin, I called a friend from the satellite phone at Minden.

'What's that noise?' she asked, struggling to hear my voice as a Warrior roared out of the patrol base gate. It was the QRF, and they were making their way to FSG Hill in preparation for supporting a foot patrol.

I watched them go as we talked, keeping my eyes on the wagon as the dismounts climbed out and began to Barma their way up the slope. I watched until the smoke of the explosion engulfed them, the roar of the IED hitting me a split second later, taking the war down the phone and into my friend's living room.

'I've got to go,' I told her, running for the ops room.

I felt sick. Having seen the explosion and the exposure of the dismounts, I was certain that they would all be dead, or fucked up into broken shapes.

The ops room had seen it all on Kill TV, and now I joined a group of other troops, from all platoons, who were pulling on kit to form an emergency reaction force.

Rifles and Vallons were grabbed, men rushing for the gate when the call began to echo around the patrol base.

'No casualties! No casualties!'

The Taliban had blown the command wire device early, the angle of the slope deflecting it from our guys. I pulled off my gear.

'I'm on R&R tomorrow,' I told the NCO spreading the news. With no intention of going back on the ground now that the all clear on casualties had been given, I moved to the safety of my cot to see out the remainder of the day.

The Chinook came in with its usual dust storm, sand whipping our exposed skin. We piled on board, the white smiles wide in dirt-encrusted faces. Cameras were pulled, men filming and photographing the moment where we began the journey to our homes.

I craned my neck to look out of the small porthole window, seeing the deep green of the wadi valley quickly turn to the barren wastes of the desert. I saw the same mountain range that I had marvelled at with Johan during that convoy from Bastion, and in twenty minutes we were touching down on that base's concrete landing pad.

Twenty minutes.

It had taken us 105 hours to make the move in vehicles from Bastion to Minden, losing two Warriors on the way, and the life of one of our men. I felt the usual disgust at how underequipped we were, but that soon faded as we began to descend from the tail ramp.

Because I saw Jake.

He had come out with the quartermaster to collect us, and I was overjoyed at seeing my friend again. We exchanged insults, and I quickly filled him in on the other members of The Firm.

'It's fucking shit here,' he told me, his wound a pink scar on the back of his neck. I smiled, glad to see that being shot had not given him a more positive outlook on life.

'I'm jealous of you arriving like this,' he added, looking at the Chinook. 'When I came in on the MERT they cut all my clothes off. Because I was CAT A half of the hospital was stood waiting, and that fucking tin-foil blanket on me went flapping all over the place in the downdraft. My cock wasn't exactly lookin' its best.'

I couldn't stop laughing. It was so good to see my brother. Back in the tents, we all took showers, long showers, and laughed and joked at the flushing toilets. For two weeks we could shit without a bag.

To be fair to Smith, he had given a 'grace period' to those about to return home, and many of us had escaped Minden with hair and sideburns longer than they should have been. We folded our sleeves halfway up our forearms, kept on our green Velcro belts, and dug out berets from our kitbags. We wanted everybody to know that we were infantry and just passing through.

A small group of us went to the NAAFI, spotting similar knots of men from other combat units. Ryder recognized a friend among one such set from the Rifles, and our two clusters merged. The rifleman was convalescing, having been shot in the back. The plate of his body armour had stopped the bullet, but the projectile travelling at supersonic speed had still caused a deal of blunt trauma, and he showed us the deep purple bruising.

Ryder's friend had had a tough tour. His platoon had lost a couple of guys, a few others losing limbs. We wouldn't have expected otherwise. The Rifles held Sangin, which seemed to have become the Taliban's main effort, and every few days there were reports that they had suffered more fatalities or life-changing injuries. The rifleman told us how the guys drew straws to decide who would walk the point on patrol, and how some men vomited before they left the camp's gates.

We knew that we had inherited a softer area of operations than the Rifles. The army is built on hierarchy, and it carried over into the way we viewed other units. We didn't believe the Rifles were any better than us, they'd just been dealt a tougher hand, but they had our respect, as did all the infantry battle groups out on the ground. In Musa Qala or Babaji, we went through the same experiences, faced the same dangers, and lost the same friends.

Some infantry units were based in places like Bastion or Kandahar Air Field, only leaving to perform operations. While they were still infantry, they sat lower on our ladder of respect as they did not have to endure the deprivations of life in a patrol base.

We were deeply envious of and impressed by the special forces. As we saw it, they led a charmed life with the greatest job in the world: shoot people in the face, then head back to base for a shower and a beer.

Those rear echelon troops who saw out the entirety of their tour in these large bases were unworthy of even being talked to by ourselves. They had access to luxuries we couldn't even dream of, their biggest risk to life coming from being run over by a shuttlebus at night as they walked back from one of the base's many internet and phone cabins. These cabins would be shut off when there was a casualty on the ground, an attempt to prevent information leaking before the family could be informed, and there were many fights between the combat troops and base-rats when someone was overheard to be complaining that the phones had been turned off once again.

The exceptions to this rule were the hospital staff, who in our eyes could do no wrong. We were awed by them, knocked over by the courage it took to deal with our horrendously wounded and dying. There were times during the infantryman's tour where he would see terrible sights. The doctors and nurses saw it on a daily basis, and it would not be an exaggeration to say that the combat troops' admiration of them went beyond respect, to love.

The REMFs of Bastion seemed to go out of their way to increase our resentment of them. The base was a huge, sprawling area, and to walk from one part to another was a hot and dusty affair. Land Rovers zipped by despite our outstretched thumbs. Aside from perhaps a rear party soldier of a combat unit, only American troops or civilian contractors stopped to collect us.

In the patrol bases we had longed for the opportunity to eat fresh, cooked food, but we were soon stripped of our enthusiasm. We were given meagre portions – 'it's a selection, not a collection', the smug-faced chefs would say – and chastised for the oil-stained state of our uniform and the length of our hair, many of us turned away at the dining facility's tented door by a greying officer. We did not bother coming back, instead paying for our food at one of the camp's many fast-food outlets or making the long walk to Leatherneck, the American portion of the base. There we were welcomed, and ate until we were on the verge of throwing up.

We were unwanted orphans in Bastion, and that was OK with us. Aside from forays for food and phones, we stuck to our tented area, our cocks stuffed into socks as we tried to gain a last-minute bronzing in the wan sun of late October.

Our transition through Bastion was a short one, though there was time to pay our respects at a vigil. This time, the service was for a well-liked and respected bomb disposal officer who been with us on our pre-deployment training.

We took the short flight to Kandahar Air Field (KAF) in that workhorse of war, the C-130 Hercules. KAF was rear echelon on a whole other level to Bastion, centred around an area known as 'the boardwalk'. It was Afghanistan's answer to Rodeo Drive, shops selling anything from fast food to carpets. There was even a TGI Fridays. Elsewhere on the base there were the usual PXs, dining facilities, and gyms. On certain days of the week there was a bazaar held by local traders.

We were told all of this by the American military policeman who had picked us up and offered to give us a tour. We drove by some members of our hierarchy, who were on foot, the OC's face dropping as he saw us in the police truck. We asked the military police officer if he could turn on the siren, but he declined, smiling.

'I've got assholes on top of me, too.'

In Kandahar, we truly began to relax. There were British troops stationed here, mostly from the RAF, but it was nominally a Canadian base. We were left to ourselves, and we liked it that way, all British transiting personnel being accommodated in a large hanger full of bunkbeds. Our contingent was the largest, and the loudest, and we were too excited and full of Mountain Dew to sleep.

'Keep the noise down!' came the shouts from the other side of the hanger.

'Fuck off!' we chorused, and nobody came over to challenge, which disappointed us.

We talked about the tour, our volume cranked to a level high enough so that the REMFs in the hanger could hear us. We wanted them to know that we were better than them. That we were soldiers and they were civilians in uniform.

Eventually we tired ourselves out, sleeping like babies on the flight that took us to Oxfordshire.

I was collected from Brize Norton by my father and youngest brother, and we drove north. I wasn't overwhelmed to be back, but I enjoyed the familiar countryside and towns that rolled by the window. We stopped at a service station for food. I was still in my faded desert uniform, my beret in the car, and a group of Scottish infanteers entered in the camouflage fatigues of a British garrison. The older among them met my eye, and we shared the slightest of nods and knowing looks.

I had no big plans for R&R. I didn't even want to drink. Of course I wanted to see my family, but the thing I desired most was to be alone. I'd spent months living in the pockets of my comrades, always a call away from some task or a duty from my commanders. Luckily, I didn't have to hurt any feelings, as my family still had to go to work or school. That gave me the daytime to be a hermit and I could enjoy their company in the evenings. During one of those nights, my mum saw me looking at a framed photo of myself that had appeared in my absence.

'They sent me that,' she told me, 'they' being the battalion.

I remembered it being taken by the company clerk at the beginning of the tour. I'd tried my best to avoid the ordered photos, knowing what they were for, but I'd finally been pinned down. In case we won the treasure hunt and were turned into IED soup, the company wanted a picture of us to release to the media. Obstinate fucker that I was, I'd not looked into the camera, grimacing as it was taken, and now I was stuck with that ugly mug on the mantelpiece. When would I learn that I couldn't beat the system?

'If anything happens to me,' I told my brother, 'do not let them use that fucking photo.'

I had never truly understood, nor had it explained to me, what our purpose was in Helmand. So far as we could see, we were holding ground that would be instantly ceded back to the Taliban the day that we left. For their part, the villagers really didn't seem to care who was in charge. They had no love for the strict Taliban, but neither were they fans of having foreign troops evicting them from their compounds and killing their relatives. Accident or not, a corpse was a corpse.

Watching the news in my living room, I now knew that the mission was hopeless. Politicians squabbled – there was nothing new there – but the entire ship of Operation Herrick seemed rudderless. The most often used argument, if it could be called that, was that we had lost so many soldiers that we must stick out the mission so that their deaths were not in vain. Easy to say that when you're in Westminster, but I was sure that the families of the next dead soldier, and the next, would think differently. I'd been through the same feelings in Iraq, seeing our meek leaders doom the efforts of the troops, and the supreme sacrifice of some. I had hoped Afghanistan would be different. It wasn't. I kept away from the news after that.

It was during my second week at home that I received a text from Ryder asking me if I had heard what had happened in Afghanistan. A story had broken about a number of Brits killed by the ANA soldiers they had been embedded to mentor, and I assumed he was talking about that.

I was wrong.

My platoon had been hit.

Ryder had received the news from the patrol base. The only thing we knew was that Johan was the most badly wounded of the victims, a broken back among other injuries, but he was expected to pull through.

I learned this in the kitchen of my grandmother's home, a place that held nothing but happy memories for me, but now I wished only to be back in Helmand and alongside my platoon. I hated that I hadn't been there. That it had happened without me. It wasn't that I thought I could have prevented it, but I wanted to have gone through it with them. To have seen Johan onto the MERT. To have cuffed my comrades around the head and told them that they'd done a good job. I wished my grandfather was alive so that I could have confided in him in that moment. I knew he would understand the desire to have been there, and why, even knowing it was irrational, I could not push the feelings down.

More information dripped in during the last few days of my R&R, which had now lost its meaning to me. It wasn't that I necessarily wanted to be back in Afghanistan – I just didn't want to be home while my friends were there.

Johan was evacuated to a hospital in the UK. Ryder and I planned on going to Birmingham to see him, but he was not in a stable enough condition for visitors. He'd been driving the QRF Warrior, and they'd hit an IED a hundred metres short of Greg's Bridge. Jake had just the day before returned from Bastion, and had been the gunner. He was understandably shaken after the hit, where he had been the first one to treat Johan. Shot in the neck on the first foot patrol south and blown up almost immediately on his return, Jake was truly living up to his nickname, 'Pinkmist'.

The final weekend of my R&R I went to Cardiff with my father to watch Wales take on the All Blacks. It was the day before Remembrance Sunday, and during the minute's silence before the game I couldn't shake the image of Hunt's broken face from my mind.

Goodbyes were never painless, but I did my best to trample my feelings and put on a mask that I hoped would reassure. It was the sixth time that I'd been through the ritual, but it wasn't something that grew easier with practice. With my brothers, I could bury the worry behind jokes and punches – 'Come back with your shield, or on it' had been my send-off since the movie *300*, during my second R&R of Iraq – but there was no such easy escape with my parents, and so I made the hugs quick and the eye contact rare. I knew that once I'd driven far enough for my headlights to be out of sight, I'd pull over and weep at the thought of never seeing them again. After telling myself to get a grip, I'd begin the journey anew.

I returned to Brize Norton, an RAF base that resembled a shitty regional airport – minus the bar – finding a mixture of the chronically hungover, depressed, and others like myself who were trapped between longing to return to the patrol base while knowing the idiocy of such a wish.

I sat down alongside Owens, whose head was in his bony hands – his girlfriend had finished things. He'd found this out when she failed to collect him from the arriving flight.

'Danny's gonna be merciless,' he said, and was right.

'You're going to the best place to feel better,' I tried to comfort him. 'Maybe you'll get to kill someone.'

It was the morning of Remembrance Day, and as we waited to taxi onto the runway, a minute's silence was held on the aircraft.

I looked around the troops of my own unit, some of them friends, some of them nothing but names to me.

The plane lurched forwards, our R&R finished along with the silence.

We were going home.

17

Aids-Gate: Part Two

The RAF wasted no time in getting us back to Afghanistan. We were only in Kandahar an hour before being loaded onto a Hercules for our flight into Bastion, arriving in the early hours. That day, there was a vigil held for the five men killed by the rogue Afghan army soldier, a sobering reminder of what we had returned to. A few hours before dawn, we were driven to the HLS to await our Chinook to Minden.

The temperature had dropped sharply in the short time we'd been away, and we huddled about a brazier like tramps. One Platoon's sergeant was with us, and he mused about life in the patrol bases.

'Bags. Everything here revolves around fucking bags. You live out of one, you eat out of one, you shit into one, and if you die, they put you in one. We'd be fucked without bags.'

After an hour spent around the embers, we finally received the news that our flights had been postponed until the afternoon. The RAF had known since the night before, but the message hadn't reached us. A thousand curses were uttered against the men in blue.

We were shuttled to the camp's dining facilities where we found the outgoing R&R, Jay and Danny among them. I joined them at the table, giving them the news on Johan from my own end.

'He's in Selly Oak, classified as critical and seriously ill, which is one below the highest, very seriously ill. He's got severe injuries that should all be survivable, but possibly life changing. He's got a broken arm and pelvis, which is really bad, and an open wound on his arm. His kidneys are damaged and there's bruising on his liver. Maybe he'll need a kidney transplant. Three of his vertebrae have popped, but they reckon he'll be able to walk.'

Danny lifted another mouthful of eggs towards his shaking head. 'His family there?'

'They flew them in from South Africa, but he has some UK family too, so they were there straight away for him. So what else is new with you?'

'We went on a night patrol.' Jay grimaced. 'The dickheads in the ANA had their own out, which nobody seemed to know a thing about. We thought we were the only friendly troops on the ground. We were patrolling through Yatimchay and then the next thing you know there's all these cunts on rooftops pointing weapons at us, cocking their guns, and fucking screaming.'

'Jesus.'

'Yeah,' Danny put in. 'We all had our safeties off and the fuckers in our sights. If one person had fired a round it would have been like one of those massacres in a cowboy film. Fucking Mexican stand off. It's a miracle no one was killed.'

I shook my head. Part of me was truly relieved. Another part . . .

'Would have been kind of cool though, wouldn't it?' I half-grinned to my friends.

Jay smiled slyly. 'Yeah,' he agreed. 'If we'd come out of it alright.'

We didn't know the ANA. We *did* know the thrill of a contact.

'Any other gen?'

Danny took another mouthful of food as he thought about it. 'HCR CO hit an IED,' he then told me, his obvious disappointment meaning that the man had survived. 'We told him not to use the wadi, too many IEDs now. I mean, we've only been here three months longer than him.'

'So he's not changed, then?'

'No. And we're only allowed to take the Warriors on Route Pink once a week now, so it doesn't get too messed up for the locals.'

'Sounds about right.'

'Turkey took a few guys on a lurk into the green zone,' Jay spoke up. 'They heard English voices, and there was no other patrols out in that area. Probably mates of that dead fucker they found with the Aston Villa tattoo a few years ago.'

It should have shocked me that we could be fighting our own 'countrymen', but it didn't – like Al Qaeda in Iraq, the Taliban were drawing recruits from all over the world.

Owens joined us, looking glum.

'Good R&R, you cunt?' Danny asked the newcomer.

'Not really,' the lanky gunner replied in his usual depressed monotone. 'Girlfriend dumped me the first day I got back. Then I see on Facebook they're engaged and expecting his baby.'

Danny's burst of laughter almost caused him to choke on his breakfast.

'No wonder she binned you,' he finally managed. 'Look at you, you hideous mess.'

'I hope your fucking plane crashes,' Owens shot back, but I interjected before the next round of insults.

'That's not the best bit, Danny. He showed me a picture of them on the Facebook, and this guy is the spitting image of him, minus the glasses!'

As Danny joined me in laughter, the sullen soldier finally spoke up.

'He's in B Company, in camp back home.'

This piece of information changed everything for Danny. He became instantly angry, all thoughts of ridicule forgotten.

'He's in the battalion?' he asked, furious on our comrade's behalf.

Danny had himself been the victim of a promiscuous partner once or twice when he was deployed. Such behaviour was to be expected of civilians, but for one of your own unit to be the culprit?

'When we get back,' he promised solemnly, 'we'll fucking kill that cunt.'

And Owens left the table with some purpose to his stride.

The Chinook flight to Minden was exhilarating. We belted low along the wadi, twisting and turning to present a hard target to

Terry below. A flock of sheep panicked and bolted beneath us, locals craning their necks at the wonder in the skies.

Sad Act was beside me on the canvas benches, and jumped out of his skin as the pilot discharged flares prior to landing, the final attempt to throw off missiles armed with tracking systems.

We piled down the tail ramp, our feet hitting the dirt once again. A sandstorm whipped about us, sand and small stones stinging skin through our clothing. Then, as quickly as we had come in, the whocka was gone.

I made my way swiftly to the Viper's Nest, anxious to find Jake and Toby.

But I was to be disappointed. They were both at Zulu, and I was to leave for DC the next day and take the position of Barma team commander on the battle group QRF. The Firm was being scattered to the winds.

I knew that the best course of action for me at Minden was to keep as low a profile as possible, lest I be pulled into some duty, and so I sat on my cot bed, reading, and listening to the conversation of the Two Platoon boys outside of my room – Robson, a young soldier well known for the size of his manhood, had an erection, and the other troops were encouraging him to display it. When he finally did, the cries of awe could have been heard in Pakistan.

Owens came to join me in the Viper's Nest, enjoying its relative comfort, insult-free now that the other members of The Firm were absent. He'd been picking up on company gossip, and told me more about the HCR CO's IED strike.

'The OC had told him it was a bad idea to use the wadi because One Platoon had found a belt of IEDs there, but he did it anyway. They weren't even clearing the route, just driving it. Boys said it was a hell of a bang. They found five more IEDs during the recovery.'

'Let's hope he finds the next one with his head.'

'You heard about Doyle and Waddle?' he asked.

I hadn't. 'They got their Aids tests back?'

'What fucking Aids? The whole thing was bullshit.'

'Fuck off! I fucking knew no one would shag those two! What happened?'

Owens didn't have the details, but these I received the next day from Jake, at Zulu. To my delight, the plan to send me to DC had been changed at the final moment.

'One of their team got hurt and Waddle came to help him. The blokes nearby wouldn't let him anywhere near the casualty in case he passed on the disease. Eventually the medic got there instead. Afterwards, one of Waddle's mates goes to see their Boss, and tells him that Waddle had confessed to him that the whole thing was a plan to get them off the tour. When his mate saw it could put someone's life in danger, he had to tell.'

'Fucking maggots,' I spat. 'What's happening to them now?'

Jake shrugged, unsure himself.

'I think they're getting charged, but I don't know, really. Waddle's hated, obviously, but everyone's been told to lay off Doyle in case he slots himself.'

'Fuck him,' I snarled, Jake nodding at the sentiment.

We took a stroll around the checkpoint. Zulu had changed a lot since my last visit. The orchard had been cleared, and two hardened accommodation areas installed. These had Hesco walls, with a metal roof for protection against mortars. Most of the courtyard had been put under a roof of corrugated iron.

'Going up in the world,' I noted to my friend.

'Hey, Gez.' I got the call from the NCO who was manning the radio. 'A Mastiff's gonna pick you up in an hour. You're going to DC.'

'Oh for fuck's sake!'

And so my stay at Zulu would last a whopping three hours. I wanted to talk to Jake about the incident with Johan, Danny having told me at Bastion that he was suffering from the experience.

We took a brew from the whistling kettle, and I asked my friend if he'd like to talk about it. He was eager to, perhaps because he knew I'd been through the same experience.

'Whenever I close my eyes,' he confessed, 'I just see Johan there, covered in blood and slumped over.'

I could sympathize with this. For almost two months after Hunt had been mortally wounded I saw the image of his jawless face as I tried to drift into sleep.

'We were heading to North Ridge when Davies told me to stop. I was the gunner, looking through the sight at two guys coming down from the high ground. Johan was driving, and tells Davies that there's a big hole in front of us. We had to move up the track, and as soon as we moved a few inches the whole front of the wagon got thrown up in the air.'

'Fuck,' I whispered. 'Did you get knocked out?'

'Yeah. I just felt numb when I came to, then I heard Davies shouting. The blast had taken our headsets off, and his helmet. Davies' wrist was fucked and he couldn't climb out the turret, so I went to check on Johan.'

As I had done with Hunt, Jake had seen the slumped over, broken form of his driver, and assumed that he was dead.

'I pushed him back so I could check his airway. Then he starts to groan,' Jake's voice began to waver as he continued, ' "Get me out of here, get me out of here." '

Jake paused in his narration, gulped at his brew, and found the resolve to continue with the account.

'Then, I almost started crying, mate. Johan was trying to crawl out himself, but his arms were just so feeble, it was like watching a baby.'

At this point, One Platoon had come under small arms contact. Some of Three Platoon's dismounts, including Fairy Eyes, had arrived to help with the casualty.

'So we finally get him out and onto the floor. His back's all swollen and all of his clothes had been ripped open at the seams.' Unexpectedly, Jake now began to smile. 'Em turns up, and she can see he has a broken pelvis, so she prods him close to his arse and asks him if he can feel it. Johan says, "Yeah, you're trying to finger my hoop." '

I burst into laughter along with my friend.

'What a fucking lad,' I said in deep admiration.

'Yeah, he's a fucking legend.' Jake smiled. 'So we're pretty sure he's got a collapsed lung, and he's having difficulty breathing, so he's automatically a CAT A casualty, yeah?'

'Yeah,' I knew this to be a fact, even from my basic level of medical training.

'Well, we got hit almost exactly the same time as the Omelette team got wiped out.'

That made sense – if the OMLT incident had occurred earlier, patrol minimize would have been enforced throughout Helmand. This restricted all units to remain within their patrol bases, an acknowledgement that we didn't have the resources to deal with two such incidents at once.

'So we're sending our nine-liners up the chain, and someone in either Bastion or DC keeps trying to reclassify him as a CAT B. We're thinking it's because the MERT are so overworked with all the casualties from the Omelette shooting. Staff Edwards and the OC stuck to their guns, and because a CAT A has to be CASEVA-Ced within the hour, eventually we had an American Pedro come to collect him.'

'It's fucking disgusting,' I said, blood boiling. 'Look at what happened with Hunt and Prosser. Just because he came out of the hatch alive doesn't mean he'll stay that way. They're such fucking cunts.'

'Gez!' came the call across the courtyard. 'Mastiffs are here!'

I put my arm over my friend's shoulder.

'If you want to talk mate, then you can always talk to me,' I told him. 'But you'll have to come to DC to do it.'

'Fuck going there. I'd rather just talk to Blake.'

We laughed, and I left him with the well-worn farewell of the infantry soldier.

'Stay low, move fast.'

18

Living With the Enemy

I wasn't thrilled to be sent to DC now that the Household Cavalry Regiment had taken command, but at least it offered the promise of cooked food and phones. The strain of providing the battle group QRF from a single platoon was too great with the R&R rotation in full swing, and so the contingent was now made up of members from every platoon in the company.

I found myself in the back of the truck belonging to Killer, his blond hair and small spectacles giving him the look of a Gestapo officer. In Three Platoon, we preferred to hand out discipline in the old school way of a clip around the head or an honest punishment like sandbag filling. We saw no need to make paperwork out of it, but the army did, giving their twenty-first century system of punishment the acronym of AGAI. I had no idea what the letters stood for, but I imagine that administration made up one of the As. Killer's propensity for handing out these formal reprimands had led to his secondary nickname from the privates of Two Platoon; Mr Me-AGAI.

I was the equal to him in rank and we had served in the same Warrior during Iraq, and so I was prepared to give him the benefit of the doubt. I asked about his R&R.

'I was in the taxi office with my brother, after going on the piss, like,' he told me. 'And there's this guy in there with a cast on his arm, giving it big licks to the girls that he got wounded in Afghan. So, me and my brother ask him what unit he was with, like.'

The imposter had answered with the name of our own.

'Did you smash him up?'

'No,' he admitted. 'I was just speechless, like.'

Despite his apparent love of discipline, Killer was quick to warn me about the pitfalls of DC now that the HCR were firmly in charge.

'Shave every day, or they'll charge you, like. But don't get caught wearing a T-shirt when you shave, they'll charge you for that, too. Obviously you need to have your weapon with you at all times, like, but keep it strapped to you if you go anywhere public. Nacho had his at the side of the sofa next to him when he was on QRF runner, and some HCR NCO was trying to sneak up behind the sofa to take it.'

'What the fuck?' I blurted, perplexed.

'Yeah, their senior NCOs try and get weapons and hand them in to the RSM, then they charge the guys. If you haven't got your weapon like literally strapped to you a hundred per cent of the time, one of the fuckers will take it.'

'That's just nuts,' I stated, but I could see that Killer was far from done.

'Yeah, I know, mate. Now if you want to go to the toilets, you need to be in full gear. If you're wearing any green kit, it has to be underneath desert camo.'

'Tactical shitting. Got it. Don't tell me, I bet everyone's just pissing behind the tent?' Killer smiled at my remark. That was exactly what was happening.

'Well that's me full of morale,' I concluded. 'Thanks for that.' But I could see he had more.

I sighed wearily. 'Go on.'

Killer told me about a piece of intelligence that had been imparted during the previous evening's powwow. A Taliban bomb maker had handed himself over to the authorities, and despite admitting to planting bombs that had killed and maimed ISAF soldiers, the man was expected to receive a mere eight to ten years in prison. It was just one more stab in the back, one more betrayal, and we lamented once again our reasons for being in that place.

The next day was Friday the thirteenth, and as we prepared our three Warriors for a resupply to one of the outlying bases the curse kicked in.

Victor – who had returned from hospital in Bastion, but still suffered back pain from the IED hit – discovered during a functions test that his Warrior's chain gun was malfunctioning. There was no chance of a replacement, and so we were a weapon system down. Then, despite having signallers crawling over them for hours, radios in two of the wagons refused to work. Victor's truck would have to be left behind, while Killer would command his Warrior with the man-pack radio I carried as Barma team commander.

Finally out on the ground, it wasn't long before Killer's truck broke down, choosing a wadi shin deep in water as the place to do it. Splashing around, we discovered that the cause was a fuel leak. That fixed, it was time to abort the mission and return to base. As our lead Warrior disappeared into a dust cloud of its own creation, the hydraulic door of our own truck's troop compartment failed to close. Killer tried calling back the lead vehicle, but the man-pack radio now decided to join the party and failed to function.

'Fuck it.'

As our comrades drove into the distance we just kicked water at each other, and laughed.

Nacho was in the base's medical centre, suffering heavily from diarrhoea and vomiting. We chastised him for his lack of attention to personal cleanliness, but had to retract our insults when we discovered the true cause of his illness.

One of the boys had thought it would be funny to rub his arsehole over the rim of Nacho's water bottle.

Clearly, the Devil was infesting idle minds, and no wonder. We were at DC with the purpose of being the battle group's quick reaction force, but the HCR seemed intent on using us for nothing more than the most mundane resupply missions. Now, they were planning on moving the QRF permanently to FOB Edinburgh, situated in the middle of the open desert. Reaction of any kind from a place so remote would be limited – we had needed the American mine-sweeping unit to break out of there in August, and look how that turned out. There would certainly be nothing quick about it.

'They just want us out of their hair,' I told Killer. 'Short as it is.'

'Don't want us stealing their thunder, like,' he agreed.

I was especially frustrated because, the night before, Three Platoon had been involved in a long-running contact. I'd expected that, as QRF, we'd be the ones putting the rounds down. Instead we spent our days in the tents, afraid to venture out and place ourselves at the mercy of what we saw as the HCR's bullshit.

We weren't the only outsiders at DC, or in the battle group, and while the HCR excelled at pushing us away, their outdated attitude provided a common ground for strangers from other units to bond over. REME, infantry, engineers; none had a good word to say about the cavalry.

'Horse-shit Cunt Regiment,' someone rumbled – the same lad who had taken down Nacho with the booby-trapped water bottle.

'Close enough,' I agreed, before laughing at the image of Nacho shitting and puking his brains out.

There'd been a scuffle in the scoff house when a group of Anglians had tabbed in from their patrol base in the north and a HCR NCO had demanded that they wash their hands for his inspection. When the infanteers' NCO had told him that they'd already done so, the cavalryman insisted that they do it again, and under his supervision. Punches flew.

A visiting REME warrant officer class one, the most senior rank among NCOs, joined us at the Warriors. He was obviously desperate for someone to talk to, even if it had to be the lower ranks who should never have heard his complaints.

'I've been all over Helmand and I've never known anywhere like this place,' he told his eager listeners. 'There's no morale. Even in the hard-up FOBs around Sangin there's craic. Here, everyone's just watching their backs, you can see it. For fuck's sake, you have to be in full dress just to take a shit in a plastic bag.'

'You're right there, sir,' one of the boys agreed. 'If the CO saw some boys in shorts kicking a ball around, he'd probably shit a Mastiff.'

And yet again at DC, there was nothing else to do but laugh.

Dressed for battle, I was making a bio-deposit into a plastic bag. Usually, it was such an effort to prepare for an outing to the toilets at DC that you would make a trip of it, perhaps reading a magazine or masturbating. Maybe both. But today I could hear gunfire in the distance. Lots of it. I reasoned that, as a member of the quick reaction force, I would soon be heading in the direction of that noise.

I ran back to the Warriors, assembling with the others. As the wagon's engines roared to life, we began to pull on body armour and ready our weapons. The rattle of gunfire showed no signs of abating, and so we waited eagerly for our orders.

Which never came.

'What the fuck is going on, Colour?' I asked the NCO in charge of our three Warriors, but he was as clueless as I was.

We climbed onto the armour for a better vantage point, shielding our eyes as we looked in the direction of the sustained contact. We stayed there for hours, hoping, and never receiving, our orders to join the fray.

The fight was in the green zone, close to a patrol base named Woqab. We had been due to go there that afternoon to collect the IEDD team, and now this same team of bomb disposal experts had come under heavy gunfire from Taliban dug into three compounds. The engineers and their infantry escorts had tried shooting their way out, mortaring their way out, and now that neither of those options had worked they would air strike their way out.

We watched as the American A-10s made two strafing runs with their 30mm nose cannons, the sound echoing across the valley, a giant buzz saw ripping the air. They followed up these attacks, dropping two 500lb bombs. Thick pillars of black smoke rose against the blue sky, and signalled the end of the shooting.

From the first shots that I heard to the dropping of the bombs, the collective blood pressure of the QRF had gotten to a point where we were in danger of collapse. We were livid.

'Why the fuck are we here?' I shouted pointlessly in the direction of the HCR's operations room.

'Gez, calm the fuck down,' the colour sergeant told me.

'I'm sorry, Colour. It's just fucking bollocks, isn't it?'

He shrugged. He shrugged to agree, but also because he had been in the army long enough to know that a lot of things are bollocks, and that's just the way it is. He had survived twenty years of the military's machinations, and you can only do that if you let things slide.

I couldn't, and I explained why to anyone who would listen.

'We're the battle group QRF, yeah? Someone in the battle group is under contact, and they don't even stand us up to immediate notice to move? Obviously they never, ever, had any intention of using us. We were supposed to go to Woqab and make the pick-up anyway, so obviously it's accessible to Warriors. We could have put thirty mil directly into those firing points! I know the rules of engagement are bollocks, but surely engaging with thirty mil from a Warrior is a better option for avoiding collateral damage than strafing runs and bombs? These cunts just don't want us stealing their thunder, and that's why they're shunting us off to fucking FOB Edi, the fucks!'

My comrades listened with tired expressions until I burned myself out. Even hours later, I was embittered (almost a decade on and writing this, I still am, the fucking cunts). This was supposed to be my tour, my war, and they were cheating me out of it.

We took a resupply to the small group of Anglian infanteers occupying Himal OP, the place we had stopped at shortly following the destruction of 1-1. We were in no hurry to leave – it wasn't like we had any other tasks to perform – and so I made the steep climb to the top of the hill.

The dust and gravel slipped away beneath my feet, and soon I was panting, my body armour constricting my breathing, a cascade of sweat on my face. As I reached the summit I removed my helmet, enjoying the meagre breeze. Perhaps I had my eyes closed in this moment of relaxation, because I didn't see the wooden beam that I walked into.

It struck my head so hard that I was put on my arse. The two infanteers inside the sangar turned to look at me, but they were so burned out from the tedium of their outpost that they didn't even smile, and simply gazed at me from hollow eyes.

I stared accusingly at the beam that had been my assassin, already feeling a lump on my forehead.

'I bet that happens all the time?' I asked them.

The reply came without a hint of a smile. 'No. You're the first.'

Blinking my eyes free of stars, I took in the scenery from behind the Hesco. It had been worth the climb, and the bump. The views were spectacular, encompassing Musa Qala and its surrounding villages, the wide wadi north and south, the desert to the west, and the sheer mountain ranges beyond. Looking into the nearest valley, along which wound Route Green, I could instantly make out where 1-1 had been hit. Through binoculars I could see the crater, and the black flag that still fluttered on the nearby compound. Seeing how visible the position of the IED was from this vantage, I became angry at how it had been possible to plant it, but these men were not the unit occupying the OP at the time and so I bit back on my comments.

I looked again to the south of the wadi. Shingle slopes grew into sheer cliff faces on its eastern side, whereas to the west the terrain was green from irrigated farmland. If this country wasn't perpetually at war the tourists would flock here, I thought.

'It's a beautiful view,' I told the two zombies beside me.

They made no comment. This was their tour; six months living inside of a dirt bunker, confined to an area the size of a small garden, staring out at an endless landscape.

Maybe living with the enemy wasn't so bad, after all.

#veteranproblems

Home, United Kingdom, 2014

I opened the desk drawer, pulled the journal from within and opened a page at random. The paper was smudged by dirty thumb-prints, the ink blurred where sweat had dripped onto the pages. The handwriting was shaky, almost illegible even to myself; my lap had been my desk. I read a page or ten at random, laughing or shaking my head at a memory forgotten.

As always, the journal led me to the staircase. I pulled open the small door beneath it, braving the spiders as I ducked within, and pulled out the black box that I'd bought in Kuwait – my campaign chest.

I took out the helmet, its interior ingrained with sand, its cover torn and bleached almost white. I felt the paintbrushes, running my fingers through the bristles as if I was caressing a lover, thinking of the art I had worked with them, a masterpiece of survival by luck. I laughed at myself.

The maps were creased from a lifetime behind body armour plates and imprisonment beneath the stairs. I told myself once again that I should frame them, but I knew that I wouldn't. What do you tell a girl when she asks about a tactical map spread onto your bedroom wall? Condoms were bad enough. I didn't want her trying to push me into a straitjacket.

I saw the sand collected in the recesses of the box and rubbed the grains between my fingers. I laughed again. Did I do this because I wanted to, or because it was expected of me, the veteran? This is what they did in the Vietnam books. This is what they did in the movies, only there should be a thick row of medals in the chest.

My own medals were in the dining room cabinet. They lay flat, masters of concealment, unseen unless you stood at arm's length from them. There were no thick rows. I failed the test as a Hollywood hero. There was my Afghan medal. My Iraq medal. I took them out. They were dirty, smudged by fingers the last time I had held them. As always, I'd forgotten the details, and was pleasantly surprised at how aesthetically pleasing they were. My precious.

I placed them back alongside the silver ring of a Roman soldier. I had been given it as a gift from my mother, and I valued it more than I did my own medals. It was a connection to a warrior of the past, and I prayed that there was some kind of Valhalla after death where warriors of all ages came together to drink and tell tales.

I closed the cabinet. The door beneath the stairs. The drawer. It was time to put them away for another year, until the nostalgia of Remembrance Sunday would compel me to go through the ritual once again.

19

The Big Push

The OC arrived at DC for his weekly orders group, transported there by the HCR's Mastiffs. There was a rumour doing the rounds that there was an op coming up, and it was expected that Victor's crew and wagon would be returning to Minden following the OC's conference with the battle group CO. But, to our surprise, a number of the company spilled out from the rear of the Mastiffs; they'd come to replace us.

As happy as I was to be heading back to The Firm and out from under the gaze of the HCR, I had to admit to myself that I was a little sorry to be leaving the phones and the food behind. Besides, it was hardly as if Minden was an oasis of tolerance and individuality.

The OC's conference concluded, we mounted up into the supposedly bombproof trucks. It was 5 p.m. as we drove out of the gates, and one of the soldiers beside me began to grumble; the scoff house was now opening.

'He could have waited twenty minutes to let us get some scoff.'

'Probably wants to get back ASAP to give his orders for this op,' I offered, though my empty stomach agreed totally with the sentiment.

'Slack fucking leadership.'

We arrived in Minden three hours later, and it had not been an enjoyable journey, the rear of the Mastiff an uncomfortable place on Afghan's rural roads. The seats fold down, meaning that they fold up whenever the wagon hits a rut or ditch, which of course was every few seconds. The worst part of this pogo was that each bump into the air pushed the lower edge of the body armour plate into a swollen bladder, and by the time we reached our patrol base I was picturing the stinking piss tubes as a man dying of thirst would imagine a waterfall.

I was reunited with my platoon, and the Boss gathered us together for orders.

'Basically,' the Boss began, 'I can't really give any orders, because no one knows what the fuck is going on. It's suck it and see. We're pushing south, with the HCR, and maybe we'll occupy a compound on the other side of the M4, or maybe not. If we do, it could be for one night, or permanently.'

'Which compound, Boss?' Toby asked. Our maps, made up from aerial photographs, showed each compound with a bright outline and number for easy identification.

'Don't know,' the Boss concluded with a shrug.

We packed the basics: ammunition, water, rations, and now warm kit for the nights, the temperature dropping steeply in the autumn dark.

'We're going back to fucking DC?' I asked Toby, incredulous.

We were. After a few hours' sleep, and for the second day in a row, we made the journey along Route Pink. We would collect elements of the HCR there, and then return to Minden the same day.

'Why the fuck can't they come to us?' I demanded of my friend. We were in the troop compartment of Sergeant Davies' wagon, accompanied by Nacho. Jake was in the turret as gunner.

'The CO's with them,' Toby answered, as if that explained everything. And it did. With us to clear and hold open the route, the CO could make the journey in next to no time.

We arrived at DC just in time to miss lunch. None had been kept behind for us.

'Says it all,' Toby spat. 'It's us and them.'

Maybe there was a reason for the oversight, but if you don't spell it out to the infantryman, then he will create his own. We saw it as a slight. An attack. We were livid.

'Stay here,' I told Nacho, before turning back to Toby. 'Let's go see if the chogi shop's open.'

The chogi shop was a small wooden hut run by the ANA, selling cans of pop and chocolate bars. We filled our pockets with enough to keep the crew of our Warrior running until evening meal, and headed back to the main gate where our vehicles were waiting.

We moved hastily through the camp, not wanting to deal with the bullshit questions about why we wore no headdress. With our eyes down, I wasn't sure how Toby spotted the open refrigerated shipping container behind the scoff house.

'Watch my back,' he told me, and slipped inside, emerging with a box under his arm.

'What you got?' I asked, and he lifted the lid to show me the sugared doughnuts.

We made it back to the truck with our prize, and despite promising ourselves that we would make the treat last for the duration of the op, we were soon licking the last of the sugar and jam off of our fingers, the confectionary all the sweeter because of its liberation from the enemy.

'Good thing we scoffed that,' Toby said, as we rolled back out of the gates and towards Minden. Yet again, we were leaving DC a few minutes before the hot meals were served. Our blood boiled.

'I don't know if they're just too thick to think about these things, or they just don't give a fuck,' I seethed.

Toby was in no doubt. 'They don't give a fuck. It's not hard to organize scoff for the troops. They can do it on the ranges at Brecon, so why can't they do it when you're starting out on an op that'll last fuck knows how long? Because they don't give a fuck, that's why.'

'I'm just sick of this place,' I moaned. 'I wish I had another doughnut.'

Toby smiled. He knew me well. 'You fucking love it.' He told me. I really did.

·

We left Minden in the darkness that night, heading east into the desert in the hope that we could skirt around the IED belts that were planted in front of the M4 wadi. But the Taliban were no amateurs, and it was only thirty minutes out of the gate before a Mastiff struck an IED.

'So much for the sneaky beaky,' Toby laughed. 'You could have heard that fucker in Swansea.'

We were alone now, Nacho moved on to another wagon, and so we stretched out onto a troop bench apiece. At one point we went wide-eyed and cursed aloud as our wagon slipped sideways on a slope, equipment scattering across the troop compartment – later, the crew of the Warrior behind would tell us that we were inches away from rolling over – and it was a while before the adrenaline had cleared out of our veins. When it did, we drifted in and out of sleep, woken only when Jake imparted information from the turret.

'We've got to wait for the QRF to come from DC and collect the Mastiff. It's fucked.'

After that delay, the battle group was on the move again, but not for long. A new route was tried to avoid the IEDs, and three Mastiffs became dug in to the mud and ditches, and had to be recovered. We were now five hours behind schedule, and a decision was made to laager up in the desert for the night. We took turns at sentry duty in the turret, snivelling and snotty with the cold. At stops like these, the dismounts would be ejected from the troop compartment to allow the crew to sleep, and so I huddled with Toby on our body armour, wrapped up beneath the raised steel of our Warrior's hull.

That morning, we took up a blocking position on a ridge known as Middle Hill. From there we were to watch over the villages of Wach Kariz and Chakaw, while other units, including the engineers, cleared Route Pink and the M4 wadi of IEDs.

I dismounted with the GPMG, Toby carrying the extra ammo that Jay would usually bring along for me, our friend still on R&R along with Danny.

'See any cover?' I asked Toby, who only laughed. The hillside was totally bare, but we were loath to spend the day in the back of the Warrior. We were joined by four dismounts from the other two wagons on the ridge line, Rabbit telling us that the MERT was on its way to extract two casualties from the EOD.

'How the fuck did that happen?' Toby asked. We'd heard no IED detonations or gunfire.

'When they were running off the Chinook, some detonators went off in one of their guy's pockets. Injured him and the bloke next to him,' Rabbit told us.

'Embarrassing,' was all Toby had to say to that.

We watched as Chinooks ferried in more troops south of the M4 Wadi, bringing the engineers, OMLT, and ANA. We could also make out Two Platoon, clearing along Route Pink with a second group of IED disposal experts. It wasn't long until The Zoo found a daisy-chain IED – several bombs linked together to one detonator, a command wire leading to a compound beside the track. The daisy-chain was made up of one 105mm artillery shell and two home-made devices packed with ball bearings to act as shrapnel. This trap had been laid with one aim in mind: to shred soldiers on foot. It was the first of some twenty IEDs that would be found that day.

We watched from our hillside, waiting for one such device to be blown in a controlled explosion. But the sound of the bang came from the wrong direction, and we turned our heads just in time to see the RPG detonating against the turret of our Warrior.

Machine gun fire now began to zip and crack about our heads, and devoid of cover we had nothing else to do but press ourselves into the stone.

'There!' Toby shouted, pointing out the firing point, identified by the small cloud of smoke drifting from the RPG's launch. 'Don't fire!' he called to the dismounts; there were friendly units between us and them.

The Warrior's turret then began to traverse, which was a relief, meaning that the men inside were unharmed. The attack lasted less than half a minute, a real tease. We dusted ourselves off and went to check up on our comrades. As we called up to the turret, Jake's livid face appeared from out of his hatch.

'They fucking blew up my GPS!' he shouted, shaking the scrambled bundle of wires and plastic in an angry fist.

Happy that our friend was himself, Toby and I returned to our vantage, a Merlin helicopter passing low over the ridge.

'They have Merlins in theatre now?' Blake asked.

Toby sneered. 'No, you cunt, you're just suffering from heatstroke.'

An Apache was the next participant in that day's air show, impressing us with its tight turns and manoeuvres above the wadi. It obviously didn't impress the enemy in the same way, because they now opened up on our company HQ. It was the same tactic, a short and sharp attack with RPGs and small arms fire. A few minutes later, and two more RPGs streaked towards the HCR Mastiffs that sat in the open wadi. Out of sight, but audible across the hillside, a unit of Jackals in one of the eastern villages came under mortar and RPG fire. Then, once again, it was the turn of the Mastiffs in the wadi to suffer the same kind of attack, but this time they would not wait in vain to identify firing points. We watched on from our ridge as they unloaded their heavy and grenade machine guns into the green zone of the west bank.

Perhaps feeling left out, our own mortars at Minden began to rain high explosive onto the treelines. It wasn't long before the 105mm guns of FOB Edinburgh also got in on the act.

Up on the ridge, we had abandoned sitting on the arse-numbing stone and stood watching the spectacle below us.

'Good this, innit?' I said, smiling at Toby.

If only we'd kept some doughnuts.

The village of Chakaw, which sat at the base of OP Hill, was cleared by the ANA and Omelette, and then our platoon moved in. No decision had yet been made on whether or not to occupy a compound, but one had been identified as a potential patrol base. Its mud walls sat on the edge of the M4, overlooking the field where Jake had been shot. It was the same building where Ratty had claimed to have dropped one of the enemy during that contact. Empty cases from the enemy's weapons were scattered about.

We spent the night in a small field beside the compound, the wagons circled and expecting Indians. Instead, only desert foxes made an appearance through the thermal scopes. I almost expected the aristocrats of the HCR to give chase to the creatures, trumpets blaring.

'They're fucking shit, the Taliban around here,' I grumbled to Toby, disappointed at the lack of action.

'Probably busy planting new IED belts further south,' he replied, impressing me with his wisdom.

I wondered if we had air assets looking for them. If we did, then we never heard about it.

As day broke, the decision had been made to occupy the compound, but this would first need to be cleared of IEDs and booby traps by our engineers. Yesterday, there hadn't been enough time to get to all of Terry's buried treasure.

'Rather them than me,' Toby said as the Royal Engineers set to their task. We were on foot, pushing out into the open ground now known as 'Pinkmist's Field'. With my GPMG and the LMG of Ginger Pubes, we were to lie in overwatch as the sappers completed their task. It was eerie to be lying in that exposed position once again, even knowing that our flank was secure. To pass the time, we retraced the steps of that day, and tried to pinpoint the position where Jake must have gone down. How much of our brass was littering this field?

We watched the engineers clear the outside of the building, sometimes blowing and sometimes recovering the IEDs that had been buried there. Some had been stepped on or driven over during the op but the detonators had not been connected to the explosives. It seemed as though we owed the HCR CO an apology. The Big Push had taken the enemy by surprise, after all.

Such was the density of IEDs that as one engineer stood and turned on his Vallon, following a break, he discovered a device a metre to the right of where he had been sitting.

As Toby and I observed, my friend passing on the information that came over his radio, we could only marvel that our patrol to this place, so early in the tour, had not resulted in a number of us going home in boxes.

Into the afternoon, our ears were ringing from so many explosions that conversation in our small party died, and so it was a welcome distraction when we saw two young children appear at the edge of the wadi nearest to us.

'What the fuck are they doing?' Toby asked, looking through the 4x zoom of his rifle's ACOG. With the GPMG, I relied on the naked eye alone.

'Are they digging?' I asked, unsure.

'I don't think they're digging, but they're definitely fucking around in the ground.'

The boys stood, something in their hands that were down by their sides, and shuffled hurriedly to the lip of the wadi, where they became hidden from sight.

'Maybe it's packages of drugs?' Ginger Pubes offered, thinking outside of the box.

We kept watching as the children shuffled back and forth.

'They look heavy,' Toby put in, and I agreed. The children's shoulders were slumping with the effort.

'Fuck!' Toby blurted, suddenly sure. 'They're mortar rounds!'

'Gen?'

'Fucking right, I saw them clearly then. They must be emptying a cache now we're here.'

With hesitation I asked, 'Should we shoot?'

'No. Warning shot, maybe?' Toby got on the radio to ask for permission to do just such a thing. From the snarl on his face, I didn't need to ask what the reply had been.

'Why?' I ventured.

'No reason. Just a no.'

We watched on as the children continued to make their shuttles, certain now that it was mortar rounds in their hands.

'Look! Look!' Ginger Pubes pointed.

A man had emerged from the brush at our side of the wadi, the children by the hole looking to him for instruction.

'Motherfucker!' Toby snorted, before getting back on the radio. 'Zero Alpha this is Three Three Charlie. There's an adult male directing these kids with the mortar rounds. We're in dead ground to them. I want to move up and apprehend him, over.'

The reply was instantaneous.

'Zero Alpha, negative, stay in your position. Out.'

And with the OC's words, we were fixed to our position. A few minutes later, the children had gone.

The cache was empty.

Later that afternoon we moved into the compound. It was the same size as Zulu, but the garden was bare. It was also on the lower end of the Afghan property ladder in comparison to Minden, with crumbling mud walls. I wondered if we'd contributed to that.

'It's in shit state,' Jake said, meaning it literally. Several of the rooms had their floors blanketed in human excrement.

'Fucking animals,' Toby growled. 'I know they don't have proper sewers like we do, but what's wrong with building an outside shitter? A burn pit or a fucking burn barrel? How do you think it's OK to just shit on the floor of your house?'

'I'm not even sure how they do it,' Jake put in. 'I mean, to actually physically squat in here and take a shit, when you're surrounded by hundreds of stinking shits. I'd be sick all over myself, like.'

'You're forgetting the best bit,' I told them. 'Someone's got to clean this up.'

'Well it ain't gonna be fucking me,' Toby said, puffing out his chest.

He needn't have worried. Like all of the shittest jobs in the army, the task would fall to the lowliest of private soldiers.

The rest of us went about selecting rooms, The Firm claiming one shit-free abode as Viper's Nest Two. We rolled out our sleeping bags on the floor and placed small wax candles in the alcoves.

'Now we're talking, boys,' Toby said with pride, lighting the final flame.

As darkness closed in and the temperature began to plummet, we huddled around a couple of candles in our warm kit, discussing our new home, and the two-day operation to take it. Our sentries posted, we drifted off to sleep.

We awoke soon after, the ground shaking, the night split.

We were being mortared.

The next day was spent turning the compound into a patrol base. It looked as if we'd be staying.

I took it upon myself to dig the burn pit in the garden, enjoying the labour. In the UK, my mum would always say that such activities were better for me than the gym, and I smiled at the irony. I was up to my waist when the CO and regimental sergeant major of our parent unit arrived on a whistle-stop visit from the UK. Luckily, I was able to avoid conversation with them as Toby entered the garden and the RSM caught sight of his bushy sideburns.

'Fuck me! I thought Elvis was dead!'

We used the spoil of the pit to fill sandbags that were placed on the rooftop to form a sangar. For some unknown reason our store of sandbags was extremely limited, and so the walls would only be two bags deep and three high.

Razor wire was rolled out around the walls, the deep recess of the M4 wadi at the back of the compound covered with trip flares and claymore mines. A toilet was constructed by placing a few of the Warriors' spare road wheels on top of one another. A piss trench was dug beside the burn pit. A number of neighbouring trees needed cutting down, but the engineers volunteered to take care of them with explosives. First, however, they needed to deal with the IED that Two Platoon had almost sat on during a patrol outside of the new base.

An explosion went off and we assumed it to be that controlled detonation, but it was instead followed by calls of 'Incoming!' from the sangars.

Our friends with the mortars were back again. Welcome to the neighbourhood. We took cover in the rooms of the compound, safe enough from anything but a direct hit. Jake looked green, but the rest of us passed the short attack with banter. Those of us who had known Iraq in 2007 – particularly veterans of Basra Palace – were well acquainted with rocket and mortar attacks, where they often occurred several times a day. After those barrages, the Taliban's attempt was treated with contempt.

Later that day, word came over the radio that the new patrol base would be known as Khabir, after an Afghan soldier who had died in the north of the battle group's area of operations the week before.

It wasn't a popular decision.

'What about our own boys?' Jake demanded.

'It's the same old story,' Toby answered. 'Our engineers clear the place, we provide the cordon, and the ANA come in and mince around the village for a bit before fucking off. Then, it's us who man the new patrol base, but we name it after them, and then it's all politically correct bullshit. The Afghans are winning the war, and we're just here to help out.'

Nobody argued with him, but the name would stick. Like the flag flying above the compound we British troops were holding, this base was all Afghan.

As our defensive stores were limited, it wasn't long until we ran out of ways to improve this new position. Like Zulu, there was nothing here to distract us, and so when not on duty in the sangars we gathered together in the small courtyard to brew up and talk.

Blake was a conversation piece the day after we moved in. During the night we'd spent outside of the compound he'd lost his thickly padded jacket. The next day, an old Afghan had been spotted walking by the new base, modelling the prized garment. We'd refused to let Blake take it back from him.

'Learn your lesson,' Toby had scolded him with delight.

There was also a stranger in our midst, an NCO who was responsible for liaison with the locals. He was already worn down by our grilling about the policy that restricted us to the IED'd tracks – as if it was born of his own decisions – and now tried to change the subject, giving us the gen about a Taliban commander who had recently switched sides.

'Now he's the district governor for Musa Qala and he wants a new wife from Kabul. She'll be his fifth. He dyes his beard this really weird orange colour because he thinks he looks great. His son is an equally fat, horrible cunt, and his dad wants him to be educated in the UK.' This brought snorts of derision from the assembly.

'What the fuck are we working with him for, anyway?' someone asked.

'Well there were two Taliban commanders with the same name. Rumour mill says the intelligence fucked up and we brought the wrong one over to our side, promising to make him governor.'

Nobody laughed at this piece of gen, and equally nobody was surprised. It was Afghanistan 101.

One of the reasons the liaison officer was present was to deal with the family who had occupied the compound before us. Yesterday, he'd had to explain to them that they were to leave within an hour, and that they would be paid a couple of hundred dollars for their troubles. Utter shithole that it was, we couldn't help but feel bad for the family who had been evicted from their front-line home, and we watched from the sangars as they set up their refuge of sticks and sheets in the open field beside our Warriors.

The Afghan family were not the only ones living outside of compounds. Part of One Platoon occupied OP Hill, the high ground that dominated Chakaw village, so named for the old Russian positions that scarred its summit. It was a testament to the perpetual war in the region, the irony not lost on us that history was repeating itself. One Platoon had two Warriors on this high ground, and were living out of the back of them. If it wasn't for the presence of their cannons we had no doubt that our new home would be hammered (when the hill was taken over by 2 Lancs the next year, who had no armoured vehicles, that is exactly what happened). The troops in these Warriors were confined to a narrow area, the engineers having to take their time in clearing the heights of the legacy mines from the former Russian occupants.

During one of the enemy's sporadic mortar attacks, the artillery based at FOB Edinburgh located the firing point using radar, and soon 105mm shells were dropping onto the position, the tremors of the impacts passing beneath our boots. Our interpreter translated the hurried messages that he received over the ICOM.

'They're firing the big shells! Get in the bunkers!'

The men on OP Hill claimed to have identified one of these bunker complexes, seeing Afghans seemingly materialize out of the ground to the south, at a position known as Lone Tree. That seemed to corroborate the intelligence gathered from locals, who told us that the next village south had upwards of eight Taliban soldiers. They added that the subsequent village along the wadi had been cleared of civilians and was now wholly Taliban.

These locals seemed apathetic about our presence, and who could blame them? Some even assumed that we were Russian, particularly when the formidable frame of Lump Head was seen patrolling their village. National affairs were not important to them, and global even less so. With OP Hill above them, the Afghans of Chakaw lived beneath a reminder of occupation, but the empty Russian positions were proof that their time here had been temporary, as our own would be. The locals knew that we'd be gone, and the Taliban would be back. Life would go on, so long as they didn't die in the crossfire in the meantime. They even held their tongues when Toby misguided a Warrior, hitting the compound wall and showering a gathering of locals and the liaison officer with dirty masonry.

Toby was in a bad mood following the incident, blaming everyone from the villagers to Gordon Brown. For my own part, I was happy. Khabir was a bullshit-free zone, exactly how I had pictured our tour to be. As more 105mm artillery rounds crumped into the earth that night, shaking the dirt beneath us, I wondered how any man could have stayed sane during the great bombardments of the

First World War trenches. It was comparing apples and oranges, I knew, but I wondered if, even in that darkest of wars, there were days when the soldiers complained about discipline or laughed at a cock joke. Without a doubt they did, I decided, proud that I could consider myself their descendent.

During the artillery strike, Jake had pulled on his helmet and body armour, pushing himself into the room's corner. Hours after the last rounds had shaken the ground, he was still wearing all of his protective gear. When he began to sleep in it we teased him about his latest eccentricity.

'What do you think that's gonna do if a shell lands on your head?'

'Fuck off.'

'When you get hit do you want us to scrape you into a jerry can or an ammo tin?'

'Fuck off.'

After a few days at Khabir the platoon was rotated, and so I led the Barma team to secure the cratered Route Pink back to Minden. One of my hedgerow men was from the cavalry; a number of HCR troopers were on loan to our company to boost numbers. Unlike their head shed, we got along just fine with these lads, though none of us could understand why anyone would want to join, or remain in, such a regiment.

Not long after we cleared our way through a wadi, the HCR trooper drew my attention to a farmer ahead, who was gesturing at us with his spade. I took a Vallon to scan in front of me and went forwards. The farmer was standing close to the track, and pointing to the corner of the field that lay alongside the wheel ruts. Unlike the rest of his land, this spot had been untouched by plough.

'IED?' I asked him, then mimed an explosion. He nodded, smiled through his few remaining teeth, and began waving his spade at the earth.

'Woah, woah, woah, mate. Careful with that,' I urged, worried he'd turn us both into pink mist. The man took my meaning and stopped his gesticulations.

I went to one knee beside the untouched earth, pulling the paint brush from my body armour. Perhaps unconvinced that I knew my trade, the farmer now moved away.

I only had to tease lightly with fingertips and the brush before I exposed the plastic wrapping on a metal object. I used the Vallon from one of my team to take a reading, confirming the high metal content. I'd seen enough to be convinced that it was an IED, placed in this position to target the outer man of the Barma team.

I called my thanks to the farmer, who waved back. I hoped for his sake that Terry wouldn't take the finding of his treasure personally and punish the man. Whether the identification of the device was a good deed on his part or he was simply pissed off at losing ground for harvest, I had no idea. Having marked the area for avoidance, we left the device for the engineers who were clearing the mines on OP Hill.

They blew it that evening, on their way back to Minden. The engineers were Gurkhas, and after a hard day's work on their bellies, they now set about butchering the chickens they had bought from the locals, turning them into the famous Gurkha curry. With these smiling Nepalese was a British ATO, and he was good enough to pass on the details of the device to me. It had been made of 15–20kg of explosive detonation cord, wrapped about a metal pot packed with shrapnel, and armed with a snap peg trigger. Without doubt, it had been planted there to take out a team of dismounts.

Many times on the tour I'd cursed the farmers and their crops, but that day it seemed as though the need for a few extra metres of agriculture had saved my life.

20

Smoke and a Pancake

A shadow was moving through the night, slipping from an alleyway between compounds, bare feet silent against the dirt.

It was a wasted effort, stealth no defence against the sentries and their night vision devices in the patrol base's sangars, and they watched the shadow, a young Afghan boy, as he placed a package alongside a break in the compound's Hesco walls.

And they did nothing.

They did nothing, and now the sergeant major emerged from this hole in the defences. He put a wad of dirty dollars into the boy's hand, the villager disappearing into the darkness before emerging again with burdens cradled in his skinny arms. The sergeant major watched him come, a collection of junior soldiers behind him to carry the midnight surprise inside.

Sacks of potatoes. Crates of coke. Boxes of Mars Bars. Packets of cheap, lung-busting cigarettes. Some of this the sergeant major would sell from the company's tuck shop, as proud of his enterprise as a first-generation corner shop owner. The potatoes would be ordered by Two Platoon, though why The Zoo needed so many was a mystery to those outside of that close band, and would not be uncovered until Christmas.

We assumed the boy was the son of a local shop owner. Selling to us openly would be a death sentence, and so orders were slipped to the shopkeeper during the roving patrols and then the exchange took place at night, the risk worth taking for the inflated prices paid in American currency. A cut-throat business, in every sense.

There were special orders, too. Eggs came before the chickens, but soon a sectioned-off area of Minden had become a petting zoo. It was Smith's baby, of course, and before long we could count a dozen poultry, a goat, and for a short time a donkey as members of the company. Temporary members at least, depending on how often we would receive fresh produce from the HCR at Musa Qala; whether they had something against us or our livestock was unclear, but the replenishments were rare. It was our Fijian butchers who snapped necks and cleaned the fowl, the task alien to we British members of the PlayStation generation; boys who had been trained to kill men – some who *had* killed men – but who shied at ending the life of a chicken.

The kitchen at Minden was made up of ammunition containers into which boiling water was placed to heat ration packs. There was one deep pan for frying the chips that came from our locally sourced potatoes, the oil recycled between the platoons. As the temperature began to drop and the fat of the greasy oil hardened, mice tap danced patterns into its grey surface.

And the mice were becoming an epidemic. We needed a cat, and so one was acquired, though no one could say from where. It was a tiny thing, a kitten, but I was confident that it would grow into a slayer of rodents. Along with a dozen other like-minded members of the company, I took to taking care of the creature when I was at Minden.

The capture of mice now became as exciting as that of the entrapment of scorpions, one soldier from The Zoo excelling at both. He became fond of placing a scorpion in an emptied water bottle before pushing the mouse inside, initiating a battle royale of insect versus mammal.

He held a bottle at head height for me, and I watched as the stinger plunged into the dirty brown fur. I watched as the mouse became still, its tiny ribcage expanding and struggling. The breaths became fewer. It died. The architect of the battle beamed, and went in search of the scorpion's next victim.

In the Viper's Nest I was woken nightly by a mouse that ran

across my face. At first the skittering movement upon my skin was enough to terrify me. When Toby caught the act in his torchlight and confirmed that it was one of our furry vermin, my relief was huge, and I almost welcomed its rapid trips through my hair. Better the devil you know.

The Viper's Nest was once again fully occupied by The Firm, as Danny and Jay returned from their R&R. As was expected of them, they'd brought baby oil and new music, but the offerings did little to enthuse us.

'Our war's fucking shit,' Danny began. 'There's no decent tunes for it.'

'Totally, mate,' I agreed. 'Look at Vietnam. Fucking music was unreal, and a lot of it was influenced by the war. I've got some awesome Vietnam music compilations. What the fuck would we have on an Afghan album in twenty years' time?'

'Some *X-Factor* cunts,' Danny sneered, face twisting at the thought.

Our war had been abandoned by culture, and so we clung on to other people's: music from the Nam era; movies of the Normandy beaches and the Arnhem bridge.

'Sign of the times,' Toby suggested. 'No one gives a fuck about stuff like politics and culture now. People live in a bubble.'

'Well the fucking music producers need to get a grip,' Danny stated with purpose, and I could only agree.

We had been raised on war films, the music as imprinted on our minds as the images of carnage we so adored. To us, 'Paint it Black' was Vietnam. 'Voodoo Chile' was Somalia. We had been taught by Hollywood that war needed a soundtrack. A soul. Shortages in equipment we could handle, but don't hold back on our album. Without it, the footage that had been rolling in our heads since the day we had wanted to kill was meaningless.

Of course, as in everything, we made do with what we had. My iPod held a playlist labelled 'war porn', filled with Hendrix, Linkin Park, Slayer, and Slipknot. Toby's taste was more Crosby and Sinatra. We could only guess at Danny's flavour of tunes. We just knew that he hated whatever anybody else tried to play. Maybe he knew what we didn't, and that even this shallow choice of soundtrack would be corrupted. I'd instructed my brother that should I win the treasure hunt, then Lostprophets' 'Last Train Home' should be played at my funeral. A few years later, and their lead singer would be convicted of conspiracy to rape a baby. When even the music of our war was polluted, it was little surprise that men's minds were the same.

Blinky, a lump of a mechanic, came into the room to find me.

'Cat's dead,' he told me, the brute trying to hide his distress. 'Somebody kicked it over the wall. It was fucked-up, so one of the lads finished it off with a spade.'

I stormed out of the room to find the killer, but no one would confess.

The kitten became just another casualty of the war.

The men of OP Hill were under siege.

The Taliban had belatedly decided to contest the occupation, perhaps realizing that it was permanent, and they had taken to sniping at the exposed position on a regular basis. It seemed as though there was one among the enemy ranks who was a crack shot with the RPG, and on consecutive days he struck a Warrior, destroying the Javelin missiles strapped to its side, and hit a sandbagged emplacement, turning the heavy machine gun into a useless lump of scrap. Somehow, One Platoon had come through both strikes without injuries.

'It's the same cunt who owes me a GPS,' Jake was certain, referring to the RPG that had struck the turret of his truck during the Big Push.

Whether it was the same gunner or not, an RPG paid a visit to Minden, smashing into the burn pit sangar. The Firm was in the Viper's Nest when it hit, and we pulled on our gear in anticipation of a further strike. There wasn't one, and instead we turned our attention to Jake, prone beneath the canvas of his cot bed.

'What fucking protection's that gonna give you?' Danny laughed at him.

'Fuck off,' came the muffled reply.

As Danny and Jay left to discover what had happened during the attack, I enticed Jake from his refuge. We stood together in the doorway, listening to automatic fire that now crackled in the distance.

'Khabir must be getting contacted,' I guessed, the attack on both patrol bases doubtless coordinated.

Suddenly we were both sent diving for cover as the booming fifty cal above our heads opened up without warning. This time there was no pulling Jake from the floor.

'You shit yourself too!' he accused me. I was laughing too hard to deny it.

Jay reappeared, informing us that there were no casualties. Behind him, in the courtyard, the panicked voice of one of company HQ's NCOs sparked up.

'Prepare to be attacked! Prepare to be attacked!'

We piled scorn on the idea, and the man. As the last of the adrenaline wore away, we climbed back onto our beds, Danny encouraging me to take photos of the sleeping form of Jake, who lay in the foetal position, encased in his body armour and helmet.

The camera flashed, we laughed, and the signs, so obvious, went unnoticed.

It was another patrol into the village of Yatimchay, recently rechristened Yatimshit, or Shatimchay by the troops. There was a new threat in this usually benign area, and it came from the backsides of the locals, who had mostly returned to their homes after the summer fighting. As winter closed in, they had ceased using the cornfields as their toilets, and now the mind of the patrolling soldier was as much on stepping in human shit as it was onto the trigger of an IED.

'What hope have we got of bringing democracy and other noble virtues to these fucking savages when they shit on their own fucking doorstep?' Danny posed to The Firm, his voice hushed in the darkness; it was a night patrol, our task to overlook a heavily IED'd stretch of track.

I was particularly strong in my agreement with my friend. The day before I had stepped in a huge human turd. Such was my anger that I had taken off after the laughing local children, but they easily escaped me, and the lumps of shit that I kicked after them. It had taken a long time, and lots of gagging, to clean the filth from the treads of my boot.

We had been in position for an hour, a dozen of us in the narrow ditch that ran alongside a compound wall, and what had started with silence had grown into hushed conversation. It began with the usual moaning about the company head shed, but soon encompassed all of the army's hierarchy, and eventually reached the pinnacle of politics.

'It's Gordon Brown's fault I got that shit on my boot,' I told my friends. 'He's the one that sent us here. This is his cluster-fuck.'

'Well technically then, it's actually Tony Blair's,' Jay corrected me. 'He was the one that started it all.'

'Well fuck them both.' I was still sore from a patrol earlier that day, where we had escorted some officers on foot to visit Khabir. Naturally, their equipment consisted of a rifle and a water bottle, whereas we were weighed down by our usual burdens. They'd made no effort to keep the patrol intact, or check on the men behind them, and so Jay and I, the machine gun duo, had finished the patrol through the village alone, enjoying the privacy of our stroll. When a round had creased the air above our heads, we hadn't even thought to bend a knee. A miss by a metre was as good as a miss by a mile. We were as salty as we were going to get.

My mention of politicians had started a new round of bitching, but this wasn't the reason why all attempts at stealth were now abandoned.

That reason was Cortez, the powerful camera system of the patrol base. It was being used to confirm all activity that we reported.

'If they can already fucking see it, then why are we out here?' Danny grumbled. 'My eyeballs don't have fucking thermal vision.'

And the thermal vision of Cortez had caught something special that week. Something that we had heard of but had disregarded as myth. Something that appalled, and intrigued, as much as the toilet habits of the Afghans.

A man had fucked a donkey.

There it was on the screens, the irrefutable evidence. The company proceeded into the camera operator's Portakabin in small groups. Some emerged disgusted, others smiling. All were glad that they'd made the effort to watch.

'Blake must have cum in his pants, seeing this shit,' Danny had remarked when our own turn had come to view the violation.

There was no doubt of what we were seeing on the screen, the man's white, thermal silhouette thrusting hard and fast into the donkey's behind. The camera panned right, zooming onto the animal rapist's accomplice. From the furious motion of his arm, he appeared to be wanking.

'I don't know what's more disturbing,' I said to my friend. 'The guy fucking an animal, or his mate watching and banging one out.'

'Neither,' Danny corrected me. 'It's the donkey. Look at it, still eating. Must have a right bucket on it, the slag.'

Copies of the video were made by filming the camera's screens. When we told this story to our civilian friends – oh, fuck, we were going to tell them this one – there would be evidence to back up our claims of witnessing a novel form of animal husbandry.

Now, in the darkness of our patrol, the donkey was on people's minds once again. We guessed at the age of her rapists.

'You don't know it was a female,' Jay observed.

'It seems to make it worse, if it was a man donkey, do you know what I mean?' Jake said, and we found ourselves agreeing. Overcoming the initial disgust, the subject now held nothing but intrigue for us.

'When does it get to the point that you think, OK, I've not got laid in a while now, I'm gonna fuck a farm animal?'

'I don't know mate,' I shrugged. 'I've not been laid in six months, and I'm still happy enough with my hands. I mean, he had his mate there, watching and wanking. If they were that desperate, you think they'd just suck each other off?'

My friends muttered agreement. The donkey fuckers would become the nail in Afghanistan's cultural coffin.

'I wasn't racist when I came here,' Jake told us. 'But how can you not get that way when you see shit like that?'

Further discourse was cut short. There were armed men in the night, and they were not British and obsessing over animal molestation.

It seemed as though our own commanders were not the only ones keen on night patrol. The snake of ANA soldiers appeared through our night vision as they wound their way along an embankment.

'Probably visiting the donkey slag,' Danny smirked in the darkness.

Turkey reported the troops' movement to the head shed. All ISAF patrols should be coordinated, but our company had not been informed, and so the OC wanted confirmation that it was indeed our Afghan allies.

'What colour camouflage are they wearing?' he asked over the radio. Turkey tried to be as patient as possible in his answer.

'You can't see colours through night vision, Zero Alpha. Everything's green, over.'

There was no reply.

It was the time of the week when the OC attended his patrol's conference at DC, and as the HCR Mastiffs were being employed on an op in another part of the AO, the battle group would have to break its rule of not using Warriors on Route Pink.

It had been raining heavily, and the usual dust of the track had attained the consistency of a thick, viscous soup. I was part of the Barma team, and we waded through the mud, too tired and angry to be concerned at stepping on anything that would tear us apart.

As well as the OC, we were clearing the route for trucks that were now returning to DC with empty shipping containers, and unlike the tracked brutes of our Warriors, these vehicles failed to cope with the deep, slippery slime. Each time one became bogged in, the

Barma team would be called from the front of the procession to attend to the stricken. Simply covering that distance was a task in itself, and then an area would need to be cleared to enable the recovery of the wagon by one of our Warriors. When this was finally done, the Barma team would trudge back to the head of the column and restart the route clearance. It took hours to cover mere kilometres of track, and by the time we remounted our Warriors, more mud than men, we were exhausted.

Usually, the final leg of the journey would then be covered in the vehicles, and so it came as a surprise when we stopped and the rear door began to open on its hydraulic jack.

'This isn't DC,' someone said, as we saw the track and the compounds behind us. The other Warriors had halted too, their engines chugging, the crews popping up and down from their hatches made anonymous by tied scarves, goggles and helmets.

I made my way out of the rear, using the bar armour to climb up alongside the turret. The intercom was fucked; I'd find out what was going on the old school way.

The Boss pulled back the ear cans of his headset so that we'd be able to talk.

'We've had a threat warning about an IED between those compounds.' He pointed ahead to where the track squeezed between two thick mudbrick walls. A choke point. A kill zone. A beautiful place for buried treasure.

I looked at the area, assessing. It would be impossible for us to isolate it as a vulnerable point, surrounded as it was by compounds. This would be a straight up the middle job, sweeping with the Vallons and ensuring there were no surprises that would ignite under the pressure of a Warrior's tracks.

Except that there was no pressure pad.

'Threat warning says it's a command wire,' the Boss told me, wincing a little.

A command wire.

Terry didn't use command wire to detonate IEDs against vehicles. Why would he, when the victim itself would oblige by rolling over a pressure pad? A command wire was used to target soldiers on foot, and my mind tracked back to the daisy-chain IED discovered on this same road during the Big Push; an artillery shell and two home-made bombs full of ball bearings.

They wanted to kill a team.

And if the intelligence was true, they would likely get their wish. There was no way to skirt this device, if it existed. For reasons unknown to us, there would be no clearing of the nearby compounds first. We were to go straight into it, and once Terry had us where he wanted, he'd send a signal down that command wire and there would be a few more bags of soldier airlifted from Bastion to the UK.

I wasn't happy about that.

'This is fucking bollocks,' I said angrily to the Boss, who did me the courtesy of not trying to disagree. 'We always drive through here. If the int is about a command wire, then why are we sending dismounts? That's what they want.'

Still, there was no argument.

'Are you saying you won't do it?' the Boss finally asked. The question was matter of fact. He was a good man. There was no judgement in his words.

'Of course I'll fucking do it,' I snarled. 'I don't have a fucking choice, do I?'

And I didn't.

That lack of choice did not come from any fear of reprisal or discipline from the army, but simply the knowledge that if I did not go ahead, then someone else would. This would not be a company or battle group commander, but a junior rank. One of my friends.

And so I had no choice.

'I'm not taking the whole team, though,' I said, and the Boss nodded as I climbed back down the bar armour.

I was livid, my earlier tiredness forgotten. I just wanted to get it over with, and then to punch some fucking officer in the mouth.

I pushed my head into the back of the Warrior.

'There's a fucking deathtrap up ahead, and we've gotta clear it. I need one of you to come and get killed with me.'

Lump Head began moving without hesitation. Unlike me, he knew enough to know that you couldn't use reason in war. Just get on with things. What's the worst that can happen?

I pointed out the task ahead.

'Let's just get it done, quick. Make sure you sweep the walls, as well as the tracks. If it is a command wire for dismounts, it could be higher up.'

I took another look at the narrow corridor that awaited us, my balls pulling up into my ribcage as I considered the implications. I didn't want to do this. I was terrified. Fucking terrified. There are days on tour, and moments in contacts, when you feel invincible, but this wasn't one of them.

I knew I was going to die.

But that fear was nothing compared to the terror of the idea that my friends would think me a coward. Pride made me walk past the lead Warrior. It was the same crushing peer pressure, the same fucked-up emotional triggers, that had men climbing trench ladders at the sound of a whistle, despite every sane sense screaming at them to stop. Pride moved my legs, and the knowledge that if I didn't do it, then one of my friends would have to. How could I live with that?

Fuck it. We'd either be fine in two minutes or we'd be dead. I took one more look at my partner, an angry troll in uniform. At least if we did die, I'd be the better looking one when our pictures hit the newspapers.

Just get it over with.

The sweep went by in a blur, throat tight, balls retracted as if protecting themselves. I'd made hundreds of sweeps like this one, but never before had I been so aware of what was at stake. Why it should happen on that day I had no idea, but the veil was lifted, and I finally realized the idiocy of my chosen profession.

Fuck. A little late in the day for a career change.

We found nothing. My balls descended. My throat loosened. My hands were shaking, and I told myself it was from anger. Before we climbed back into the steel womb of our truck, I raised my two fingers to the vehicles behind us. Such defiance.

We made it to DC for the OC's conference. A few hours later we turned around and began the journey anew. Irrigation ditches had burst beneath our tracks on the northern leg, and the mud of the morning was now an overflowing quagmire. The sun went down. We slipped, floundered, and cursed. We pulled each other out when the gloop held our boots fast. We waved our Vallons around. Some ran out of battery, but at that point, who cared? We could find anything with our feet as well as with a metal detector.

We passed an Afghan army base. Perhaps they saw the Warriors, and the men lurching in front of them, and decided that we needed some encouragement. They were good enough to shoot at us.

They were as bad with their aim as the Taliban, and we made it to Minden looking like exhausted apparitions from some ghastly swamp. Like dogs, we then waited for our pat from the master. A tally-ho for the job well done.

We waited in vain, and then we slept.

I crouched in the ditch that ran alongside the compound, the four members of my team scattered to the corners of a bare field. It was Minden's helicopter landing site, and we were waiting for a Chinook to bring us mail.

The village kids who gathered about the burn pit now spotted easier targets and came to throng about me.

'Choc-oh-late. Bis-queet,' they chirped.

I gave them what I had and, finally satisfied that I wasn't holding back, some dispersed. Others squatted beside me, their faces dirty, open, and inquisitive. *Oliver* with olive skin.

'Helicopter?' one boy of perhaps ten asked. He mimed the whirling of rotors, and I smiled to myself. If the kids knew what was on the way, how would we ever surprise Terry? How were we even still standing in this war?

The kid began to point to my body armour, where the green shape of a smoke grenade was hooked into the loops. When the chopper was close, I'd pop that smoke, the pilot coming in when he confirmed the colour. If we said we'd popped purple and he saw green, he'd know the Taliban were trying to lure him into an ambush. It was a tactic that went back to the Vietcong.

The kid pointed again at the smoke, and I guessed that he wanted to know the name of the object.

'Smoke,' I told him.

'Schmoke,' he repeated, sounding like the *Austin Powers* character, Goldmember.

'Schmoke and a pancake,' I replied, reciting a line from the movie, the children copying and affecting the Dutch accent. Soon they were shouting it, and I joined in too. Why the fuck not? What would the head shed do? Sack me from being the man in charge of pulling a pin?

The beat of the Chinook's heavy blades became audible, and I shooed the kids away, but they returned as soon as my back was turned.

'Schmoke and a pancake!' They cheered as I threw the signal, their words drowned out as the whocka descended onto the field, scattering my smoke and dust in every direction. My eyes were covered by goggles and still I was forced to turn my head, seeing the children squatting, watching the whirling beast, dark eyes squinting through the sandstorm, their billowing shirts pulled up over their faces.

'Schmoke and a pancake!' I shouted against the tempest.

I had always thought that to the Afghans we British would all look alike, particularly when we were clad from head to toe in protective gear, our faces hidden by helmets, bandanas, and sunglasses.

But I was wrong.

For the rest of the tour, whenever I set foot outside of the patrol base, I would be assailed by cries of 'Smoke and a pancake!' It became the most welcome sound, greeting me at the end of every dreary patrol. Already weighed down by kit, the urchins would take hold of the sling of my gimpy, chanting our mantra as I dragged them along.

'Smoke and a pancake.' Meaningless words that came to hold for me all of the best memories of those children.

How would they look back on their younger days, spent begging beside a pit where shit burned? The days where they would be called to carry the Taliban dead from beneath our sights. The brown-eyed brood had been destined to grow up on the front line not only of a war of insurgency, but one of culture, religion, and ideologies. The universe is fickle, and it had been their lot to be born into that place, and that war.

Smoke and a fucking pancake.

#veteranproblems

Home, United Kingdom, 2014

The final British troops were pulling out of Afghanistan.

It had been the headline all week, and tonight I chewed on my dinner as I watched the news with my mother, talking through a mouthful as I saw the shoulder tabs of the hated RAF Regiment.

'What the fuck are they talking to them, for?'

My mum pulled a face at the language and told me not to be so angry.

The national news finished, and the regional began. Usually, I enjoyed this section, laughing at the banality of Wales, but tonight they'd set an ambush.

Following the news of the cessation of the Afghan mission, the regional station was running a story about the Welsh soldiers who had lost their lives, and I found myself looking at the familiar faces of H, Prosser, and Hunt.

I forced down the food that now felt like lead in my throat. My mum was no idiot, and she knew that some of the faces on the screen were known to me. After my breakdown one night, she knew that I'd been the first to come across one of them.

The remote was sitting astride the television, and I was trapped. I ground my jaw tight, forced my eyes onto the screen, determined not to show any weakness. The pictures disappeared, and I began to cut another mouthful, my appetite gone, but my stubborn pride intact.

But there was more to come – an interview with a familiar face, the mother of Prosser. She'd always been vocal about the circumstances in which her son had died, and five years had not changed that. How she held it together on camera I did not know, another mother as much of a warrior as her son.

I tried not to look at my own mother beside me. How could I have been so selfish that I could have put her in that possible position, and for what? No one was even trying to make the argument that the mission had been a success. Politicians talked about groundwork, and giving the Afghans the ability to determine their own future. They had that before the bombs began to drop. Oh, how the goal posts could change in politics, but there was no changing the numbers that mattered. No changing this mother's future without a son.

What was my own mother thinking, watching that interview? Relief, maybe. Compassion, certainly. Whatever it was, she held the thoughts to herself.

The rotting carcass of the war had joined us for dinner that night. We could not help but breathe in its stink, but we could both pretend that we didn't see it.

'Pudding?'

21

Flesh Wounds and Haircuts

Middle Hill, a windswept desolation that lay between OP Hill and a long ridge, known as Dickers, was to be cleared of IEDs.

Those at the bottom of the food chain didn't know why, though that hardly seemed to matter. A few of the NCOs questioned why we were interested in that space, as it offered the same views to the west and south as our newly occupied OP Hill and the western views were more limited than those from Dickers itself, but we were not clued into the thinking of battle group HQ. We could only guess that because the IEDD team and the engineers had been sent to us, by the logic of our leaders it would be a waste not to use them.

I was part of the QRF, along with Toby, and we sat on the turret of our Warrior, parked up in a muddy field outside of Khabir. With us was Smith in his own truck, and in the event of any casualties we would move forward to collect them, before making the dirty dash back to Khabir, where they could be CASEVACed from an emergency helicopter landing site (EHLS).

The Zoo were the platoon accompanying the engineers, and at first all had been peaceful. For a while there was the usual ICOM chatter about attacking this, and Allah that, but then it had all gone quiet.

It wasn't quiet now.

The Zoo were returning fire onto the villages to the south, and I watched with Toby as the tiny figures darted back and forth across the bare hilltop.

'Gunfire sounds different in winter, don't you reckon?' I asked my friend.

'Yeah. More crisp, like.'

We spent the afternoon sitting in the December sun, enjoying the fact that we were not called forwards, but nor could we be called away for any bullshit tasks, in case a casualty was taken. Eventually the contact died away, but it had delayed the operation enough that the engineers would now have to call it a day and resume their work in the morning.

The rule of law from Minden was steadily trickling down to Khabir, and the sergeant major had seen to it that his journey south was accompanied by a set of hair clippers. I grumbled as Danny put these through my locks, a grade four on the sides and trimmed on top. It was the length I had when on garrison duty in the UK, and looking into my reflection in the wash bowl of a Javelin end cap, I had to admit my friend had done a good job.

'There's hope for you in civvie street yet, mate,' I thanked him.

In the morning, the task to clear the hill began anew. Zoo were once again the IEDD team's guardians, while we waited at Khabir as the cavalry. To the east, the ANA and their OMLT mentors spread out across Dickers Ridge.

It wasn't long before the inevitable happened, and as we had done the day before I enjoyed the view with Toby from the armoured seat of our Warrior. But today, there would be a twist to the action.

'Got a casualty!' Sergeant Davies shouted to us as he scrambled into the turret. I made for the rear door with Toby, but we were gestured by the sergeant major towards his own wagon.

'Help me with these,' he told us, and we removed the sacks of potatoes that had been occupying the vehicle's stretcher.

Spudless and mounted, our two Warriors roared their way to the base of OP Hill. It was a short trip, as far as we could go without clearing the route ahead.

The Zoo's Warriors were in action, 30mm cannons booming. I dismounted with Toby and the rest of our team, and we began clearing a lane up the slope towards the firing forms of Zoo, forcing

Patrolling south of Minden, doing my best for the battlefield fashion catwalk by mixing up green and desert camo, with a few forbidden morale patches on my sleeve.

Jason, a good friend from Iraq, in his 81mm mortar pit at Patrol Base Minden. Terry often got the good news dropped on him from these tubes.

Sometimes the simplest way to dispose of an IED was to set them off. This is a controlled explosion of one at Patrol Base Khabir.

Below This hill had the Russians on it, then the Taliban, and then us. Behind me is the Musa Qala wadi, and an area that has known constant fighting for years. For the locals who live in these compounds, war is just a part of life.

Pinkmist during an attack on Minden, trying to use his bed as hard cover. He would later go to sleep curled up in full battle gear. We just laughed. The signs of his troubles, so obvious, went unnoticed.

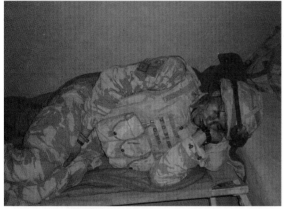

Below With Pinkmist (left) at Khabir. A few days later, my close friend would never be the same.

Above Inside a sangar at Khabir, a regular spot for tit for tat exchanges with Terry.
Below In the foreground are the banks of the M4 wadi, with Mount Doom looming
in the background. Everything in this photo was nominally under ISAF control,
but IEDs or attacks could occur at any time, in any place.

Above A patrol in the green zone – the area of dense vegetation and irrigated farmland that was perfect cover for the enemy to lay IEDs and ambushes.
Below The company taking a break at FOB Edinburgh. This FOB was home to the 105mm guns of the Royal Artillery, who joined our own mortars in smashing the enemy.

'Ho ho ho you cunts! Merry Christmas!' On Christmas Day, Santa – the Zoo platoon sergeant – brought us the kind of gifts every soldier wants: ammunition and water.

Above A sunset view of the Musa Qala wadi, where the fighting was going on, from the rear sangar at Zulu. Looks peaceful, but this was often the time of day when things would kick off. *Below* On the move down to Round Hill, where we took contact. Almost at the end of our tour, this was our last dance with Terry.

Above Back in Bastion at the end of the tour, with Jay. We made it.
Below I know little of war, but I know a great deal about soldiers. The thought of never soldiering again can leave me angry, numb, or in tears. But I've taken the road out of the darkness – and never intend to go back.

ourselves to take our time and to do the job properly. Still there was no name or status for the casualty, and so we prayed for our friends, and prepared ourselves for the worst.

Reaching the top of the hill, Two Platoon's sergeant called to us over the sound of the gunfire and revving engines.

'Clear a lane to my boys! They're bringing the casualty from Dickers!'

Dickers. So the casualty would not be a friend. We breathed a little easier, and saw the stretcher party working its way through the valley below us, two men ahead of them sweeping the route for traps. We were in dead ground to the contact, and the snap and crack of the rounds went high above us. We could afford to forget the shooters and concentrate on surprises in the soil.

As we closed with the casualty, we could make out the faces of his bearers twisted in exertion. The stretcher was no solid construction, but a lightweight kind, a sheet attached to small lengths of rope with wooden toggles.

'Swap! Swap!' we shouted to the guys as our parties met. Ally Man took my rifle as I gripped a toggle, and disappeared with it before I could take it back with my left hand.

'Let's go!' Toby called beside me, and we lifted the load of the man off the ground.

It was like carrying a fridge, the dead weight sinking into the centre of the stretcher, straining our shoulders against sockets. It was an uphill struggle, and after mere metres our chests were heaving, finding no give from the thick plates of our body armour. Sweat poured and stung our eyes, and still the Warrior and respite were hundreds of metres away. During training, stretcher races had been a form of competition, and we had run and dragged our logs to victory. But we had not been encumbered by body armour then – there weren't enough sets to cover units in training and those in deployment – or the equipment that now burned into our shoulders. The heat of the day felt like the scorch of summer had returned, each breath rasping. A gasp. Teeth gritted against the voice in your head saying, *Fuck it. Give up. Let someone else carry the fucker.*

I was so tired that it was some time before I even looked at the casualty. He was one of the OMLT, naked thighs thick with field dressings. A round had gone clean through one leg and lodged in the other. We later found out that, soon exhausted, the ANA soldiers that he mentored had refused to participate any more in his evacuation, and that's why a section of The Zoo had been sent to the rescue. He was a big man, a Yorkshire soldier. Why couldn't it have been their dainty, female medic who got hit? As we struggled, men changing on the corners at a frequent rate, the stretcher scraped and bounced on the hard dirt floor. The man made no complaints – he was high on morphine, a serene look on his pale face.

I refused to swap out, a stubborn mule. A rigid stretcher made its way to join us, and we lifted the casualty onto it, the going easier from that point. Up ahead, an NCO of Zoo was pushing men up onto the hillside.

'Oi!' Toby called at him. 'That's not been cleared you dickhead! Get them back! That's not been cleared!'

The NCO ignored him, pushing more of his men out. They hesitated, hearing Toby, and knowing he was right, but they moved up onto the slope anyway. I winced, expecting an explosion at any moment, and saw Toby go after the man with murder in his eyes. At that moment the air tore apart, but it was no IED. A French fighter jet split the sky, hurtling between Middle and OP Hill, sending some men scattering and leaving others open mouthed in awe.

We placed the stretcher into the sergeant major's Warrior, bleeding man now resting where the spuds had been, and I went in search of my weapon, taking it back from Ally Man. We were too tired to speak, and loosened the sides of our body armour so that we could gulp down air.

'Mount up!' came the order, and we of the QRF left The Zoo to continue their exchange of gunfire with Terry.

We'd expected to have the casualty extracted from the EHLS at Khabir, but word had reached us that a unit of ANA elsewhere had been involved in a fuck fest, and had sustained fifteen casualties, ranging from dead to walking wounded. The MERT had their hands full, and yet again it seemed that Task Force Helmand lacked the medical resources to deal with two incidents at once. We'd take our wounded Omelette to Minden, and ask the Americans if they'd be kind enough to collect him.

We waited beside Minden's HLS, the OMLT members who had accompanied their wounded comrade saying their goodbyes. The casualty was too high to make sense of any of it, and smiled peacefully at the good-natured insults. It was the same scene as when we had said goodbye to Jake. It was the same scene for every evacuated soldier with a non-lethal wound. I imagine it had been this way since war began, and would be forever.

The Black Hawks of the Pedro swooped in over our heads, majestic, giving us a moment to indulge in the fantasy of our personal war movies. Two medics jumped out, beckoning us over, and we ran through the smoke and dust, desperate not to catch our feet on the rutted ground and send our litter spilling.

As we slid the stretcher onto the metal deck, I noticed the cockpit, the door removed. The pilot, hidden behind his black visor, was talking into his radio, words lost in the tempest, and I was hit by envy of this man who hurtled across the country, nothing between him and the deck but air.

An empty stretcher was handed out to us, and we ran back to the compound, the Black Hawk rising behind, and then dipping low over the treetops.

The engineers were the next to leave from the HLS, their job of clearing Middle Hill accomplished. I'd meet one of them a couple of years later, and he laughed as he remembered the Two Platoon soldiers launching themselves from the safety of the Warriors with whoops and cheers, desperate to get into the fight once the bullets began to fly.

The excitement of the day over, and with all troops off of the ground, the QRF was stood down.

Carrying the stretcher had drained me physically. In our own soldierly language, I'd been hanging out of my arse, and chin-strapped. But despite the earlier exhaustion, I now had an overwhelming desire to use the gym. Whether the urge came from body dysmorphia or the need to blow off steam after the evacuation, I didn't know, but soon I was lifting weights in Minden's makeshift gym, my mind at ease within my comfort zone.

I was alone, which was how I liked it, until Owens came to find me.

'Sergeant major says you've gotta get a haircut.'

That was fair enough. My hair had been a little on the ragged side until Danny had cut it the night before, and the only time Smith had seen me since, my head had been tucked into my helmet.

'Tell him I've had one, mate,' I replied. My lanky comrade shrugged and left, only to reappear moments later.

'He says he wants to see you. Now.'

I threw the weights to the floor. 'For fuck's sake.'

I found Smith outside of the ops room.

'Sir,' I reported.

'You need to get a haircut.'

Maybe the confusion showed on my face, because he went on.

'Everybody's got to get US Marine Corps style jarheads.'

I thought he was winding me up, and laughed. He wasn't.

'But I'm not in the US Marine Corps, sir.'

'Doesn't matter. You're getting one.'

And for some reason, it was this trivial matter that finally snapped me.

'I'm fucking not,' I told him like a petulant school boy, and walked away, back to my weights. I continued with my workout, knowing that the army's discipline would be moments away.

Fuck them. I was finishing my session. I wanted out of this halfway house between war and the parade ground, and like a naughty child runs away from his parents I sought a doomed refuge in the sanctuary of the dusty tent.

Turkey was there moments later, and didn't give me a second to explain. Why should he? I'd refused an order and walked away from a sergeant major. Regardless of reason, I was in the wrong.

'Who the fuck do you think you are?'

'I'm not in the Marine Corps, that's who I—'

'Shut the fuck up!' he cut me off. 'It's a fucking haircut. Grow up.'

Maybe he saw something in my demeanour, because his tone changed and he was once again the calm voice of Three Platoon.

'What's the problem, Gez?' he asked me, now man to man, not sergeant to lance corporal.

And I told him.

'It's just fucking bollocks, mate. This morning, we're in a fucking contact, extracting casualties, and doing what we're supposed to be doing, and then two hours later I'm getting told I need to have my hair cut like some military I don't even belong too. I've just had enough. This whole place is a joke. I don't care how many extra guard duties I get. I've had enough. I'm not getting it done.'

'He'll pin you down if he has to.'

'Then I'll punch the cunt,' I said, hearing the futility even as I spoke the words. 'Look, mate, I try to play the game. Danny cut my hair last night. I'm just fed up.'

And I was, but why? We had the same bullshit in the UK, and no matter how unwillingly I'd stuck to the rules. What had changed? Why had I decided to make a simple haircut my Thermopylae?

I saw the answer clearly enough, though it was never one I could have translated to my commanders or even many of my peers. Afghanistan was not what I'd expected it to be. It was the same bullshit as garrison duty back home, only now we could be killed or maimed on any given day. It was too much of a juxtaposition for me to handle, and it had come to a head with a simple order. I had volunteered for Helmand, and this war, believing that it would grant me the highest of freedoms, and instead I felt robbed of any. Unless I was dispatched by another's orders, I was confined. The threat of death and injury was present every day, and even if I did my drills perfectly I could still become a victim. No human, no matter their occupation, can control life and death, but we can give ourselves the comforting illusion that we do through making smaller choices on a daily basis. Here, even those simple decisions were denied. I would eat whatever it was that was handed to me from a cardboard ration

box. I would sleep when I was told I could sleep. I would wash when
I was told I could wash. I would walk when and where I was told I
could walk, and return to the confinement of the camp when I was
so ordered. I could ask for the use of a phone, and I could be
denied on a whim. Orders needed no explanation, only to be followed. Appearance was not a choice, it was a uniform after all. Even
attempts to wear 'green' winter trousers to protect against the cold
were stopped. The final thing in my life that I thought I held control
over was my hair. No longer.

I knew I was in the wrong.

'I'll get it cut,' I told him. 'But not a jarhead.'

I tracked down Ratty, who owned clippers, and he put a grade
seven over the top. It was the shortest I'd had my hair in years, and
all of that time the army had taken no issue with my appearance. I
reported to Smith to apologize, and to show him that I'd bent the
knee.

'Not short enough,' he told me, but without malice. 'Look, I'll
show you the email.'

And he did. It was from the HCR, and in black and white it
instructed all members of the battle group to have Marine Corps
style haircuts.

'But if it's not in our regulations, then how can he order us to do
it?' I pleaded, Smith giving me a patient shrug. He must have known
the hypocrisy of the order himself. The HCR officers had hair that
would shame an eighties' rocker.

Eventually we compromised on a four on the top, and a two on
the sides.

'That's better,' Smith told me on my third inspection.

'I'm sorry for being a dickhead, sir,' I apologized. 'But I think the
whole thing's ridiculous.'

I couldn't let it go, and back in the Viper's Nest, Toby had enough
of my whining.

'You think you're fucking special, that's your problem,' he told me
that evening. 'We've all had to do it, but you're the only one who
had to fucking moan.'

That wasn't especially true, and I told him so.

'Look, Toby. Maybe it's because I've spent more time in civvie street than you, but I just can't accept this shit when it's obviously bollocks. You tell me that I'm not good at what I do,' I challenged him. 'I'm not having it made out that I'm a shit soldier because I want orders to make sense.'

'You just think you're fucking special,' he repeated.

It was a lovers' tiff, and we soon burned ourselves out, apologizing with handshakes first, and hugs second. I was polygamous, Toby was one spouse of mine, and the army another – but one where I feared divorce was hurtling towards us.

Toby was right. By the army's definition I did think that I was special. I couldn't slope my shoulders and let the bullshit run off. I saw an order to 500 men of a battle group as a personal affront, and I responded that way. If I wanted reason, I was in the wrong place, and I was slowly beginning to realize that truth. It did not mean that I'd accept it.

'You joined the army, the army didn't join you,' Toby told me that night.

He was right. Of course he was right. I'd entered into the marriage as a willing, loving partner, but now I was bitter, and wished only to discover the embrace of a new lover.

I didn't sleep that night, because I had no idea where to find her.

22

The Kid

'He's not going to make it,' Jay said.

Looking at the kid's wounds, I found it hard to disagree. He was maybe ten years old, lying in a wheelbarrow that his father had pushed to the patrol base. Deep purple burns dotted his face and covered his thin legs.

'We do this?' I asked Emily. She shook her head as she assessed the wounds, the kid hardly moving as she touched him, a bad sign.

'He did it himself, fucking around with petrol.'

Jay and I shared a look, shame averted.

'He's dead without a hospital,' Emily said, looking for the interpreter. 'Tell his dad we need to send him to a hospital.' She turned to me. 'Gez, hold his leg up.'

I held it as Emily plied her trade, covering the wound in ointment and clingfilm.

'When did this happen?' she asked the father.

'Three days ago,' came the reply, via the terp.

'What? What's taken him so long?' The question came from all of us, with varying degrees of incredulity and accusation. The terp shrugged as he answered.

'His father is scared of your hospital. He's scared he won't see his son again.'

'Fucking asshole,' Jay spat under his breath.

As word of the injured child spread, more and more of the company came to see him, doting on the youngster. In no time the wheelbarrow was a manger of biscuits and candy.

The kid's eyes were huge ink spots, doped, but he tracked our movements. For four hours he watched strange foreign soldiers brood over him, argue and joke among themselves, while all the time his elder brother wept beside him.

Requests went out for a medical evacuation, and were granted. The father took more persuading, but eventually agreed to the hospitalization if his eldest son could accompany the child.

I was told to prepare the HLS. By now the kid was all wrapped up, only his eyes and nose poking out from his blankets. I gave him a thumbs up, his wide eyes giving me nothing back.

'We've got a Pedro coming in,' I was told, and I took a smoke grenade from my gear in preparation. Outside the Hesco, the usual fan club was present, greeting me with cries of 'smoke and a pancake!'

I heard the rotors beating in the distance before the Black Hawks roared across the patrol base, taking the dust from the rooftops, and ignoring the forward air controller's advisement to stay clear of the villages to the south.

Bursts of automatic fire now erupted from those enemy held areas, the Black Hawks banking, returning it, and heading north in a hurry. They came onto the radio net, advising that they needed to return to Bastion due to 'technical difficulties'. There would be no pick up.

'Stupid fuckers got hit.' It was Staff Edwards, our head medical honcho. I nodded, and asked about the kid's chances.

'Probably lose the leg,' he said, then smiled, shaking his head. 'Can you believe that chopper got hit?'

They came back later that night. The kid left us.

I hope that he lived.

23

Head Gone

The frosted dirt cracked beneath our boots, a sign that deep winter was upon us, bringing with it a new twist to the treasure hunt. The ground was hard, digging in bombs harder, but if they could do it before the ice set then winter would provide the cloak to cover Terry's night-time activities.

The distant mountains were snowcapped now, their usually harsh outlines suddenly inviting.

'I want to go skiing,' I told Danny, my eyes on the faraway ranges. We were at a halt on our move to Khabir, the prospect of relaxed discipline enough to put even the most bitter of us in a good mood.

'You'll never ski again,' he replied, slyly. I raised an eyebrow, expecting the next words, and they came as inevitably as the cold season had done. 'Got at least another six weeks to go. Plenty of time to lose your legs.'

'Cheers.'

'Don't worry,' he reassured me. 'I can always just strap your body to a snowboard and push you down the slope.'

'You're a good mate. I don't know why any of your girlfriends wanted to fuck other blokes.'

'Cunt.'

We moved onwards. Closer to Khabir now, the trail winding beside compounds. It was here that a daisy-chain IED had been discovered, linked to a command wire. Terry was a visitor to these homes, and their high, thick walls.

Over which came a surprise.

I caught the movement in the air, my first instinct to shout 'Grenade!', but something gave me reason to keep my mouth shut, and stay standing. The object landed on the frost with an almost silent finality.

It was a kitten. A dead kitten. A strand of cord, two feet long, was tied about its neck.

A cluster of Afghan kids appeared, running towards me. The kitten was their toy.

I hit the first boy around the head with an open palm, furious.

'What are you little cunts doing?' I chastised them in a language they did not understand, upset at the death of the innocent feline. In that moment the irony was lost on me that I stood there with a machine gun across my chest, ammunition dripping off of me as I went in search of my own prey. How could these children be expected to value life, any life, when they saw it snuffed out in front of their eyes by our rifles, Apaches, and mortars?

Fuck, it was less than 300 metres from here that I had cheered ending the life of another human being, and now I was angry at these children for killing a cat? Protector of animals, and killer of men. There had to be something stronger than a double standard, and I was it, the twisted hypocrite, with Widowmaker cradled in my arms.

'Get the fuck out of here,' I snarled at the children, swiping my boot towards them to get the message across.

Arriving at Khabir, we found the builders of the Royal Engineers had been hard at work. They were still at it, a truck and a tractor with them to build the Hesco walls, and a prefabricated sangar that would face south across the village.

OP Hill was also being hardened, and that afternoon I made the trip up its steep slope on a patrol to deliver mail and a sat phone, reaching the summit with my lungs dragging somewhere behind me.

It was a bizarre feeling to be on the spot from where the enemy had tracked our movements, and it was little wonder that they, and the Russians before them, had used this position as an observation point. The views were open in all directions, the white house of

Musa Qala DC visible through binoculars, the irrepressible Mount Doom behind it. Further to the north and east lay the frosted mountain ranges, the wide gravel wadi shimmering silver now that water ran along its course. To the south were the villages held by the Taliban, bandit country all the way to Sangin, where the brave men of the Rifles paid a high price to hold on to the town.

I removed my helmet and laid my weapon down, pacing about the perimeter to take pictures of the sweeping vista. The Firm, Toby absent now that his R&R had begun, posed for a photo on the lip of an IED crater. I lingered longest outside the Hesco to admire the view, and was rewarded by a round that cracked by my head from one of the southern villages.

'Fucker shot at me,' I told the men we were relieving.

'Yeah. They do that.'

The spot of war tourism over, Jay and I made our way with half of the platoon to Khabir, the others remaining on the hill. Jake and Danny were with them to man the turrets of the two Warriors that stood sentinel on the heights, their armoured silhouettes imposing against the landscape as the sun began to drop away, and the valleys turned orange with the dusk.

From Khabir we sent out patrols along the steep-sided gorge of the M4 wadi. Mud and water seeped beneath our boots as we swept the depths of the ravine for IEDs.

'Stinks of shit down here,' I said to Jay behind me.

'Because it is shit.' He grimaced as we continued to pick our way through what passed as a sewerage system in Afghanistan.

One of our patrols led out into the wide gravel of the wadi. Perhaps our commanders were bored, because they pushed us out into the open, an inviting target to the Taliban in the opposite treeline. We didn't mind. We wanted the chance to put rounds down, and so we pranced up and down on the lip of a depression, appealing to Terry to fire.

He declined. Killjoy. Perhaps he was busy elsewhere, as in the distance we heard the echo of a large explosion. That was nothing new, the distant rumble of guns and bombs a part of daily life. Most went unremarked. The bigger ones would provoke a generic, 'I wouldn't wanna be on the end of that.'

During our evening briefing, the source of that day's far-off explosion was revealed. It had been a suicide bomber, targeting a cafe in Musa Qula that was frequented by Afghan security forces. Jay told me that I should record such incidents and the number of casualties we British were sustaining in my journal. For a few days I did, but the practice struck me as macabre, and I gave up with the tally at ten CAT As, and the same again in Bs and Cs – the Guards' battle group had been smashed.

The nights were freezing, and as I took my turn on the radio stag I pulled on every layer I could find, a perennial brew in my hands as I listened to Fairy Eyes on OP Hill.

Watching through the Warrior's thermal sight, he'd seen men appear from the Taliban bunker complex at Lone Tree. He claimed to have seen one with an RPG, before the fighter had covered it with a cloak. He was requesting permission to fire, and having it denied by the OC. It was obvious from his tone that our commander had been dragged from bed for the conversation.

It made me think about the rules of the war. Though I wanted to see bombs blow compounds to bits, I realized that policy would be counterproductive if we actually wanted the locals on our side. Still, I found it perplexing that we could not fire even warning shots at men who were standing next to a known bunker complex, in the dead of night. By contrast, our enemy that day had walked into a civilian cafe and blown the patrons apart. I didn't want to resort to their level, but surely there was a way to meet their aggression in the middle? It seemed as though we were allowing the enemy to dictate terms, and surrendering the initiative was the first step to failure.

The cold was an excellent distraction from such thoughts. I lit the hexi blocks, and set to making to making myself another brew.

•

Bash, our interpreter, was under attack.

Like any group of young men, soldiers enjoy winding each other up, and no more so than when their victim bites. We'd discovered that Bash was finicky about food and would only eat one kind of ration pack – for reasons of flavour rather than religion – and so we ensured that there were never any to be had. He'd have to sit, complaining, while he watched us eat. We also renamed him, turning his surname Ahmed to Ham Head, not something that a devout Muslim enjoyed. Any of the men who were particularly keen to needle the Afghan would question his faith, breaking into fits of laughter as the interpreter wound himself up into an incandescent rage.

'I tell you again!' he protested. 'The Taliban did some good!'

'What about the women they killed in the stadiums?' Jay asked him, without heat.

'Ah!' Bash put up a finger, coming to our enemy's defence. 'That is because the women were cutting out the hearts of the babies!'

We had no reply. There was no sign of disbelief in his eyes. He was a twenty-five-year-old man, allegedly one of those on the side of progress in Afghanistan, and he believed every word of the extremist bile.

'The Taliban are just a gang, like anyone else who sells drugs,' I tried.

'No!' he countered, vehement spittle flying. 'They are holy men!

'Oh, fuck off, you mong,' Jay dismissed him, finally tired of the conversation, and the Afghan slunk away to the other side of the compound.

I also took my leave. It was my turn in the low, sandbagged sangar that overlooked the M4 and what had become known as Pinkmist's field. I watched as One Platoon and two of their Warriors patrolled along Route Pink towards us, bringing a resupply. As they began to cross the ditch of the wadi, I spotted my friend Ryder in the Barma team.

'Alright, you fucker?' I called down to him.

I didn't hear the reply, because at that moment Terry opened up from the opposite side of the wadi, just as they had done the day Jake was hit. The crack and thump of rounds began to fill the air.

I had the gimpy up to my shoulder in an instant, no thought of identifying targets. I let rip, traversing along the treeline. The Warriors of One Platoon swung their turrets outwards, adding their own fire as the dismounts ran for cover. Rounds pounded the air above my head, but they were mostly heavy and heading in the enemy's direction, the western-facing Warrior on OP Hill smashing high explosive into trees and compounds.

In seconds the afternoon had gone from peace to an orgy of small arms and cannon fire.

A whoosh announced the launch of a Javelin missile from OP Hill. Not to be outdone, Lump Head fired his own from the rooftop of Khabir. The engineers stopped their work and formed a personal cheerleading section for the big man, whooping and yelling as a second missile followed the first, Lump Head blowing through over a hundred grand's worth of weaponry in five minutes.

Another GPMG joined me in the sangar, the noise from our combined fire deafening, our ears ringing after mere moments. I saw Turkey appear on the rooftop, but he was forced to quickly dive down, puffs of smoke sprouting on the wall beside him from the enemy's fire. I was having such fun that I'd almost forgotten there was a purpose to our overkill.

Below us, a machine-gunner of One Platoon let rip a hundred round belt in one burst. It was the signal that the fire had gotten out of control, and Turkey screamed himself hoarse.

'Cease fire! Oi, you cunts! Cease fucking fire!'

Eventually the fire died away, and the only sound was the chugging of the Warrior's engines, and the excited laughter of the troops.

It could never stay that way.

Somebody pulled a trigger, and before Turkey could stop it the fuck fest was in full swing once again.

'Identify your targets!' an NCO shouted.

Fat fucking chance.

An irrigation pump was hit by high explosive, water spewing into the air. A body lay face down beside it.

'Is he dead?' Ratty asked beside me.

'If he wasn't, he's drowned by now.'

Time and again the firing died away only to begin anew when a giggling, mischievous soldier claimed to spot armed men in the treeline. There was plenty of movement, but likely it was the local farmers running for their lives and cursing the infidel fucks who treated their home like an arcade game.

The barrel of my gimpy glowed hot. I should have had a spare one to swap in. We should have had a lot of things. Instead, I pulled the working parts to the rear, and opened the top cover, an attempt to let the air cool the metal. I looked at the piles of empty casings about us, taking a handful and throwing them at Ryder in the wadi below me.

After a few hours to ensure that we were done with our mayhem, the locals came out to collect bodies. There were a few of them, including the body beside the broken pump, the water now silver in the dying light.

He was Danny's kill, I found out that night, as our dark hours patrol took a diversion to visit our friends on Op Hill.

'You enjoyed yourself, then?' I asked him.

'Yeah, but Jake didn't leave the Warrior all the way through it. He's still sitting in there now,' he added, and I found our friend clad in his helmet and body armour, hours after the last round had been fired.

'Alright, mate?' I greeted him.

'Yeah,' he answered without conviction. He saw the look I gave his protective gear, and smiled. 'I'm not stepping out of this truck until we get back to Bastion.'

'Here,' I told him, handing over a photograph, 'Johan sent these.' Ryder had passed them on to me following the afternoon's shoot 'em up. The picture was of our South African friend in his hospital bed, giving a thumbs up and smiling. On the back of each was a personalized insult.

We compared abuse, and then it was time to leave. I gave my friend a pat on the leg.

It would be a long time until I saw him again.

Staff Edwards was with us at Khabir, and once again I found myself having to answer questions on Sniper Hunt and the day that we'd been hit in 1-1.

The reason for this was that Corporal Bailey had recently been returned to the UK, following an assault on a private in his platoon. He'd caught the soldier asleep in the sangar and kicked his sleeping form in the mouth, knocking out teeth. Many of us had no issue with the punishment he'd meted out – the soldier had been putting his comrades' lives at risk after all, and less than a century ago he'd have been shot for the same offence – but that was beside the point. Bailey was facing severe disciplinary action, and his defence was to claim post-traumatic stress disorder. As I had been there when he handled Sniper Hunt, I was asked whether or not he'd seemed to be traumatized.

'You were there too.' I said to the medic. 'What do you think?'

'I don't know,' he shrugged.

'Well there you go then. Put that.'

Turkey gathered ten of us together. We were to patrol the local village and visit a mosque where the Pakistani members of the Taliban had apparently held a meeting with villagers a few days before, despite our new checkpoint being on its doorstep.

Bang.

We were barely out of the gate when the small explosion sounded a few hundred metres away at the foot of Middle Hill. A tired column of dust rose from behind a compound where a decrepit tractor was chugging along, its driver unconcerned, or perhaps oblivious to the explosion hidden behind the sound of his struggling engine.

'Must have hit an old mine,' Turkey shrugged, and we paid it no more mind, threading our way into the network of compounds.

Bang.

The same sized explosion, maybe within fifty metres, but separated from us by at least two compound walls. We looked at each other.

'What the fuck's going on? Is someone throwing grenades?' I offered, knowing it was a weak possibility.

'Fuck it. Let's go back in and see what's going on,' Turkey ordered, and we turned on our heels.

Bang.

This one was clear for us to see, as it struck above the compounds on the slope of OP Hill.

'Light mortar, maybe?' someone guessed. We felt safe enough in the alleyways, and there was little concern in the voice.

We arrived at the gates of Khabir. I paused with Turkey, turning our attention back to the village.

Bang, Bang.

Two more explosions, their dirty smudges again on the slope, but higher this time. A burst of automatic gunfire echoed a split second later.

I pulled a face and looked at Turkey. 'This is fucking weird, mate.'

'Roger that.'

Bang.

Another on the slope.

Bang.

This one lost to our sight. Eventually, we caught a glimpse of the drifting smoke.

'They're bracketing the hill,' Turkey realized.

Whatever was firing was aiming short, then long. Now they should be able to guess the distance of their quarry by splitting that difference. The next round should be bang on.

Bang.

It was, striking the Hesco baskets of the hill.

Bang.

A second round struck the side of a Warrior.

'I bet Jake's enjoying this,' I laughed.

Bang, Bang, Bang.

Three more strikes.

'Fuck,' Turkey grimaced as news came over the radio. 'Two casualties.'

'Bad?' I asked him, smile gone, my stomach instantly churning.

'Cat C,' he told me. 'Light shrapnel.'

And then the fire died away. Another burst came across the radio.

'They're gonna try and draw the fire so the artillery radar can locate it,' Turkey said, clearly not in love with the idea.

We watched a figure dart between the Warriors on either end of the slope.

Bang.

The first dash drew a round, but further shuttle runs proved futile.

'At least the Boss is getting some exercise,' I said to Turkey, who laughed.

'Three Three Alpha is on his way to get the casualties.'

That was the sergeant major's callsign, and to cover the extraction the mortar platoon laid down a screen of smoke shells across the wadi.

I watched the Warriors climb the hill, then saw them disappear towards Minden and the darkness.

It wasn't until the morning and a patrol to the hill that I got the full story. The story of one of my closest friends.

Pinkmist was 'head gone'.

It was Danny who told me. He wasn't one to show emotion, but a lack of insults and his usual banter was the surest sign that he was hurting inside.

'As soon as those rounds started bracketing the hill, that was it. He was in the back of the truck and he just went foetal. It was like he had rigor mortis he was so stiff, and there was no moving him. I had to get up to the turret, so we sent Wayne in to talk to him.'

That had been a mistake. Wayne was a soft touch, and seeing the distress Jake was suffering, he was soon in tears himself.

'That new fat private got hit in the face with shrapnel, and starts moaning,' Danny went on. 'We were just telling him to shut the fuck up, so we could concentrate on Jake.'

The private had been evacuated to Minden, but a trip to Bastion was not necessary.

'Smith gets here in his truck, and Jake's still like a solid lump, but he'd started crying, too. He just kept repeating, "I'm sorry, I'm sorry." Me and Fairy Eyes were with him now and we told him he didn't have anythin' to be sorry about, then Smith turns up and starts giving him the tough love. "Don't think you're getting off the ground." And all that shit.'

'Cunt,' I spat, but Danny shrugged in the sergeant major's defence.

'I dunno. I think he was trying to help, in his own way. Anyway, when he gets here, we have to cross deck Jake, but we can't get him out. His fingers were like fucking vices and he wouldn't let go of the truck. I don't think he was even trying to do it, because he was still saying sorry, but it was like his body had just taken over from his head.'

He was flown to Bastion. 'I've never seen anything like that,' the twelve-year veteran confided in me as he concluded the story.

None of us had, and Pinkmist's breakdown left us more shaken than any physical wound could have done.

'You think he'll be OK?' Danny asked me.

I shrugged. I had no idea.

There was no chance of him rejoining us on the ground for the remaining few weeks of the tour. Jake would ask to be sent home to the UK, wanting the eternal comfort that all broken soldiers seek: his mother. But this he was denied, causing the rest of us to curse the army's spite.

Our friend was CASEVACed, but his body was intact. It didn't feel right to call it an injury, but what else could it be? Mental trauma? Wasn't that just a head injury? How many of us were carrying that inside our skulls? Would it manifest itself in me, and if so, when? The thought of breaking down in front of my comrades was more terrifying than any flesh wound.

For a soldier, ego was all. We could scoff and ooze bravado, perpetuating a myth that we were men without limits.

No more.

The strength of Jake's will had been pulled and snapped. There could be no denying that our minds were as vulnerable as our flesh. Nothing was sacred. The war, if it chose, could take anything, and all.

Who was next?

24

Merry Christmas

For me, Christmas came early.

I was staying on at Khabir with The Zoo while the rest of Three Platoon took their turn at sangar bashing in Minden, and with the prospect of no shaving and the regular contacts from the sangars, I felt like dreams really did come true.

One crisp December morning the platoon was split into two, and now half of the platoon was under contact in the village of Wach Kariz. The ANA and OMLT were with them, and though the fight was in dead ground to us, we could tell the nationality of the firers by the length of their automatic bursts.

Air cover arrived in the shape of an American A-10, a snarling shark's mouth painted on its ugly nose, the beast jinking and banking its way along the valley, enemy tracer following it into the sky. Our war boners were solid that day.

The contact died away, and the OC, watching the sport from his Warrior atop of FSG Hill, decided that he would push Zoo further south and onto Dickers Ridge. Under the command of Zoo's boss, and with ten other men, the remainder of us moved out from Chakaw to provide the men on the high ground with flank protection.

I wondered if The Zoo would be singing 'Men of Harlech' today. In the middle of the tour, their platoon had occupied a compound with the intention of goading Terry into attacking by having the terp hurl insults at him through a megaphone. It had worked, and as the rounds came in, one of The Zoo's most eccentric NCOs had let loose in baritone as though he were on the walls of Rorke's Drift.

The first few soldiers of Zoo were now cresting the summit of Dickers, others strung out along a path on its protected rear, their silhouettes conspicuous against the bare ass hillside.

'Bring the PKs,' came over the ICOM, the Taliban ordering their machine guns forward.

And they used them, the initial rate of fire heavy and accurate, rounds splashing at the feet and cracking by the heads of the few men who'd crested the ridge. Those who were strung out along its reverse slope now began the sprint upwards, adrenaline some small consolation against lung-bursting effort.

In our blocking position there was little to do but listen to the breathless radio communications and enjoy the satisfying crackle of gunfire on a winter's day. The Taliban went to ground in two compounds, and Zoo kept up their fire to fix them in position until missile strikes could be called in.

Like the Tomahawk missiles made famous in the Gulf War, the Exactors were equipped with cameras. Moments before impact a parachute would be deployed, allowing the artillery operators at FOB Edi to make minute adjustments to the weapon's course, and to bring it down into the throats of the Taliban fighters.

The first missile struck, the compound walls bulging but not breaking, dust blown outwards like the ring of a giant cigar.

Our terps were able to distinguish the enemy's individual accents. One Taliban commander was particularly vocal on the ICOM, 'Allahu Akbar' accompanying his every order, but once the second missile struck he was never heard on the airwaves again.

As the dust of that impact settled, all went quiet. It was time to pull back The Zoo, and they came quickly, leaving Dickers Ridge littered with empty cases and taking up new positions along the M4 Wadi.

You had to admire Terry. He followed on bikes, three shooters appearing on the ridge where our own men had been minutes before. They used the high ground well, shooting down into the wadi, but now our Warriors on FSG Hill had their targets, and 30mm cannon began to smack into the slope.

'Is that a head or a rock?' I asked the big Fijian, Siki, beside me. Rounds were slapping about it, and I couldn't believe that someone would keep themselves exposed under such fire. But it was no rock. It was one of the Taliban fighters, and though he was in range of the gimpy it seemed a pointless effort to pull the trigger with such a weight of fire coming from our trucks.

'Fuck it,' I told my comrade. 'We'll only have to clean it if we do shoot.'

Instead I settled for a different kind of shooting, and pulled the digital camera from my pocket. I set it to video, and was tracking back and forth from FSG Hill to Dickers Ridge when the slope suddenly disappeared in a razorback of smoke.

A split second later, the air tore apart in a deafening roar.

From out of nowhere an A-10 banked hard left, leaving a trail of destruction in its wake, the echo of its nose cannon sounding as if some god of war had split the realm between heaven and earth.

My eyes and ears took a second to process what had happened, and then I whooped with pure joy.

'Fuck me,' Siki whispered beside me, awestruck.

'God bless the USA,' I said in my best Texas drawl, and we began to pray for a second strafing run.

That was not to be, the Taliban on the ridgeline reduced to scraps of meat. The pilot claimed three kills. We weren't about to argue with him.

We pulled back to our patrol bases, not envying the task of the children who would be sent in to recover the leftovers of humanity now spread across the rocks.

As we pushed back through the wadi, the ICOM scanner buzzed to life once again.

'*Allahu Akbar!* They are retreating! God is great!'

We shook our heads. What else could we do? We'd pummelled them with small arms, hit them with missiles, and then obliterated their friends with a gun run, and yet still they cheered and claimed victory.

How do you beat an enemy like that?

Life on tour left a man lonely, and so I took a well-thumbed copy of a lad's magazine and made my way to the relative privacy of the wooden toilet shack.

The deed done, I was enjoying the serenity of my condor moment when a bang sounded from the opposite side of the wadi.

I knew exactly what it was.

'RPG!' the sentries called out.

I was trapped, milliseconds to decide if I should pile out of the exposed shack, cock in hand, to find cover, or if I should stoically wait it out and pray that I would not become the man remembered as the pink mist masturbator.

I waited.

I heard the whoosh of the rocket as it passed by, but there was no explosion, only a dull thump. The round was a dud, but the contact would not end there.

Our sentries could identify the firing point from the telltale smudge of smoke and as I pulled up my pants and ran for the sangar, gunfire was beginning to crisscross the wadi.

Ratty was there, nestling in behind my gimpy. I yanked him away by the scruff of his body armour. 'I carry it, I fire it.'

I pulled back on the cocking handle, and looked through the weapons iron sight.

Then I blew my second load of the morning.

'I hope the HCR CO's wife cheats on him while he's out here,' Danny told us. 'Then gives him syphilis when he gets home.'

'You don't know if he's married,' I pointed out.

'They all are, these fucking aristocrats.' He laughed darkly. 'Got to keep the bloodlines pure.'

It was Christmas Eve, and he wasn't in a good mood. The latest 'briefings' had been passed along to us from our battle group, and as usual it was a bullet point list of bullshit. One item of hot debate was the order that no civilian clothing could be worn at any time.

'Clearly the fucker's never stood still in a sangar for three hours at night,' I chewed, eyeing Danny's padded North Face jacket. 'If the shit they issue us isn't up to the job, why should we suffer?'

'It's this fucking visit that grips me,' Jay put in, referring to a planned Christmas Day call to Minden by a general. 'Who the fuck does he think he is? Is he that deluded that he thinks we want to see the cunt?'

Danny began to wobble his head, and affected the accent of the aristocracy.

'Oh, how the ranks will be lifted by a visit from their commander. Never mind that they will be buried under a ton of bullshit for days before my five-minute visit. Tally-ho! Over the top!'

'He'll be telling stories to his other general mates about how he spent Christmas Day at a patrol base,' I grumbled.

'Cunt,' came the chorus.

'Well,' Danny began, looking for a silver lining, 'if he does come, we can always hope he steps on an IED.'

We moaned, but in truth we were happy. Three Platoon had won the lottery, and we would be the ones holding the more informal Khabir over the Christmas and New Year period. Whatever bullshit they had planned at Minden, we would escape most of it.

I reclined back onto my 'sofa', which had been constructed by bending back the wire frame of a Hesco basket. Danny's own chair was a lot more chic, a wire-framed armchair, with a foam roll mat for added comfort. I looked up into the empty blue sky, and heard Danny clear his throat. His morning rant was not finished, and now he had a notebook in his hand. He recited the list as if he were an officer in the trenches.

'Helmets or berets to be worn at all times. No Santa hats.' He looked at me as he added the last part – I had one pulled down below my ears.

'Tell him to not give us such stupid fucking haircuts, then,' I said with a laugh. 'It's the only thing I've got to keep my head warm.'

Danny continued with his list, losing his affected accent a little as he was riled by the final item.

'Desert pattern boots only. Fucking desert boots? Has he seen the state of the place down here? It's a mud fucking swamp! Fucking desert boots?'

We'd all been wearing our leather pattern boots for months, collected when we'd been home during our R&R. Many guys had also brought wellingtons for wearing around the patrol base. Siki wore them on patrol, but the big Fijian was a law unto himself. No officer dared question the soldier who managed to remain imposing in green gardening footwear.

'All this hate towards Christmas,' Danny smiled mischievously. 'You reckon the HCR CO is actually a hardline Muslim in disguise?'

Our bile vented, I helped Danny rig a set of field-telephones to the checkpoint's sangars. It was a nice change to see a tangible result for our labour, and to test the new lines a happy Danny called the sentries to deliver a threat warning.

'Lads, we've had some int that there's a Taliban fighter in the area who may try and infiltrate the base tonight. He's described as having black boots, a red suit, and white beard. If you see him, you're cleared to shoot on sight.'

A few hours later, when Sad Act took over sangar duty from Ginger Pubes, a deadly serious Ginge asked his friend, 'Have you heard about the new threat warning?'

At quarter to midnight on Christmas Eve, I was awoken by a bell ringing in my face. It was Danny, his Grinch-like features smiling in the darkness.

'Wake up you cunt. You're on stag.'

I dragged myself out of my sleeping bag and into the cold air. I was tired. Earlier in the night Danny had been playing porn loudly from an iPod, despite my pleas for him to stop. Unable to get back to sleep, I knew what needed to be done, and so I tried the noise-reducing technique Jay had told me about: raising the knees inside the sleeping bag to reduce rustle.

It didn't work.

'Gez, are you wanking?' Sad Act had asked, the man beside me shining a torch beam into my eyes.

'Maybe.'

He turned off the torch, and I took that as permission to finish.

I saw in Christmas with Danny. We stood in the courtyard of Khabir, where my friend had prepared drinks for us. Some good-natured souls had snuck miniatures into our care packages, and the whisky and Coke was divine as it slipped inside our cold bodies.

After daylight, we got together around a few bowls of tepid water for a communal shave. It was a precaution against a visit from Minden, and our only bullshit of the day. We loved our Boss.

I used a bayonet to cut open the presents I'd been sent from home, mostly functional items such as scarves, socks, and food. Ginger Pubes had acquired trick balloons, and formed a cock out of one and a vagina out of another. I took a break from reading my cards to watch him try and fuck Sad Act with the squeaking latex.

An iPod and speaker were set up in the courtyard, and Christmas jingles played. In the UK I hated such music, but in the dirt of Khabir it somehow felt right.

We each took turns to use the satellite phone, brief calls home just to say 'Merry Christmas, I love you'. When my own home's phone rang out, I tried my grandmother. My family were in the car on their way to hers, she told me. Typical timing on my part. When Danny had finished his turn, the unloved bastard took a lot of flak.

'Who were you calling? A sexline?'

'The speaking clock?'

'Suicide hotline?'

Two Warriors from Minden brought us a resupply. In the turret of the lead truck was Zoo platoon's sergeant, clad from head to toe in a Santa outfit, white beard thick beneath the mic of his radio headset. About the Warrior's cannon was wrapped a stream of tinsel. He pulled to a stop outside of our sangar.

'Ho ho ho you cunts! Merry Christmas! I've brought gifts for everyone!'

The kind of gifts every soldier wants: ammunition and water.

The head shed had been watching the resupply on Cortez and losing their hair over the costume.

'Fuck them,' the sergeant snorted. Now sitting on the turret of the Warrior, he'd lost the beard so that he could smoke. 'It's so fucking shit up there. I'm telling him our trucks broke down, so we can stay here,' he joked.

We amused ourselves by cornering Bash, our interpreter, and calling him a heathen savage. As it was our Holy Day, not his, we joked that he could perform all of the burdensome tasks, such as disposing of rubbish and loading the empty jerry cans onto the trucks for their return to Minden.

The war didn't stop for Christmas, and we had a threat warning that Pakistani members of the Taliban had placed a command wire IED on the corner of one of the village's compounds. So began an hour of clearance, balls in throat, nobody wanting to be the one who burdened his family with a death on Christmas Day.

Nothing was found. Then it was up the slope to OP Hill and a chance to spread Christmas cheer with our friends there. We posed for photos, my forbidden Santa hat worn like a badge of honour. I'd made sure it had accompanied me on the patrol.

Back at Khabir, Turkey had bought potatoes for the troops, and these we sliced and cooked in oil, chips serving in place of our Christmas dinners. Only two servings could be cooked at a time, and so it was a drawn-out process to feed all eighteen of us at the base, but no one complained. I kept the fire going with Jay, the pair of us sharing headphones to watch *Family Guy* on his iPod. We'd tried to hold back ration packs that fitted the Christmas bill as closely as possible, and my chicken and herb dumplings proved an adequate substitute for turkey and roast vegetables. As ever on Christmas Day, it was the company that mattered. Jake was in Bastion, Toby on OP

Hill, but I had Danny and Jay with me, and if these two were not my brothers then who was family?

We cracked more of the miniatures, mixing them with the soft drinks we'd bought from the locals. Months of sobriety meant that we soon became tipsy.

One of our soldiers finished his phone call to the family, and we laughed as he imparted the information passed on by his mother.

'She said on the news that some army spokesman was saying we all got delivered a Christmas dinner!'

That statement would get under our skin in the following days, but at that moment we laughed it away. We had good company and drink in our veins. We were alive, and with brothers.

Nothing else mattered.

Between Boxing Day and New Year's we at Khabir fell into a comfortable routine. Each morning and afternoon a patrol was sent into the local area. Overstretch meant that only four to six soldiers were left at the checkpoint during these outings, and so men were eager to be the ones heading out of the gate – no one wanted to be the man snatched from a lonely sangar and beheaded on YouTube. Some IEDs were found on these patrols, and often we did not report them higher up the chain, knowing that to do so would mean an operation to recover and destroy them, and so we simply informed the others who would be patrolling in that area. If a local should step on it then tough shit, but they were usually the best informed about what treasure was buried where.

With the end of tour getting closer, there was also plenty of work to do on our Warriors, and the labour proved a welcome distraction from the monotony of sentry duty.

On Boxing Day, we heard that a major newspaper was about to run a story on our company, and not the kind that the army liked.

In preparation for the general's visit on Christmas Day, the head shed at Minden had gotten rid of all of the cooking utensils at the patrol base's 'kitchen'. These dirty bowls and ammunition boxes were all the troops had to fry or to heat rations – supplies of hexi had run out, and had been replaced with wood – and so the men ate their food cold from the packets. Someone's father had heard Prime Minister Gordon Brown's declaration that each man in Helmand had received a hot Christmas dinner delivered from Bastion, and when his son in the company had told him the truth of the matter the angry parent had gone to the paper to expose the lie.

Those of us in the ranks hoped that the story would run. None of us expected to receive a Christmas dinner when we didn't even have the resources to collect our own wounded, but if politicians and commanders were going to make hay by spreading a lie that we were being looked after in that way, then we wanted it exposed for the fantasy that it was.

But the story didn't run. The MOD quashed it, seeming as reluctant as ever to release a balanced account of goings on in Helmand.

Perhaps a better story to have run was that of the ingenuity of the British soldier, especially those in The Zoo, and Bungle in particular. The man had set up a still, explaining why Zoo had been purchasing such a quantity of potatoes, and on Christmas Day the men of that platoon had been paralytic from moonshine.

On New Year's Eve I sat with Danny on Khabir's rooftop, finishing what was left of our own alcohol stores. As the clock struck midnight we fired illumination rounds into the sky. The mortars at Minden did the same, as did OP Hill and every other British-held base in the area. Flares shot up all over the horizon, giving us an indication of where our comrades were doubtless sipping their own whisky and Coke, wrapped up from head to toe against the winter, and enjoying their own moment with a brother in arms.

#veteranproblems

Home, United Kingdom, 2014

I woke shivering, the sheets about me soaked in clammy sweat. I'd been home from the Gulf of Aden a week following a security job, and my body's thermostat seemed to be struggling to cope. I gave up on sleep and went to my laptop.

I read the early chapters of this book, the pages fresh, but the stories well worn and familiar. I felt like I needed a new set of eyes and so I sent a text to Pinkmist, my confidant, asking if he'd take a look. Of all my comrades, he was the one I felt I could be totally candid with. There was no need for me to put up a front; to wear the poker face of the veteran. Maybe this was because I'd seen him snap, head gone, and I still loved and respected him, so surely it was safe for me to show my own cracks in the armour?

He got back to me later that day, agreeing to read them, and I asked how things were with him. He told me that he'd been to see a doctor, thinking that he was coming down with a bug because he kept waking in the nights soaked in sweat and shivering. That sounded familiar. The doctor had asked him if he'd suffered any traumatic experiences – I laughed at that – and then told Jake that he was suffering from nightmares that his memory was suppressing. I told him about my own night sweats, and now it all made sense – they'd begun the day I'd started writing.

Jake told me that he'd agreed to give a talk to a meeting of eighty people about the struggles facing veterans and their reintegration into civil society. He was already regretting it, and I laughed when he told me that he was supposed to talk to his audience for thirty minutes.

'Just do a fat line of coke,' was my advice. 'They'll never get you off the stage.'

'I'm just gonna get up there, talk shit, then probably get angry and punch someone.'

I smiled at the image, half certain that he was joking.

He texted me a few hours later, having read what I'd sent him.

'This brings it back,' he typed. 'Thanks for reminding me about the medic's balls in my face. I'd almost managed to forget about that.'

I told him that if it wasn't for him and his misfortune, I'd be struggling for creative influence.

'I was supposed to die there. I'm sure of that,' he said, and I found it hard to disagree, but there was only one reply to give, and only one thing that mattered.

'But you didn't.'

25

Last Dance

There was time for one final push south.

The Firm didn't know the purpose of the reinforced patrol but nor did we care – it just seemed like a good way to stir up a hornet's nest. Our days in Helmand were growing few. We weren't out of the war yet, but we were already beginning to miss it.

The objective was Round Hill and the small village that lay on its slope. OP Hill had taken fire from these compounds, but usually the single shot kind. We suspected the Taliban were visitors rather than occupants.

The patrol itself consisted of three Warriors, a recovery vehicle, and a variety of dismounts with an even greater variety of acronyms: FOO, FAC, MFC, ECM, and the GPMG carried by myself.

One Platoon at Khabir pushed one of their own Warriors onto Middle Hill as a support group, while the sergeant major's wagon held the junction between OP Hill and Khabir. To the east, OMLT and the ANA would operate in the area of Dickers Ridge.

We left Minden with the dismounts spread out between the wagons, enjoying the winter walk along Route Pink. The OC was with us – he'd be overseeing the chess game from OP Hill but was now at the rear of the formation, up the arse of the man in front of him.

Danny saw, and turned to look at me. Once he'd caught my eye, he shook his head. I returned the gesture.

Having passed Khabir, the patrol broke up into its various parts.

As gimpy gunner, I'd be hanging back behind the trucks as our Barma team cleared a route to Round Hill. Once we were there, I'd break off with Turkey and a number of others and we'd poke our noses among the compounds.

The going south was easy enough. Miraculously, no IEDs were found by either the Barma team or the tracks of our trucks. This was likely down to the fact that we were free from being restricted to the dirt tracks and instead we made our way across bare fields that had cultivated poppies in the summer.

The ICOM buzzed, but Bash, our terp, heard nothing that he thought needed passing along. That was until we came to a halt, and the suddenly animated Afghan called out, 'Incoming!'

Only Rabbit bit on the trick, hurling himself to the deck. Bash became helpless with laughter.

An old man in the fields, perhaps confident because we were hidden from sight by the banks of a wadi, warned us that the low ground ahead held belts of IEDs and that the Taliban were active in the area. It was decided that there was nothing to be gained by pushing the Warriors further south, and so they were left in a position of overwatch as the dismounts made their way towards the compounds.

On the right-hand side of the village, standing alone, was a breeze-block construction. None of us could guess its purpose, but we could figure out well enough why a pair of military-aged males alongside it were watching us – we were being dicked.

We walked the alleyways between the compounds, confident enough that there would be no IEDs lurking there. Scotty, our MFC, found an empty 7.62mm case. It was in a position that offered an excellent view of OP Hill. I wondered if it could have been from the same weapon and firer that had taken a potshot at me as I'd admired the views from the top of that vantage point.

Few villagers wanted to talk to us and we had no cause to move inside the compounds, and so the patrol was over quickly. We were at the lower end of the village, and Turkey decided that we'd take a smoke break in the shade of a compound wall before collapsing back northwards.

As we were finding a comfortable place to park our arses, a few shots echoed in the distance. It came over the radio that they'd been aimed at the Warrior placed on Middle Hill, but that was an end to the matter.

A creaking metal door in a compound wall opened, and an old man came out to talk. Perhaps he wanted to know how the Russian's war was going. He talked to Turkey through Bash as I chatted shit with Scotty, looking westwards at the imposing shapes of our Warriors.

Who knows what sixth sense civilians developed living in a war zone, but when the old man said suddenly, 'I don't feel safe. I'm going,' we knew that kick-off was a few moments away.

Sure enough, Jay came over the net from the turret of his Warrior, reporting movement to the west of the village. Further north, the sergeant major reported seeing civilians hurriedly leaving compounds along the big Wadi's edge. The tranquillity of the winter's day was about to be shattered.

'Let's go,' Turkey ordered, and we headed across the decaying fields towards the safety of a narrow wadi. I was last man, repeatedly checking that my belt of ammunition was clear of dirt and kinks.

An RPG started it all. Jay saw the man firing, but his gunner was looking the other way, and by the time they were shooting back the RPG team had dropped into cover.

A weight of automatic fire followed immediately, but we were in the depression of the small wadi now and it passed over our heads. We heard the sergeant major's truck open up to the north, as well as the Warriors that had accompanied us south, and machine gun and cannon fire began to crisscross above our heads.

'I hope our guys' sights are on,' Scotty smiled at me – a dropped 30mm shell into our refuge would not be welcome.

We ran along the depression, moving closer to our Warriors so that they could carry us away in their metal wombs. As we waited for our battlefield taxis, I pleaded with Turkey to let me push up the bank and engage with my gimpy. He refused – my fire would make no difference to the weight that was coming from the turrets of our trucks. I knew as much, but I just wanted to get in on the gang bang.

Bash, listening in on the ICOM, reported that the Taliban on the west bank of the wadi were preparing to join in the fight. At that moment a Warrior lurched to a stop on the ground above us, and we ran towards it as the hydraulic ram pushed back the door of the troop compartment.

The Barma team were already crammed inside, room for one more only. Danny took the spot as rounds began to zip and buzz about our ears. The Taliban to the west had got stuck in, and we, the perfect targets standing in the open ground, were for some reason laughing hysterically.

Giggling as we ran through the crashing rounds, we came to a second Warrior, finding its troop compartment empty, but awash with diesel.

Any port in a storm.

We piled in: me, Turkey, Bash, Rabbit, Nacho, and Fairy Eyes. Barrels of weapons poked and jabbed into our flesh as we struggled to arrange ourselves, and still we were laughing.

As our wagons lurched and roared north, Turkey informed us from his radio that Khabir was now also in contact – the madness was spreading.

We pulled to a stop alongside the sergeant major's truck at the base of OP Hill and Turkey ran off to get his orders. Rounds were still cracking back and forth, and Rabbit wanted the door closed. I was happier to take my chances with the bullets than with the stinking fumes of the diesel that was soaking into our boots.

With Turkey back we crossed the M4 wadi, coming to a stop about fifty metres north of Khabir. Turkey took off again, this time with Bash, who he had to leave at the smaller patrol base.

'Stay here!' he told us.

In the turret, Jay and Wayne continued their fire.

'Smash,' Jay ordered.

'Smashing now,' Wayne replied, booms of the cannon following.

'Stay here,' Turkey had said.

Fat chance.

I climbed out into the sunlight, seeing the sangars of Khabir putting down a weight of fire across the wadi. Our mortars were pounding the far bank, accompanied in their destruction by an Exactor missile.

I set my GPMG up at the lip of the track and joined the fuck fest. The gun struggled at first, the diesel and crap from the deck of the truck clogging the link, but soon she was singing.

The others from the truck decided I had the right idea and spread out to my left. The range was too far for rifles, but they fired anyway.

The ANA had appeared from somewhere and they joined our line on the track. The morning was turning into a fucked-up range day, nobody worried about targets, only triggers. From the booming cannon to my right, to the line of machine guns to my left, the noise was unreal.

The weight of fire was a blanket, the opposing treeline and cliffs turned into a boiling sea of bullet and shell strikes. This wasn't a firefight any longer. It had nothing to do with the rounds that had been coming our way. This was six months of anxiety and frustration unleashed. We weren't just shooting up the people and the countryside of Afghanistan, we were pinning it down by the throat and cumming on its face. This gunfire was our moment of domination. Our reprisal for the buried bombs, our broken friends, and the bullshit of our leaders.

It couldn't last forever. Order was restored. Jay was given permission to target a fighter seen among the smoke, hitting the area dead on with cannon fire. The rest of us watched, stretched out in the sunshine, engorged.

The ANA were the first to leave the orgy. Theirs was a piratical look, crossed belts of ammunition and missing teeth. One hard-looking bastard said something to me. The only word I caught was 'Taliban', but the brute was smiling, and so I smiled back, miming a throat slitting gesture with my thumb. He liked that.

When it came time for our own move back, my sling was soaked in diesel, and so I carried my gun over my shoulder as I'd seen them do in the Vietnam movies. The O C was behind me.

'I don't like the way you're carrying that weapon, Corporal Jones,' our leader told me. 'It's pointing straight at me.'

'It's not loaded, sir.' Following the gang bang, I'd not bothered to load another belt of ammunition. Terry was done for the day, I was sure.

'Yeah, cheers for that'.

I wanted to remind him it wasn't me who'd accidentally fired his weapon during the tour, but I kept quiet like a good soldier.

As we closed up to Minden my cheerleading squad spotted me, cries of 'Smoke and a pancake!' welcoming me back. I used my free hand to high five and shadow box with the kids.

That evening I went with Danny to relive the day's events via the screens of Cortez. Our favourite piece of footage was of a Taliban fighter shooting over the top of a wall. A cannon round smashed into his upper body, spreading him across the compound.

He was the company's final kill of the tour.

26

Decompression

The end of tour – so eagerly anticipated and yet equally feared – came in a blur.

There was the incessant itching in my wrists and crotch, a family of parasites having made me their home. There was the Warrior maintenance, tough love for our armoured steeds. By the army's logic, now that the tour was over we could re-equip our perennially broken-down wagons with the spares we'd been begging for since summer. From dawn to dusk, men broke and hauled track, fitted road wheels, and the more skilled lurked in the murky depths of engine compartments. Toes and fingers were jammed, Toby's wedding ring crushed into flesh by a missed swing of a sledgehammer. We were sent out on patrols that we knew by now to be futile. Nobody was in the mood for the game. Good officers took us instead to OP Hill, where we drank brews and sent in bogus grid references.

During a break on patrol, one of The Zoo sat on a used needle, opiates a favoured pastime of the locals, our enemies and allies alike. He was evacuated to Camp Bastion for blood work, testing positive for hepatitis.

The ANA and OMLT were contacted in a drive-by shooting from a pickup truck. We hoped this would allow us to be able to turn the tour into an LA-inspired turf war.

An Afghan man hit a child for the shame of him begging for biscuits, and it took three of us to hold back an enraged Sergeant Davies.

IEDs were found and destroyed. One had been ingeniously placed in a patch of dead ground between Minden and Khabir. They must have crawled out to bury it, using the cover of a shallow haystack. It had a low metal content reading, but a sharp-eyed private had spotted the disturbed earth. With days left on the ground, this wasn't the time to die.

There was a patrol south onto Middle Hill, accompanied by an FST of American marines. Our area of operations was being handed over to the USMC – I'd meet one of them in a bar in LA – and the group of stern-faced soldiers sat among a nest of antennas in the shallow remains of a Russian trench. Binoculars and weapon sights were glued to their eyes, radios to the ears. In the shell scrape beside them, I exchanged a barrage of stones with Scotty, our MFC. Maybe Terry was busy fucking around with his own friends, because there was no shooting that day. I was a fan of American football and asked the marines who had made the playoffs. None had any idea. Jay found they were equally useless with the ice hockey.

'So what do you guys play?' he asked.

With an excited smile, their captain answered, 'Ping-pong!'

The next day, and with seven others, I was whisked away to the local ANA base, having been informed a few hours earlier that we would be taking over from the Yorkshire Omelette, and performing their task for a few weeks until the replacements for the next tour arrived. I was glad of the posting, already homesick for Afghanistan, the chance to work with the ANA a guarantee that there would be some more shooting to do before we left the ground. We just needed to heed the advice of the men we were relieving to never wash or be naked in front of the Afghan soldiers, as they'd happily watch and rub themselves through the pockets of their grubby trousers.

That first night with the Yorkshire men we set our own guards, not trusting the Afghan sentries in their sandbagged sangars. The distinctive stink of weed drifted across the compound – little wonder they'd shot at our Warriors.

We exchanged videos with the OMLT. I came into possession of one clip that showed their comrade being shot through the legs; the same man I had helped carry away from the fight and onto the chopper. Throughout the video there was only laughter.

The Afghan commander of the base was a stout major who looked like a Pashtun Joe Pesci, short and angry. During contacts, he'd strut up and down in the open, extorting his men and defying the bullets that danced around him. He'd been shot several times, by several enemies, beginning with the Russians. What if he should be killed?

'*Inshallah.*' As God wills. With all those scars, perhaps God was telling him to take a fucking firing position.

The Yorkshire Reg' OMLT left us in the morning. We were the embedded now, and enjoyed a game of football with the Afghans on the patrol base's dirt courtyard. The OMLT had left their gym equipment behind, and we laughed at the Afghans who couldn't perform a single repetition with the weights. We watched helicopters come in and out of Minden, ferrying kit back to Bastion. We heard the Taliban's attempts to hit them, Battleshock Blake shitting himself at each new burst of fire.

This was a good home. No bullshit, and the chance of regular contacts. It could never last, and it didn't.

Twelve hours later the plan changed – we'd head to Bastion with the rest of the company, and so we were returned to Minden.

The HCR flew in their men who would be holding the base until 2 Lancs, and eventually the Marine Corps, took over. The hair of the HCR men was long, their equipment non-issue, forbidden badges on their Velcro patches. It seemed the classic scenario of 'do as I say, not as I do'.

There was no sad farewell when we left Minden. Glad to see the back of the bullshit we piled with speed into the Warriors and roared out the gate. Though we had the desire for combat, we were repelled by the presence of our 'adoptive' unit. We were as unwanted as a ginger step-child, and so we left without a backwards glance.

I was with Toby, a troop compartment to ourselves. By virtue of being with the short-lived OMLT I had escaped being drafted into any of the Barma teams that would clear the route to Bastion. I had nothing to do for the journey except snore, and talk to my friend. Jay and Sergeant Davies were in the turret, smiles hidden behind their facemasks.

The company pulled to a stop in the gravel wadi outside of Musa Qala DC, home of the hated HCR. There was some kind of livestock market taking place in the dry riverbed, the locals parading skinny-legged ponies with brightly coloured blankets laid across their backs. Goats and mangy sheep were in abundance.

'Looks like an Afghan brothel,' Toby laughed.

We posed for photos in front of the scene, and the familiar, block-like headquarters building behind us, decorated as it was by the painted emblems of the battle groups who had passed through this area of operations. As we mounted up and lurched away, the HCR's leaders were treated to a salute of two fingers from the turrets. Terry would be getting an invitation to our reunion before the cavalry did.

We spent the first night at FOB Edi. There was a huge tent there that provided shelter for a makeshift workshop, and we amused ourselves by climbing to the top of the canvas and sliding back down on our arses. Beneath it, six months earlier, Sniper Hunt had danced along the Warrior tracks the day before we'd been hit, a moment that now seemed a lifetime away.

Leaving Edi, on the home stretch, I was oblivious to our last contact of the tour. So had Jay been, until the rounds began to ping off the turret hatch behind him.

'Probably some pissed off farmer,' he shrugged. What was the bullet that didn't hit you?

Our wagon broke down and we had to be towed. Tracked vehicles do not tow as elegantly as those that are wheeled, the final twelve hours spent like a baby tossed around in a particularly loud and angry washing machine. After one violent bump the vehicle's fire extinguishers were set off. Despite the powder in our throats, Toby and I were helpless with laughter.

The swift return journey to Bastion was everything that our journey out had not been, and we emerged, incredulous, within the wire and Hesco of the huge camp. We posed for photos, almost stunned to realize that we would be going home alive and with all limbs accounted for.

Smith gathered us together for another inspirational speech. The gist was that it had been a good tour, but all that counted for nothing if we didn't shave now that we were in Bastion.

Weapons went into the armoury. We showered, water splashing back and forth between laughing soldiers. We ate hot, fresh scoff, and then it was the food that was thrown.

We were happy. Relieved. Alive.

We'd made it.

The Firm was reunited. We had survived the war, and with the exception of Jake's mind and neck tissue, we were mostly intact. Once again we were inseparable. We scoffed, showered, slept, and shit together. We had all been on tour before, and we knew that once we arrived in the UK things would not be the same again. We would always be friends, but the bonds would be looser. How could it be any other way? Our relationships would be concerned with talk about rugby and women, not life and death. We knew this, and we feared it. Like lovers on a summer holiday, our affair was finite, and so we spent every minute in each other's presence, basking in that unspeakable comradeship for every second that we could.

For Jake, his second convalescence at Bastion had been as frustrating as his first. He was caught between two worlds and part of neither. He told us how he'd been racked with guilt that he was safe behind the lines while we were still on the ground. He wanted to be with his family, be that the family of his blood or the battlefield.

The army wanted 'battle shock' casualties kept as close to the front lines as possible. This made sense if the aim was to allow the soldier to rejoin his unit, particularly in the classic rotation of units to the front as dictated by the First and Second World Wars, but in Afghanistan there was no rotation. Jake languished in Bastion until our own tour was over, and his guilt crushed him, no matter that none of us were harmed, nor blamed him.

He was also forced to see a mental health specialist, an overweight RAF officer who Jake despised for his lack of experience on the ground. The presumption of a combat virgin to tell Jake why and what he was feeling irked Pinkmist, who became confrontational. The RAF shrink called the regimental sergeant major in the UK, describing Jake as 'angry and aggressive'.

'He's an infantry soldier,' the RSM had replied. 'He's supposed to be angry and aggressive.'

We began the final maintenance on the Warriors, The Firm forming its own elite team for track bashing. Sad Act and Ginger Pubes somehow acquired an RAF firefighting truck, the water cannon blasting the dust from our wagons. They asked for money out of the company funds we paid into to buy the firefighters a crate of Coke. A thank you for saving us possibly days of work. They were told no, so our platoon pranksters took care of it themselves.

After a few days, the sergeant major was bored. He got us on parade.

'Right, there's a few things that are going wrong.' He paused, and we could see that he was desperate to think of something. 'I've seen people walking around carrying brews,' he finally managed, as if it were a capital crime. 'That's got to stop. No hands in your pockets, either.' He seemed oblivious to the fact that behind him all three platoon sergeants had their hands either glued inside of their trousers or clasped about steaming cups of tea.

Our tent was a hundred metres from the helicopter flight line. During daylight hours we got goosebumps watching the Apaches take to the air, visiting Terry with their payloads of murder. At night-time, however, we cursed the pilots and prayed that they'd crash, the roar of blades making sleep impossible. A further two hundred metres away was the base's main runway, which was now the fifth busiest UK-run airport. To avoid a nasty surprise by Terry, almost all flights came and went during the hours of darkness.

Monotony soon set in. Once the Warriors, weapons, and ammunition had been taken care of, there was nothing for us to do, but the RAF was so overstretched that there were no flights to get us out of the country. Instead, we were consigned to a corner of the huge camp, out of sight and out of mind.

The war was over for us, but not for units in the field. There were more vigils, though the number of deaths had fallen since our arrival in the summer – little consolation for those who died, and their families.

Our regiment's 1st Battalion were now in Bastion, operating from there in helicopter-borne ops, and with about half a dozen other men I volunteered to stay on with them for the final four months of their tour. I was already missing the ground, and the idea of never being in contact again left me feeling hollow. It seemed that the unit was keen to have us, and the prospects of staying in country looked good. As I walked out of the gym one day, angry music blaring in my headphones, a Black Hawk helicopter roared low above my head and sent shivers of excitement down my spine – fuck, I did not want to leave Afghanistan.

I tracked down my friends in the 1st Battalion. They were enjoying their tour, whisked in and out of Bastion by helicopters, contacts followed by hot showers, food and the gym. A charmed life. Grimes had been my driver in Iraq, as well as a hometown friend. He took me to meet his sergeant major, who promised to get me into his company and Grimes's platoon when our tour extensions had been confirmed.

I ate with Grimes in his own unit's dining facilities, and it was there that we saw Pete. He'd been a young private in our platoon during Iraq, but now he'd achieved his dream of becoming an officer. He'd only just arrived in theatre, and had yet to be on the ground. He took our banter well, forgetting rank, and joined us to eat.

'You ever find that shit Dai put in your bergen?' I asked him. When Pete had left Iraq early to return to university, his tormentor in the platoon had left a clingfilm-wrapped surprise in his kit.

He grimaced at the memory. 'Yeah. After about a month.'

We finished dinner and said our goodbyes. A couple of weeks later Pete would finally realize his ambition of being a platoon commander at war. A few days after getting on the ground he'd step on a mine, the shrapnel stripping his legs of most of their flesh. He'd keep the limbs, but he'd never be able to cope with the rigours of the army again. Pete would be medically discharged, his dream career cut short by thirty years.

I visited Grimes a few more times between his operations. He told me about an IED they'd found, dug in on the side of a track beside a canal, the aim of the explosion being to tip the Mastiff into the water. If Terry couldn't kill the crew of the bombproof trucks with shrapnel, then he'd drown them.

There was a further vigil for more riflemen killed in Sangin. It was almost the end of the Rifles' tour, and the caskets kept coming. Tales from the rumour mill reached us about men so worn down by the war that they no longer cleared the tracks ahead of them. Like the ANA major, they put their fate in the hands of a higher power. *Inshallah*.

To my dismay, the request to stay on with the 1st Battalion was denied. The reason we heard was that the battalion commanding officers had a spat over what should happen with the medal ceremony, after which our own CO refused to allow any of us to stay on with our sister unit. Obviously, we affected individuals were not asked for our opinions.

I paid a final visit to Grimes, who was gearing up with his unit to take part in the biggest helicopter assault since Vietnam. I felt physically sick to not be a part of it. Sick with jealousy, and sick with hate for the men who had made my decision for me. I hate them still. More so than the enemy. At least with Terry, I knew where I stood. I posed for a photo with my old comrade and I thought we were smiling happily. Looking back at it years later, our faces seem empty.

'Stay low, move fast,' I told him.

I would have traded places with him in an instant if I could.

Instead I was to go home 'home'.

I was to leave Afghanistan.

•

After weeks in Bastion we did not know how to feel when our flight arrived. We'd been in purgatory, and the initial grateful excitement that we had felt at leaving the ground was over. Many of us were desperate to return to it.

We were flown out of the country and spent a night in Cyprus at Camp Bloodhound, for what the army termed 'decompression'. We'd been in this same place following Iraq, and that trip lived in infamy.

The idea of decompression was one of the army's better ones. Like Wellington, some of our commanders must have thought of us as 'the scum of the earth'. They knew that, unleashed onto the streets of the UK and with a skin full of drink, we would be looking to fight, and would be a general public nuisance.

And so, as the war in Iraq had intensified, Camp Bloodhound, a tiny remote place in the hills of Cyprus, had been set aside for the returning soldiers. Beer was limitless. Entertainment was provided by lewd comedians. Men could settle scores, and get the worst of their alcohol-induced emotions out of their system. During our post-Iraq decompression, unfortunate signallers attached to our own unit had been held down and hosed with piss. Portaloos had been knocked over, showering the occupants with shit. Men had each other's balls, cocks, and sick in their mouths. As the smoke cleared, a hundred comatosed men had been herded onto the flight to the UK, made docile by epic hangovers. They left behind a wake of vomit and pissed beds, but they had decompressed. Mission accomplished.

Not so following Afghanistan. Perhaps the generals had had cause to visit the site. Perhaps the cleaners had gone on strike or were suffering from PTSD. Whatever the reason, two years following our last visit, we were told that we were to be limited to two cans of beer a man.

We took this as an insult and a waste of our time. Better to just get us home if that was the case. The comedians did their best, but we were in a sour mood, and a poor audience. We amused ourselves by collecting what beer we had and forcing it down the throats of some of the younger privates. Even their drunkenness soon bored us and we went to bed. We were not decompressed, only bitter, and the streets of our hometowns could suffer the consequences.

The one highlight of the visit had been a brief moment at a go-karting circuit. Nacho believed he'd been overtaken in the pit lane, and not to be outdone, he stomped on the gas, terrified track workers leaping for cover behind the walls of tyres.

The next day we landed in Oxfordshire, and were taken by bus to our camp in Wiltshire. Many families were waiting. I'd told mine not to come. The tour was over. They'd see me soon enough.

We were formed up in ranks outside of the camp, and marched through the gates behind a Warrior, the assembled families clapping, smiling, and crying.

I felt no such relief, or elation. My war was over and for the first time I could see no future tours. Our battalion was slated for none, and President Obama had already declared that the US would start pulling their troops out of the wars the following year. No further opportunities to pull the trigger and become the soldier that I had always longed to be. I'd had my chances, they had slipped by, and here I was, the same person I'd been before I first set foot in these countries.

I collected my car keys from the guardroom and drove home. I was bitter, angry, and lost.

But most of all, I was mistaken.

HOME

27

Prodigal Son

When the weather's cold, my big toe hurts. It hurts because I broke it. It hurts because I broke it trying to kick down a door. I'd like to say that it was during an operation in Iraq or Afghanistan, but it was inside my own home, and there were no insurgents on the other side of the wood. There was only my mother, moved to terror and tears by her own son.

Most of what happened at the beginning of my return home is a blur to me now. I can't tell you if I was a cunt from the moment I landed back in the UK or if it took time for that egg to hatch.

I do remember my first night out with civilian friends. One of them asked me if I had lost comrades, and I had tried to tell him about Hunt. It didn't go well. Aside from the investigating military policewoman at Zulu – when I'd still been numb and convinced of my own end – it was the first time I'd ever tried to speak about it in any depth, and with the first words came tears. One of my friends noticed and made a joke. I threw my glass at his face and then I left the bar. Walking alone in the town, I eventually came across a friend who had been a para. He was also known for trouble, and was barred from most of the pubs and clubs.

'I'll get you in,' I promised, and did, but we had barely walked up the club's stairs and onto the dancefloor when someone bumped hard into my friend and gave him a shitty look. I didn't wait to see what happened next. I just hit the guy. A second later there was a bouncer's arm around my throat, and I let myself get dragged back down the staircase.

'You're fucking kidding me?' the bouncer on the front door said, shaking his head. He'd allowed me in only thirty seconds earlier after ten minutes of me assuring him that I would control my friend.

'I'm sorry,' I told him, and meant it. 'I'm sorry.'

I'm not really certain what happened next. At some point I found myself tucked behind a set of bins, crying uncontrollably. I called a friend. Against my wishes they called my mum. She arrived to collect me, and I knew at that point that I had failed as a soldier. I had failed as a man. I was still the toddler that cried for its mother when it fell down. When the drink and the tears cleared my system, I simply felt hollow. I knew what I was. Weak and pathetic.

I was also angry. So angry.

Like the thrown glass at my friend's face or the punch in the club, that anger could boil over from nothing in an instant. It was as if almost all of the gears had been taken out of my emotional engine and I was left with two to choose from – apathy or anger. I was either the most relaxed man in the room or I was throwing insults, punches, and furniture.

I was angry at so many things. The people back home for one. I was angry because they didn't understand the reality of the situation in Afghanistan, or they simply didn't care. They lived in a bubble that, at that time, I was convinced was provided by the sacrifice of soldiers in that war and Iraq. To see them oblivious to that made me want to beat them bloody until they understood. I didn't recognize the irony that I wanted to harm them because they did not acknowledge that we protected them.

I was also angry at the government and the army. I knew things were not going well in Afghanistan. I knew they could be handled better. I knew, even back then, that people had died in vain, or at least due to poor decision making and equipment. In February, one of the soldiers who now held PB Minden was killed during a night patrol, a death by friendly fire from the Afghan army. As on our own tour, the Brits had come across armed Afghans in the night. This time, however, the uncoordinated ANA patrol had opened fire. The Brits had returned it with deadly effect, killing two ANA soldiers.

Lessons had either not been learned, or not been passed on from our own experience in that location, and as a result, a nineteen-year-old British soldier and two of his Afghan allies now lay dead. I fumed at such a preventable waste of life. This anger towards our 'leaders' did not diminish as time went by. In fact it grew. I was choked with hate when I heard of six soldiers dying in a Warrior in 2012 – the vehicles, so unsuited to that theatre and the IED threat, were still being used there two years after we left. I wanted to find the people who made these decisions, and stamp on their fucking faces until their skulls shattered.

But, more often than not, my anger was directed at myself. I was angry that I showed weakness. I was angry that I hadn't done more on tour. I was angry that I felt apathetic about being home. I wanted to feel gratitude and love to be back among family and friends. Instead, for the majority of the time I felt numb, and from that emptiness would suddenly come anger.

Sometimes my family were the ones to suffer this rage. Sometimes they were the ones I was trying to protect. A honked horn at my mother would see me fly out of the car door, begging the other driver to get out the car and fight. Once, I found myself stared at by a busload of frightened pensioners – the bus driver had been riding the bumper of my brother's car. I guess he was in a rush. He wasn't in a rush to get out when I appeared next to him, trying to grab his throat through a tiny open window.

A sly glance towards one of my friends was usually enough for me to expect violence, and to pre-empt it. The need to 'shoot' before the 'enemy' did leaked into every aspect of my life, and I began to imagine sneaky words and looks even in previously safe havens of mine; like the gym, where my paranoia would see me explode in a rage that had people no doubt thinking I was sticking myself full of dangerous levels of testosterone. In the months following my return to the UK I was argumentative, violent, and unpredictable.

And I was lost. The truth was that I had no desire to be home. I wanted to be in Afghanistan. I missed it, and I ached to be back in those summer months where we had leaned against sandbags and watched tracer arc up against pink skies.

At least I could be among comrades. After a couple of months of leave, we returned to our garrison. Though camp duties were a far cry from our deployment, it was a joy to be reunited with my brothers. With the majority of Three Platoon, I left A Company and took a place in the Recce Platoon. I couldn't have been happier with this. We had the same leadership as we had on tour, the Boss and Turkey, and though The Firm was split up between Anti-Tank and Recce platoons, we were still close together in Support Company. Pinkmist lived in the same flat as I did – imagine university accommodation but with occasional weapons and much more vulgarity – and we spent a lot of time in each other's company. It wasn't long until almost every man in the accommodation had bought himself a PlayStation and *Call of Duty*, and we took our war online, raging with fury as we were picked apart by twelve-year-old kids on the other side of the planet. 'You little cunt! I'd like to see you do that in a real war! Arghhhhhh!'

I'm not sure if this compulsive shoot 'em up playing was a good thing or bad, but there was no denying that it was a rampant addiction for us during our first few months back in the country, and then in barracks. Eventually it tailed off, and for myself at least I have never played a similar game since.

It was hard to fit back into the routine of barracks after being on deployment. We were salty, and questioned much of the wisdom of what we were doing. In my own mind, I railed against the time-wasting aspect of it all. Much of our day was spent waiting to go from one parade to another, where we would be told to wait for the next parade. Perhaps it was because Afghanistan had taught me that life could end at any time and so time should not be wasted, but I chaffed during these seemingly meaningless days. The Boss came to my rescue and put me forward for the army's physical training instructor course, a ten-week stint in Aldershot. I would be responsible for the unit's PT on my return. I loved it, not only for the physical challenge, but because it brought me into contact with other soldiers from all kinds of cap badges and backgrounds. Many were infantry who had served in Afghanistan, and inevitably we formed the closest groups. In particular, I became very close to two 1 PARA soldiers, and I began toying with the idea of transferring to a unit where I could see more deployments, and combat.

There was no sign of that on the horizon with the Royal Welsh. Instead there was a trip to the Falkland Islands, where the Support Company soldiers who had deployed with A Company would now miss their second Christmas in a row. This included Toby, who was red with rage that he would be pulled away from his family so quickly after returning to them.

It was halfway through my PTI course when I realized just how much I had grown to hate the army – and by that, I mean hate in the same way that a husband may come to detest his wife while still acknowledging a deep-rooted love for her.

I had been called into the course coordinator's office, and now stood to attention in front of his desk.

'You need to call your unit,' the PT corps officer told me.

I asked for permission to step outside and make the call – phone use was not allowed at Fox Lines, except for in the NAAFI. The officer nodded. I stepped outside and took out my phone. It was barely out of my pocket when a red-faced NCO screamed at me. 'Oi! You! Get off your fucking phone!'

'I've got to call my battalion, Staff,' I explained.

'Well you can't do it here!'

'The course coordinator said I could.'

I could see this threw the NCO. The man was his superior, but then there was the no phones rule to adhere to. I could see the battle rage behind his brainwashed eyes.

'Well,' he began, 'you've got to play the game, yeah?'

'Yes, Staff,' I agreed.

You've got to play the game.

We stood facing one another, the phone in my hand. Finally, with confusion etched into his features, the NCO went on his way and I made my call.

I soon wished that I hadn't.

'I've got to go to an inquest, sir,' I explained to the course coordinator. 'It's in Birmingham.'

'What dates?'

I told him. He frowned.

'You may have to drop out of the course then.'

'I'm sorry, sir?'

'I don't know if we can give you two days off the course and still pass you. Do you think you can get out of going?'

I didn't know what to say. I would like to tell to you that in that moment I calmly thought 'To be fair, I don't know what he has been through in his own life or his army career,' or, 'I'm sure he didn't mean to upset me'. But I fucking didn't. I just wanted to smash his face in. To scream at him: Are you fucking serious? One of my boys died on tour, and this is the inquest into his death! Do you think me throwing logs over my head and climbing over walls is more important than this? How fucking sheltered are you here in your office you little prick? Have you ever even set foot on the ground? Have you ever fired your weapon? Have you ever been certain that you would die on the other side of the world? THAT is what being a soldier means! THAT is why we have an army!

Instead I said, 'No sir, I can't.'

'Well, we'll see if we can let you stay.' He dismissed me.

I called back to my company after that. I let them know that I would likely be dumped off the course and the Boss lost his shit for the same reasons as I had.

'I'll talk to the cunt,' he promised, and he was true to his word, because I was granted the two days away from the course.

I would go to Hunt's inquest.

The inquest was to be held in Birmingham Magistrates' Court. I was told to wear my Number 2 dress uniform, the first time I had worn it since the funeral of my friend Jamie on the day I'd flown to Afghanistan.

We were put up in a hotel, and in the morning I met with A Company's OC, One Platoon's commander, and Emily. The OC explained why we were there. Because Afghanistan was not legally a war, and because Hunt was killed by terrorists, rather than an enemy combatant, then there had to be an inquest into his death. As he died in Selly Oak hospital, then it was to take place here.

Birmingham. I would like to say that our uniforms did not draw contemptuous looks as we walked from the hotel to the courts, but that would be a lie. In London the sight of a soldier in uniform drew smiles and requests for photos. Here there was apathy at best, and many scowls. By the time we reached our destination my anger was fighting against my nerves for control of my shaking limbs.

I was terrified, and nervous. Nervous because I was going to have to take the stand and testify. Terrified because I would be coming face-to-face with Hunt's family.

'They can ask you questions,' the liaison officer explained. He was a para whose ribbons stretched back to the Falklands campaign, and his manner was as steady and solid as the British line at Waterloo. Little wonder he had been chosen as the man to guide young soldiers before they took the stand. I was in awe of this warrior, and there was no way I would let him down.

'The reason you're here,' he explained to me and Em, 'is that there's some discrepancies in the written statements between you guys and the medics on the chopper, so we just wanted to get that cleared up.'

'OK, sir.' I swallowed, trying to appear stoic.

'Now look,' the career soldier went on. 'The judge is going to ask you things. He's a good bloke, so don't expect a grilling like the movies. He will make it easy, and then the family get to ask their questions.'

We said nothing. For a moment, neither did he.

'There was an inquest I did once for a Fijian lad,' the old soldier then explained, reading my mind. 'His section commander was giving evidence, and the Fijian's father asked about his son's injuries.

'The corporal looked the man's father straight in the eyes, and said, "Sir, when I got to your son, he was in a very bad way."'

I swallowed the lump in my throat, and nodded. 'And if they press for an answer after that, sir?' I asked, memorizing the words should I need them myself.

'Then tell them the truth,' the man told me, and I felt as though someone was reaching into my stomach and trying to pull it out through my face.

'Come on,' the para encouraged. 'Let's go.'

I don't remember much of what happened inside that courtroom. At one point I was called to the stand. As I got up one of the shoe-laces came out of my boot and I stopped to tuck it in, going red in the face. I had borrowed the boots and they were too big. I walked like a clown, terrified I would trip.

I don't remember the judge's face, just his tone – calm and patient. A reassuring presence. He led me through the events of the day when we had been blown up, and I confirmed the statements I had made while in theatre. I don't know if this lasted two minutes or twenty, but I do remember the moment when the judge told the family that they would now be able to ask their questions.

I turned to face them. It was less than a decade ago, but the memory is haze now. It was haze the moment I left the courtroom. The faintest vision of benches and the blurred faces of Hunt's family. I stood trembling, fighting back the urges to cry and vomit.

But they had no questions.

I sagged with relief, and walked from the stand with my hands pressed to my side to hide nerves, my stomach still in my mouth. I was present for the rest of the proceedings but my mind was distant. I remember an expert witness explaining that Hunt's brain injuries were not survivable. More witnesses came and went. I fought a running battle to control tapping feet and shaking hands. Eventually it was over.

Tea. What else would a British soldier do after an event like that but grab a brew? There was a room set aside for the military witnesses. Myself. One Platoon's Commander. Emily. The OC. I looked over at the others, all moved by the event. Here again I saw that the company commander was a good man. We talked among ourselves, animated now as the relief flooded through us that it was over. Finally, I was calming.

And then Hunt's family appeared in the doorway.

It was his mother who spoke, her words cutting into my heart to leave the one thing that I can remember from that day with absolute clarity.

'I'm glad he had friends with him at the end,' she told us, pushing back tears. Beside her, Hunt's father stood as if shell-shocked, no obvious emotion on his face, only the numbing astonishment that appears when a person is thrown into a situation that they could never contemplate, nor accept.

They did not stay for long. I expected that the uniforms and our faces were bringing forth uncontrollable emotions. It was the last time I saw them in person, but I have thought about those words almost every day since, the picture of his mother's face a vision I have never been able to forget. Some days I draw strength from her own, and on others despair. I felt as though I was a liar. A fraud. I had not been his friend. I had been his comrade, and despite what the expert witness had said about his injuries not being survivable, I knew that in some way I had failed him.

I don't remember what happened after that. I don't remember leaving the court. I just remember being back in the hotel, and wishing it was me who was dead.

28

Friendly Neighbourhood Killers

You wouldn't think that he's a killer. With his ripped jeans, long T-shirts, and the bracelets on his wrists, he looks more like a skater than a soldier.

But he was.

His war is invisible to you, but it's etched inside of his skull, jagged and violent. It slips beneath the surface of his life like an alligator, that primordial entity that will snatch from the banks anyone too stupid or lazy to keep out of its way. The killer may look like a skater, a suit, or a homeless man, but he was a soldier, and that means that he will forever be a soldier. In that past life, every panted breath he took, every drop of blood he gave, every bead of sweat that he perspired, it was for him to live, you to thrive, and the enemy to die.

There are many of these killers among you.

They repair your car. They train you at the gym. They live on your streets. But they are here. In a country where most men have never thrown a punch, there are thousands of killers. The fortunate ones killed the enemy and look back on those memories fondly. Some made mistakes and destroyed families; they try to not look back at all.

Don't think that because you drink your frappu-fucking-chinos and order your food through a phone that the world is not a savage place, and that savages do not walk among you. You are lucky to have them there. Fucking lucky, because these savages are the ones who lick their lips at the idea of kicking in doors and pulling bad guys from their beds – or better yet, putting a double tap into their faces. The world needs bad men who will carry out painful deeds against worse men, because a good world does not exist – it is a dark, insidious place. If you are reading this, then the probability is that you live in one of its lighter corners, where the blood and sweat of noble savages has bought you the illusion that we can all live together.

Wrong.

So fucking wrong, because there are people in this world who will kill a woman for having an opinion. Wrong, because there are people who will behead a man for speaking out against an ancient book. Wrong, because some of the strong will always prey on the weak, and for these reasons you should be glad that killers walk among you. You should drop to your fucking knees and thank them. Thank them that the blood on their hands keeps yours clean. Thank them that you will never have to endure the sight of your family being butchered with machetes in the streets, or herded screaming into gas chambers. Thank them that their nightmares have bought your nights of sound sleep. Thank them that their friends died, so that you could laugh with yours.

Perhaps you think that I'm overstating, and that the world is not as dark as I paint it.

Wrong again.

Wrong, because I am a middle-class university graduate who loses sleep over the number of Taliban I *didn't* kill. Wrong, because if you had handed me the bomb maker who killed Hunt, I would have dragged his death out over days. This is not written for dramatic effect, but a statement of fact. I am telling you this as an acknowledgement that there is darkness inside of everyone, and that there is an incident that can unleash it. If you acknowledge it, then you can face it, and challenge it. You only need to look at what is popular in our culture – people do not tune into *Game of Thrones* by the tens of millions because they want to see castles; they want to see blood, guts, and above all revenge. If you want to pretend that life is sunshine and rainbows, then the darkness will creep up on you and slit your throat. No one is immune, but many are spared. They are spared because *your* killers are better than theirs. They have killed on your behalf, and continue to do so. Uncomfortable thought, isn't it?

'I didn't ask them to do it,' you say.

Fuck off.

Your frappu-fucking-chino asked them to do it. Your Range Rover asked them to do it. Your bag full of shopping from Primark asked them to do it. Your bottomless mimosas asked them to do it. Your cocaine asked them to do it. You enjoy a safe affluent life because somewhere a price has been, and is still being paid. War is part of the machinery that treats you to the Western delights. Sometimes it is a necessary thing, good against evil, but more often than not it is tied to greed and wealth. As a British citizen, you have benefitted from war your entire life. An empire fought for by men in pith helmets now replaced by those in Kevlar. You've been on the winning side of history, and so next time you're enjoying that Sunday brunch, thank a killer.

There's probably one in the bar.

29

Out

I don't know exactly when I first thought about killing myself. There's no marked front line between me wanting to be a part of the world and wanting to be out of it, but one memory has stuck with me vividly – I was driving along the Pacific Coast Highway in Malibu, California, and wondering if I had the balls to roll the car off the road. It would be a tragic end, but the one that would perhaps spare my family the knowledge that I had taken my own life . . .

Yeah. That was the first distinct thought I can remember about killing myself. It was not the last. I worry that writing about it is self-indulgent at best and toxic at worst, but if I have learned anything over the last few years it is that there is no such thing as a unique thought, and so, if I write my own journey, perhaps some other soldier will identify with it, and I can steer them from the pitfalls to the better place that I've found now.

And so back to the army days.

Following completion of my PTI course, I was sent to work in the garrison's gym and escaped the Falklands deployment. This was due to a kindly officer. I told him that I would not be extending my contract and staying on with the battalion. I would leave in April 2011, and until that point I was allowed to work out of the gym. It was a job that I enjoyed immensely, and I would have stayed on for a further few years had I been allowed to remain in that position. However, the army in its wisdom dictated that, should I remain, I would have to return to a rifle platoon. After war, I had no interest in spending my life on exercise – from combat to the training area felt like going from sex with a beauty to masturbation with a sock – and so with conflicting emotions I said goodbye to my comrades and returned to my family.

The six months following my departure from the battalion were a very happy time for me. I took a job working as a personal trainer, made a lot of new friends, had a lot of sex, and a lot of fun. I was cocky, confident, and though I'm sure there were times when I lost my temper, I was on the whole free of any consequence of my tour. I remember one minor breakdown in a pub toilet, but considering what was to come, that was nothing. Looking back, I can see that was because I had done an excellent job of pushing it down inside of me, trying to forget that it had happened.

Only once did I return to the battalion. They were holding a families day, and my good friend Jason invited me along. I couldn't have been happier to see the old faces, and for a moment I regretted leaving.

That feeling didn't last for long. Captain Daniels, who had known me in Iraq and Afghanistan, came to grumble about a hundred quid I supposedly owed the corporal's mess club.

'You're not welcome here,' he told me.

Funny. With the dozens of handshakes I'd received in the past twenty minutes, I felt pretty welcome.

'Where are you staying?' he grilled me.

'A hotel in Salisbury,' I lied. I was staying with Danny in the barracks, which no doubt he had expected and was hoping to foil in revenge for the mess club.

'Don't hang around,' said the officer who had congratulated me when I received an award in Iraq.

I didn't. So much for the regimental family.

•

Pricks like Captain Daniels did everything to convince me that leaving the army behind was a good idea, and gym life was great for me until the one morning when I arrived for work and found that the doors had been padlocked. The owners had not paid their rent, and I was out of work. Fortunately my friend Rhino, formerly of the 1st Battalion, offered me a lucrative solution – to work armed security with him, protecting ships from Somalian pirates.

How could I say no to that?

I spent the next few years flying around Asia and the Middle East to pick up ships and escort them across the high-risk area where pirates stalked and hijacked vulnerable civilian shipping. The money was good, the weather was better, but best of all was the fact that I was once again working with British soldiers. We may no longer have been serving, but we were the same people, with the same mindsets, the same humour, and the same stories. These came to the fore whenever we had chance for a drink, which thankfully was quite often. We talked about the things we had done, the things we had seen, but most often we talked about the comrades we had served alongside.

It was at this time that I first put pen to paper, and began to work at my dream of becoming a writer, trying my hand at screenplays before I eventually began to expand on the journals that I kept on tour – the pages that would eventually become this book. It was also when I developed a love affair with California. Following a short trip there with an old friend and without considering such things as 'budget' and 'cash forecast', I rented a room in a Malibu beach house that I could use as a vacation pad. It was beautiful, the weather was beautiful, and the women were beautiful. It should have been everything I wanted.

Except it wasn't.

I felt numb. I felt empty. The feeling had come over me slowly, like a glacier, but by the end of 2012 I was firmly beneath the ice, and depression could hit me at any moment. So it was that I found myself behind the wheel of that car, thinking about flipping it off the road and into the rocks. I had hit a crossroads in my life, and with no idea how to proceed I reached out to the constant saviour of the lost and the pained.

I turned to drugs.

#veteranproblems

Wrexham, Wales, 2013

I pounded back the shots with Rhino. It was rare that we were in our hometown together, our security work taking us to different pastures, and we were making up for lost time. Behind the luminescent bar, *Transformers* played on a flat screen.

'Bring the rain!' we shouted, echoing the actor's line as the A-10 unloaded its missile and nose cannon onto the thrashing Decepticon.

Rhino swept his arm out to encompass the bar, drink splashing across his hand. 'How many people in here can say they've seen that?' he asked me.

'Bring the rain!' I answered, hoisting another shot, affirming the line as that night's beer-soaked battle cry.

The night went on. More rain, and with it blurred eyes, but there was no difficulty in making out our fellow veteran when he entered the bar. He was being pushed in a wheelchair, both legs and an arm absent.

He couldn't have been older than twenty-one.

It was a small town, and we knew who he was. He didn't know us, and now, vodka pulsing through my veins, I felt as though he should. Surely he was a friend through shared experience?

Shared experience – how could I even begin to understand his?

But I was drunk, and I wanted to.

'We should talk to him,' I nudged Rhino, the look of my friend telling me he thought it was a bad idea. I thought I knew best.

'He's from your battalion,' I insisted. 'Come on.'

I stuck out a hand to the man who was living my nightmare.

'Alright mate? I'm Gez, from the 2nd Battalion. This is Rhino, he's from the 1st.'

The soldier wouldn't look at me. His friend moved from behind the wheelchair. 'Don't be a dickhead. They're just trying to say hello.'

He wouldn't raise his head.

After a moment of silence we slinked away, ashamed to have intruded on the boy's night, bringing Afghanistan with us. On a night where he just wanted to be a young man, he didn't need us pushing the war in his face.

'I told you,' Rhino shrugged.

'Let's go home,' I suggested.

But where was that?

30

The Hollywood Machine-Gunner

I didn't ever think I'd be a drug addict.

Looking now at those shameful words on the page, I still can't accept it, even if I can't deny it. I have become a member of the group most reviled, most loathed in society. I have become one of those people that my parents warned me about. The type of person they promised me would be excommunicated from the family should I ever fall so low.

Well, Mum and Dad. I fell. I fell fucking hard.

It didn't start when I was in uniform. I may have been a lot of things as a soldier, and I railed against many rules, but the zero-tolerance policy on drugs was not one of them. I held the line.

Then, in the summer of 2011 when I was working at the gym, I began to dabble in tiny amounts. A bump from a key here, or a half a line there. Hardly enough to touch me, but enough that my mentality switched from strongly opposed to open.

And then, two years after leaving the battalion, there was Malibu.

Then, there was cocaine.

My next-door neighbour smoked all day and snorted all night. He was successful – very successful – and perhaps I didn't see the danger. No. That's stupid, *of course* I didn't. But I did see the opportunity.

And what opportunity was that?

To feel *something*. To overcome the nagging malaise that was telling me my life was run, that I would never experience highs like I had done in the military, and in combat. To feel *confident*, and not be so on edge in public that my back and shoulders ached with tension. And most of all *to talk*. All the things I wanted to talk about – all the things I had pressed down into my stomach – were threatening to come out. Any attempt at talking about them sober or with booze had led to me breaking down in tears, but with cocaine I now had an outlet to talk and talk and talk, and I would never break down.

It was for that reason that I used to say that cocaine saved my life. I don't really believe that anymore – and if it did save it, then it also tried to take it – but it did allow me to uncork the bottle where I was holding in my hurt. It did allow me to talk.

But at what cost? To be left wide-eyed the next morning, when all your 'friends' have gone? To be staring at the ceiling, replaying those images and thoughts in your mind again and again? I thought a lot about Hunt, of course I did, but I was blind and thought that drugs were the answer.

And let's not kid ourselves that the highs were not enjoyable – they fucking were. All of a sudden I had the confidence to be in busy public places, and I was on top of my game. Meeting women was easy. Making friends was easy. If the crash the next day had not been worth it, then in the early days I would have stopped doing it, before it became a compulsion, a tradition, an . . .

Addiction.

I don't think that point came for a few years. I could take or leave coke up until that point; if it was on offer I would take it, but I made no effort to seek it out. Like many people unhappy with their lives, alcohol was doing a good job of drowning out the noise – and don't go kidding yourselves that alcohol is not a drug. You think it's so popular because we enjoy throwing up and pissing ourselves?

That happened to me a lot more than my civilian friends in LA. They put it down to me being a hard-drinking Brit. There's some truth in that. As a nation we don't know when to stop. That's re-inforced further in the army, and it's pushed further still when you're trying to cope with things in your head that you don't want to deal with.

What were those things?

Honestly, at the time, they were vaguely formed visions and impressions. Feelings that, though distant, could quickly pull me down into depression. Only looking back now with a few years' hindsight can I pick them apart.

Of course there were the vivid images of Hunt, and the knowledge that other comrades had died. Then there was the sense that I was drifting, devoid of all purpose now that my short combat career had come to an end and I would never soldier again. I missed my friends and comrades, but above all my depression came from the fact that I hated myself. I hated myself because I was staying often on the beach in Malibu, I was making decent money from the anti-piracy work, and I had a steady stream of beautiful women interested in me. And what was I doing?

Feeling fucking sorry for myself.

It felt like a betrayal of Hunt. It felt like a betrayal of all my comrades, living or dead. How dare I feel sorry for myself when this amazing life was laid out in front of me?

And so I took drugs. I took drugs and I nosedived.

When I left the army in April 2011 I had been full of confidence, and I had worked my way through the women of my hometown like the flu. By the spring of 2014 I had almost given up on taking girls home. This wasn't due to an enlightened attitude towards casual sex, but because I failed to perform most of the time. My self-loathing reached the point where I could talk myself out of any sexual engagement. A gorgeous woman could be throwing herself at me and I would convince myself that I was unworthy: Why the fuck would she be interested in you? You're weak. You're pathetic. If you were a man then you wouldn't be thinking this way. Hunt wouldn't bother you. None of it would bother you. You're no soldier. You're no man.

Such was the track that played on loop inside of my mind. It convinced me that I was nothing but a drain and a burden on those that mattered, and so I realized finally that drugs were not the only option open to me.

There was suicide.

31

Living the Dream

I should have been an actor, not a writer. Ask anybody who knew or met me between 2015 and 2017, and they'd have told you that I was living the dream. I could hardly blame them. Seen through a snapshot of Facebook statuses and Snapchat stories, my life looked like this: Vegas, Hollywood, Miami, women, parties that raged for days, and stories.

And there were some good fucking stories in there. They were good days, in a lot of ways. If those thirty second videos were a true depiction of my life, then there probably wouldn't have been a happier guy on the planet, but here's what they didn't show: the debt that sat on my chest like an elephant; drinking vodka like water; the coke, the MDMA, the weed, the ketamine; the dark thoughts in my head; the reason *why* I spent my waking moments partying, and drug-fuelled.

It's hard to feel sorry for someone whose lowest point in life was spent backstage at clubs around the world or in Hollywood Hills after-parties. Good. I don't want any of that, but I do want to give you some understanding because this could be happening to someone you know in your hometown. Think carefully, and you may recognize that there is something deeper going on in the mind of your friend the veteran. You know him. He's the guy who always suggests shots when you go for a quiet drink. He's the one who pulls out a handful of drugs when you turn up for a dinner party. You always laugh it off, thinking that he's just a fun-loving guy, living for the moment, but have you ever wondered why he's so desperate to get off his face?

Don't be fooled by the act.

I suppose I'm more self-loathing than the next guy. There was a tiny part of me that must have known what I was doing was wrong, and that it had to come to an end in one shape or another. I didn't look at my pile of credit card debt and smile. But I also didn't think about how I would wake weak and lonely, picturing that first line of coke and the vodka that would wash it down. I wanted to be off my face 24/7, living in that land of cocaine confidence and the uplifting embrace of pills, but I could *never* be that guy who sat home alone, drinking in front of the TV. Nah, that was not a veteran caricature that suited me, thank you very much. But the guy who hits clubs every night? The guy who rubs shoulders with celebs, pro athletes, and beautiful women? Sign me up for that. My friends will think I'm a legend and I can get as fucked-up as I want. Even if people back home know about the drugs, they'll just think it's a phase, and in that they're right – I'm not stopping until I'm out of credit or I'm dead.

'Why didn't you just stop at the time?' That's probably what you're asking me right now. Well, I didn't see it with the clarity that I do as I'm writing this, a year after the point where it all came crashing down. I couldn't fully realize it then, I honestly couldn't. Whenever the reality of the situation poked its head up, I beat it down with powder and booze. When that didn't work . . .

Yeah, back to the Snapchat stories. See me partying. See me jumping around. See me smiling, more MDMA than man. Maybe what would have made better viewing was the stuff that came after. Me, leaning over Vegas balconies, thinking of how easy it would be to up and over. Hotel rooms and apartments, crying like a pathetic little baby, counting down the hours until it was acceptable to be in the company of others and the legitimacy that their presence offered. Hey, if everyone else is doing it, then it's fine for me to do too, right?

With hindsight, I could see that I was lost. The part of me that knew what I was doing was not allowed to surface, and when it did

the truth was so painful that the only solution I could see was suicide, and despite some pains I still loved life. I loved my family. I
didn't want to die, and so instead I tried to bury the voice that told
me I was a burden. That told me I was a weak, pathetic piece of shit.
I tried to bury it, I tried to run from it, but reality caught me in a
pincer move.

Two things happening simultaneously took my legs from under
me.

It happened in Ibiza, in June of 2016. There are worse places for a
breakdown, right? Long since unable to afford extended vacations
in LA, I'd come back home to the UK, and Ibiza offered the promise of cheap flights, readily available drugs, and better yet the excuse
to take them.

It was the day before my flight that I heard the news that Corporal Bailey had killed himself. I can't remember how, exactly. I was
probably off my face. Details were sketchy, but it seemed as though
the police had tasered him for his own safety. It hadn't worked, and
the guy who had finally been run out of the army for drug use had
slit his own throat.

Slit his own throat.

What drives a man to do that? I knew Bailey was troubled. In
Iraq, he had tried and failed to save the life of his closest friend. I
thought back to Afghanistan, where he had helped me with Hunt.
That effort too had proved futile. Bailey had quietly told me as much
at the time, hoping to prepare me for the worst. I hadn't listened,
and I was wrong. Hunt died. Now, after a long fight with heroin
that came from the same fields where we had fought, Bailey was
gone too, and at his own hand.

It shook me. It shook me harder than I could have ever imagined
it would. He was not a close friend, and there had been times where
I even disliked him, but he was a comrade, there was no doubt about
that. He had been alongside me in a dark moment and that counted
for something.

He was no stranger to drugs, I knew that, but neither was I. For
the first time, I realized that suicide was not a single choice. It was

the culmination of choices and events that happened over years, making the end inevitable. I thought about suicide daily, but did I *want* to die? No! But . . . but a few years ago, it was a thought that had never entered my mind. Now, unless I clouded it with drugs, it was ever-present. Where would my mind be in a year? Two years? I was terrified then. I knew that most veterans kill themselves years after service. It may not be my time, but with these thoughts in my head, and drugs and debt as my lifestyle, then how did I expect it would turn out?

I didn't deal with this revelation well. Instead, I went through with my two-day trip to Ibiza. When my friends left, I stayed. I stayed for twelve days, begging, borrowing, and stealing so that I could get my hands on whatever was cheapest. The pretence of only doing drugs with others was long gone, and I spent most of my time alone, drifting in and out of a tranquilized stupor. In my lucid moments, I thought only of death. I knew that, worse than doing wrong by my own self, I had done wrong by my family and friends. They had worked hard to provide for me with love and money, and here I was, a pathetic druggy who couldn't even muster up the decency to kill himself and spare them the further burden.

Burden. That word and its connotation was burned into my brain now. I knew what I was. I knew that, regardless of my next actions, there was no way to move forward without remaining one. Get clean, work on my debt, and tackle my problems? I'd still need help. I'd need a roof over my head. I'd need food. I couldn't afford any of that myself, and so I would be a burden. A pathetic, miserable, burden.

So kill myself then? And then what? I wasn't stupid. I knew that my death would scar my family. Possibly break my mother. I would be dead, but I would be no less a burden. I would hang around my family's neck for life, dragging them down with me.

In 2015, a comrade from the TA died of wounds he had sustained years earlier in Afghanistan. Affectionately known as Pudding, this warrior had faced surgery after surgery with the same bravery as he'd faced the enemy. He had fought for life, and here I was, waving the white flag on my own.

My cowardice made me want to puke. I had to do something.

I stayed in Ibiza until my money ran out. There was no other option, now. I did not want to die like Bailey, and so I would go home.

I would beg for help.

32

Admission of Guilt

In the weeks after Ibiza, there were no drugs, booze, or parties. In their place were dark thoughts, soaked bed sheets, and screams. Sleeping before dawn was not a possibility for me, no matter how early I went to bed or how tired I was. Any sleep before first light was guaranteed to end in my screaming, my bed drenched with sweat as if I'd had a bucket poured over me. I'd rise late, causing friction with my mother.

'You need to get into a proper routine,' she'd tell me, and then I'd lose my temper, telling her that soaked bedsheets and screaming in my sleep had nothing to do with a change in time zone. I think she knew – I think she knew everything – but she didn't want to admit that her boy's head had cracked open. Who would?

It went on like that for a while. I googled the symptoms, and saw that I was suffering the effects of PTSD. For the first time I consciously accepted that I likely had the condition. Doing so caused me to feel weak and wretched, and in those moments when I wasn't soaking sheets and waking up gasping for air, I thought about killing myself. In ten months or twenty years, I knew it was only a matter of time until I went out like Bailey, and that thought only doubled my misery.

I didn't want to die. I wanted to live, and I wanted to live happily. I wanted to be the crutch, not the burden. I wanted to be strong, not pathetic.

And so I texted Jake.

Me:
You still get them night sweats mate?

Jake:
Yeah bro, I'm going away to Telford for 2 weeks in September for therapy. My mother and missus staged like a fucking intervention and contacted Combat Stress. Give them a call mate. I went off the rails a little bit a few months back. Since I've started this process with Combat Stress I feel as though there may be a glimmer of light at the end of the tunnel.

Me:
Talk to me next time you knob. Although saying that I didn't talk to anybody so I know what it's like.

Jake:
You're mad dude. Seriously give them a ring. There's no shame in it. That's what my mother and missus said 'I never speak to them about anything that happened'. I started getting random thoughts about doing it then for some reason.

Me:

I had it around 2012 then it stopped and has come back since xmas. I honestly think its when the Taliban took back Musa Qala and they admitted it was all for nothing. I been doing mdma most days since feb. Only time I can speak about it face to face is if I've smashed a gram of coke.

Jake:

Seriously man you've got my number. You know you can buzz me any time you want to blow some steam off. Throwing that shit into your system just makes things worse. I felt completely demoralized when I heard they had retaken msq.

Me:

Fuck me I literally have every one of the symptoms listed on their website. Got to just admit it to myself that I have it.

Jake:

The quack was trying to pry the shit out of me when I seen him. He said I've got serious underlying problems. They scored me a 3 out of 3 on the whack job scale. I've been taking 40mg of Valium every night for the past 2 months just to try and get some sleep.

> **Me:**
> I'm laughing and crying mate. Our heads are scrambled.

I called the number on the Combat Stress website. It took me four or five attempts, as I choked each time they answered and hung up. Finally, I held the line.

'Hello, Combat Stress?'

'Hi. My friend . . . my friend said that I should try and call you.'

That was about as far as I got before I burst into tears. Through my sniffling, I don't know how the woman heard my details and made me an appointment to be triaged over the phone by a mental health nurse. I only gave a few details of my service, but the thought of asking for help and the admission that was brought me to my knees. By the time that I got off the phone I was shattered. I cried uncontrollably for a while. I had begged them for help, telling them that 'I don't want to die like Bailey.' After some time, I texted Jake.

> **Me:**
> I called them. If all this therapy is as hard then I'm just gonna do myself in now. I gotta wait for the triage nurse to call me. Triage – like my leg's hanging off lol.

> **Jake:**
> Don't hold back like I did dude, it just delays things. Tell them everything. They ask you about drug use. They will probably wonder how you're not dead already.

I was laughing at myself then, elated that I had made the first call and taken the first step. Weight off your shoulders is a cliché, but that was exactly how I felt, like an oppressive force had been lifted because I had bawled down the phone to a stranger, and she had offered me hope.

Jake was my confidant at this time. Relieved as I was to be asking for help, I still felt that I was a pathetic creature to be needing it, unfit to be called a soldier and man, and so, besides Jake, there was only one other person who knew everything. She was a girl that I had met in America, and our first few weekends together were a blur of arguments and drug use. I don't know why she stuck around, but maybe she saw past what had been the drunken British party boy. She had cussed me out for my indulgence, going as far as to take my wallet so that I was stopped from buying more drugs and booze, and I had grabbed at her company like a drowning sailor clutching wreckage. Somehow, I had convinced her to come and see me in the UK.

She arrived from America on 4 July 2016. To celebrate, I took her drinking in Manchester. It was a good night, and I texted Jake to tell him as much.

> life is good bro. no matter how many headfucks or night sweats we get we experienced something hardly any man ever does, and we got family and friends who worship us. Lets get our scrambled egg brains fixed for them haha.

Shame that mood only lasted for an hour.

> I said all that and then went and had a mini meltdown after. Fuck my life hahahahha.

That mini-meltdown was me bursting into tears in front of my American girl. I don't remember the trigger, but before I knew it I was awash in self-loathing and shame. She helped to pull me out of it, but it wasn't the first or last time. July was a roller coaster for me, elation followed by deep depression. The thought of ending it all was never far away, and I expect that a lot of these mood swings were a result of the recalibration of my brain as it began to get used to life without drugs. Or at least, life without them daily. A few quiet drinks still turned into me drinking to the point that I'd puke or black out. Toilet stalls were still visited to snort lines from off my phone's screen, but discreetly, because it was forbidden by my American girl – how could I tell her that I didn't feel comfortable in busy spaces without it? That I was too anxious to be able to stand at a bar in comfort without coke in my brain to inspire fraudulent confidence?

American girl went back to the States, and my appointment with Combat Stress arrived. It was over a month since my first phone call to them, which spoke to their backlog. Somehow, knowing that there were so many other veterans requiring their help made me feel better. I wasn't alone.

The location of the session was on the grounds of an old country estate on the outskirts of Wrexham. To get there I had to drive along a lane that took me by the rugby club where I had played in my childhood. The sense of nostalgia and sadness was heavy as I passed. How had I gone from junior rugby and the blank slate of childhood to the nervous mess whose hands were shaking on the steering wheel? The steering wheel of my mother's car, my own long since sold to pay for drink and drugs. What the fuck was wrong with me?

I pulled up at a new building, pale brown brick surrounded by the trees of the old estate. Dappled light fell across me, the location serene. It did little to help the churning in my stomach. The dryness of my throat. I was as scared as I had ever been when I was looking for IEDs, but I was stubborn, and the pride that had kept me from asking for help now meant that I would see it through once I had committed myself. I was already convinced that I was a waste, but someone had set time aside for me, and I would not rob them of it, even if I was unworthy. And so I stepped from the car, walked the few steps to the door, and rang the buzzer.

Don't cry, I said to myself. Don't fucking cry.

The woman who answered was in her forties, plump and friendly. Her name was Sue. As I walked into the treatment centre I saw white walls and blue carpet, with the same polished scent of any new offices, bright sunlight reflecting from the pale wood effect of the doors.

Sue took me into an office and gestured for me to take a seat. It was thin, and I bounced nervously against its weight.

'Want me to close the blinds?' Sue asked, seeing me shoot nervous looks towards the glass. I did.

It was easy enough at first. She asked me the basics. Who I had been with and where I had been. Then we began to talk about tours, fishing for the incidents that had lodged inside of my mind. Fishing for the things that had me snorting powder and soaking the bedsheets with sweat. It was all going well, and my confidence was growing. I could do this. There wasn't even a tremor in my voice. Not even when we started to talk about Afghanistan. Not until I told her about the IED that hit us.

'I opened the driver's hatch . . .' And that was as far as I could get. I could feel it about to break, the dam of my grief and emotion. I fought to hold it back.

'He was . . .' I tried. 'He was . . .'

The next word broke me. There was no more facade, now. The worst thing I could have pictured had happened. My biggest fear. I had broken down in front of a stranger, and now I was crying uncontrollably, my face pressed into my hands. With each sob came more shame, and I knew that I had made the wrong choice in coming here. I was a miserable piece of shit and nothing but a drain on others. Now even strangers had to clean up my mess. I should have had the decency to die in Afghanistan, and if not there then by my own hand.

'Seven years feels like nothing, does it?' I heard her say through my self-pity, and something in those words pulled me back from my recrimination. They were simple words, and in them I heard no judgement or condemnation. I heard only the desire to help me.

'I'm sorry,' I blubbered through my fingers.

'Would you like a minute?'

I nodded yes, and Sue left the room.

I don't know if she was gone for one minute or five, but in that time I fought to master my emotions. I beat them down, telling myself that the worst was over. I'd cried in front of her, and it could only get better from here. There was nothing left to be afraid of, at least in this meeting.

'I'm sorry,' I told her as she came back into the room, glasses of water in hand. 'I'm OK now.'

She smiled, and we went on. I didn't cry again. By the time that we were finished with the assessment, I felt drained. Sue outlined what would be the next steps in the treatment programme. Possibly they could get me on a residential course in April.

That was nine months away.

'I don't know if I can last that long,' I told her honestly. 'I'm not saying I'll do myself in, but I'm worried I'll just slip back with the drugs.'

And so Sue offered me an alternative – therapy sessions with NHS Veterans Wales.

'There's a waiting list for that, too,' she told me, 'but it will be faster than this. It's not an intense, residential course like ours, but you'll get to speak with a therapist. I can put you forward for that, if you like?'

I told her yes. Now that I had taken a sip from the offered cup, I wanted to gulp as much of it as I could. I wanted help. I wanted to get better.

Sue showed me to the door. She put out her hand. I hugged her instead. I began to thank her, but I felt the tears coming back.

'Are you going to be OK to drive?' she asked me.

I told her yes. After twenty minutes of sitting behind the wheel, attempting to master my racing breath, I was.

> **Me:**
> Fuck me bro that was intense. Cried like a fucking baby. Biggest lesson for me today is how angry I am at our leaders.

> **Jake:**
> That was my biggest lesson as well mate. It's their fault I got shot lol.

> **Me:**
> That was fun tho.

> **Jake:**
> Yeah, even tho it stung a little. Looking back now, it was the most exhilarating experience of my life.

> **Me:**
> Fuck yeah. Best day of my life that was man. Sorry about your neck tho lol.

What else could I say? It had been.

33

Facing It

It was never going to end well.

I woke in my own sick. It was bright red from the wine. Someone was shouting at me. It was my brother and my American girl.

'What the fuck is wrong with you?'

She left that day. I didn't think she'd come back. She did, and she had videos. She wanted me to see what had happened the night before.

It started with a happy reunion. I was visiting the city to see my brother, and made plans to meet with One Platoon's former commander – the man who had looked back on my wagon when we hit the IED and I had stood over Hunt, waving my hand across my neck to signal that he was dead. He had been sir, then. Now he was Justin.

I hadn't seen him in years. A lot had happened in that time. I knew I was ripped at the seams; I'd find out that he was fraying, too.

But first there was laughter. First there were happy stories. First there were photos and smiles. Justin made me look great, and I saw my brother and girlfriend looking on at me with pride. They probably didn't notice that the two former soldiers were finishing three drinks for every one of theirs.

'Will you share a bottle of wine with me?' Justin asked.

We shared three, with shots to go with it. Eventually, Justin was ready to tell me what he had been holding in for years.

He blamed himself for Hunt's death.

I told him it was bullshit. It was bollocks. I told him he had been a great boss and I would still follow him into battle, and gladly. I meant every word, but he didn't hear it, self-recrimination thick around a soul left lonely in London's faceless churn, no comrades, no brothers to talk to.

'You should have fucking spoke to me!' I raged.

'You should have talked to me! Fucking suicide?'

I'd told him about the last few years. I shouldn't have done. Great man that he was, he took it as a failing on his own part.

I'm not sure when we started fighting.

It was mostly verbal, my brother tells me, and it was a fight born of love. He shouted that he was a failure as a commander and was to blame for Hunt's death. I swore into his face and told him that he was a hero. I meant it then, and I mean it now.

I don't remember going our separate ways. I do remember walking straight out into the London traffic. I was selfish in my grief, selfish and childish, and I didn't care if I was hit. My brother wrestled me to the pavement. I tried to fight him. I could hardly stand, and he beat me easily.

My girlfriend watched and recorded with her camera. She knew that I needed to see this. She knew that I needed to hear the slurred words coming out of my mouth.

'I want to be dead. I want to be dead. I'm fucked up. I want to be dead.'

My brother wrestled with me until my anger turned to shame and self-pity. I begged him to leave me on the street. I wasn't worthy of him, or my girlfriend. He put me over his shoulder and carried me home. It was a few hours later that I woke spewing crimson.

I spent the next day alone, scrubbing Malbec from the carpet. Eventually my girlfriend came back, and showed me the videos. I promised her that it would never happen again.

That was a lie.

I walked alone across the movie studio, passing empty stages and full tour buses. I was in Hollywood, on one of my regular trips back and forth to the states to visit my girlfriend, and to dream of a life of sunshine and riches. I was a working writer in the UK now, a few publications beneath my belt, and with the help of family and publishers, I was on my way to clearing the debt that I had saddled myself with. On this day I was making my way to a screening of *Thank You For Your Service*, a movie that tells the tale of a group of young soldiers who come back from Iraq and then fall apart. I found a lonely seat in an empty aisle and slid into it.

I'll say this for the director – he nailed Iraq. As the men patrolled through the narrow streets and locals eyed them with scorn, I felt as though I was back there. I could feel my heart race. My throat tighten. When the rounds started to fly, I wanted to be there, in amongst it, lighting the enemy up.

Then the guys came home. They came home, and it wasn't long until one of them blew his brains out because his girlfriend had left him. It didn't get any better from there.

Thoughts of suicide. Rage. Seeking and consuming drugs. It was all too familiar, too close to home. When I saw the story from the family's side, I hated myself for what I had put my own through.

The movie ended. There was no glimmer of hope. The story I – and the audience – was being told was that at best we broken soldiers could hope to *control* what was in our heads. There was no way to conquer it. No way to come out thriving. As we had needed to survive the war, now we must survive the peace.

I didn't like that.

It was a long drive back to Orange County, where I was staying with friends. I tried to put the movie out of my mind. I thought that I had.

I met up with my girlfriend and friends from the Marine Corps. We went out and started drinking. I'm not sure when I got to the point of blacking out. I'm not sure when I bought the drugs. I'm not sure when it all hit me, and I started looking for my friend's gun. I can't even tell you if it was a cry for help or if I fully intended on pulling the trigger.

What I can tell you is that I found myself on the balcony, snot thick on my shirt, eyes and throat red and raw. I wanted it to be over. I either wanted to be normal or I wanted it to be over. I didn't want to live the rest of my life with my head this way. My girlfriend tried to talk to me, but I didn't want her, I wanted my friends – marines. People who could maybe understand. She didn't like that, and so she left. When she came back and found that I had taken LSD to try and get out of my mind, she left for good. I could hardly blame her. Thoughts of suicide and getting high were all intended to take me away from myself – how could I hold it against anyone who wanted to get away from me, when *I* wanted to do the same?

But for some reason, my friends stayed with me. There was no hiding my feelings from them. They'd known me for years. Seen my slide. I think I wanted them to know. As I drowned in the dark waters of my own creation, I wanted them to throw me a line. If it was all a cry for help, then my shameful call was answered, again and again and again.

It was days before I got sober. When I did, I knew that I would never allow myself to fall into a suicidal state again.

And I haven't (not quite). I can thank my friends for that.

34

Diagnosis: PTSD

Pork and chips. All told it was a solid meal. The meat was a little fatty, but the thick chips had been cooked to golden brown perfection, and went well with the cheesy sauce of the cauliflower and broccoli. It was the kind of meal I usually wolfed down in moments in my mother's home, but instead I simply looked at my plate, unable to force more than a few lonely chips down my throat.

The reason wasn't the company. To my left was my long-suffering mother; as strong as Thatcher, as kind as Mother Teresa. To my right was my youngest brother, best friend and comic. I couldn't ask for better company. I really couldn't.

So why was I looking at the knife in my hand and thinking about ramming it into my own throat?

I didn't want that thought, but it wouldn't leave me. I looked from my food to my family, and hated myself more than ever. I was as blessed as it was possible to be, and in a moment that should have been nothing but joy I could only think of killing myself.

Shame and sadness overcame me. I tried to speak, to join in the conversation, but all that came out was a choke. I knew then that I was about to be overwhelmed, and so I moved quickly away from the table, touching my mum on the shoulder to let her know the reason why. She understood – it wasn't the first time this had happened.

I went upstairs into the darkness, closing the door to the landing and sitting back against it. In the black, I cried. Realizing that I was a cliché, a smile almost broke out.

But mostly I cried.

The day of my NHS therapy sessions quite often ended like this. That's no surprise – the whole point of going is to dig up uncomfortable memories – but today had been different; never in the sessions had I felt so empty of hope.

I don't know why I was surprised. Monday morning had not been an auspicious start. I had tried to work things out by calling my ex in the States, but my promises of change didn't cut it, and so I had responded in the best way I knew how – through taking drugs and pretending that I was happy. So it was that that on Monday morning I had awoken fully clothed down to my shoes, and a good thing too – I had my official PTSD assessment in thirty minutes, a forty-minute drive away.

I made it, and I expect I looked the part as I walked into the clinic – my nose was running like a tap, my eyes were red-rimmed and heavy, my limbs had leaned out from a weekend of not eating. Doubtless the stink of booze and cigarettes hung to me like a shameful cape.

I didn't enjoy what followed. I felt like a fraud. I hated myself. I was so terrified I'd lose my shit and cry that I dug my nails into my arm until the pain gave me some distraction. I shifted and fidgeted like a crackhead. During all this the shrink asked me about my upbringing, family, service, and career since the army. With each answer I gave, I knew what a creature I was – I could not ask for a better life, and yet here I was, with thoughts flickering between taking my own life and getting off my face with more drugs.

'Why haven't you tried antidepressants?' the doctor asked me.

'Because I don't want to get addicted to them,' I told him honestly, hearing the irony in every word.

The doc explained to me then that they would take the edge off my anxiety in public places. Less anxiety = less desire to drink. Less drink = no drugs. No drugs = less depression. Less depression = less suicidal thoughts. Less suicidal thoughts = don't end up killing myself. It sounded like a pretty straightforward formula – no one chases the dragon when everything is going great. I didn't think it strange then that he didn't bring up the medicine that *would* eventually save me. He was doing his job and his job told him to prescribe pills. Not time in the mountains. Not meditation.

'Well,' the kindly shrink said, 'there's no doubt that you have PTSD.'

I almost smiled at that – I was now officially headfucked.

I left that clinic desperate for a shower, but I wasn't ready to go home. Fraud and coward that I was, how could I face my family? Instead I drove aimlessly through the countryside for a while, and then I remembered that my body had barely known food in three days. I stopped at a pub, and was proud that I could stare down the drinks that waved invitingly to me from behind the bar. My self-loathing that morning was overwhelming, and I was in the stage of my drug use cycle where I was promising that I would never shame myself or my family with such abuse again.

After filling my belly I went home, found one of the family's cats and clutched it to my chest. I lay on the sofa with it for hours. No phone, no TV, just holding the cat. The poor thing probably needs its own counselling now, but it helped me – I could feel its heartbeat. I could look it in the eyes and see something there. I don't know what, but *something*. Whatever it was then pushed me to be outside, among nature. I went and tried to marvel at trees, birds, and animals. For the most part it worked. I felt myself bobbing above the depression, not free of the fear of drowning, but hopeful. When my mum asked me how the visit to the shrink had gone, I'd told her 'alright'.

'Are you alright?' she tried me.

'I am.'

'You're not, are you?'

I shrugged. I knew one word would break me. Instead I went to sleep.

I screamed a lot in my dreams in the weeks after my girlfriend left me. I don't know what she had to do with creeping mortar barrages and having my face cut off (by a friend no less), but it taught me something to do with the nature of PTSD. At least in my own experi-ence, the condition is not a war hammer banging at the shield of my mind; rather it is an insidious virus that seeps in through cracks in the armour. When life hands out the shit sandwiches that every sin-gle human being must deal with, PTSD is there to capitalize on the misery. Since being made single, not one dream I had directly related to our break-up. What I did have was terrifying dreams about death and combat. In the weeks preceding the split, when all in life was going well, I could not recall a single nightmare.

I'm afraid that this insight doesn't help with dealing with the dis-order: 'Don't want your PTSD to flare up? Just go through life with no setbacks! Easy-peasy!' Not going to fucking happen, is it?

The one thing I can say – and I have tested this extensively – is that when something bad happens, it does no help to reach for the bottle, pill, or rolled-up note. It's going to be a hard ride anyway, and you don't need to make it harder. Granted, through drugs you'll get relief for a short time, but then you're left with only two options – feel even worse or keep going. Neither of those stories has a happy ending, and I believe that those *are* out there, if you're willing to look, and work for them.

35

Get Over It

I'm fortunate that I survived a period of my life where I was doing everything I could do destroy my body and mind. Some people don't come through that. Some people don't want to.

I did.

I did, and I was only able to do so because of family, friends, counselling, and comrades. I hope that any soldier reading this is in a similar position, but if you are – don't become complacent. I did, and before I knew it I had fallen back into bad habits. It lasted a few days before the fog cleared and I realized what a huge mistake I was making. I got on the phone to apologize to the people that support me, including my mother.

'At least you realize you made a mistake,' she told me.

And I did. I truly did.

That doesn't mean that I'll never make another one, but that's the aim. It has to be. Drugs are a temporary release, but their interest rates are high – you'll pay back a lot for the relief that they give you, and that payment comes in the form of further misery. On one of my final binges, I had a new girl come and stay with me.

'What do you think of Gez?' my buddy Seabass asked her later that week.

'He screams a lot in his sleep.'

Not true. He screams a lot in his sleep when he's been doing drugs. Most nights, he's just fine . . .

I think. There's always that fear that if I fall asleep in public I'll wake up screaming the place down. I know I'm not the only veteran who's anxious about this. Seabass had done it himself on a flight into Vegas. Once, I woke with a start and knocked a drink over the passenger next to me. He was good enough to laugh. I nodded off again, and this second time I hit him across his chest as I came to.

I got myself a coffee after that.

But anyway, I'm proud to say that I have found some light at the end of the tunnel – a huge fucking floodlight actually – and the entire purpose of the previous self-indulgent chapters is so that you can see what a low place I was in, so that the solutions I can offer now will carry some weight. Soldier, if you are in a similar place, then please pay as much attention now as if you were sweeping a dirt track for IEDs. It may well save your life, and I can say that because it is not hubris on my part. What I am about to share I learned from a man named Nate Boyer.

Nate Boyer is one of those people in life that you just have to envy, and love. Nate spent ten years in the Green Berets – including five years where he played American football for the University of Texas in the winters, and deployed overseas in the summers. He then went on to become the oldest rookie to ever play in the NFL, at thirty-four. Having already done more than most people do in a lifetime, Nate began an acting career, and was soon appearing alongside names like Gerard Butler and 50 Cent. As if that wasn't enough, Nate was the man who convinced NFL quarterback Colin Kaepernick to get off the bench and take a knee during the national anthem. As more players took to adopting the peaceful protest, Nate found himself on national media on an almost daily basis, a patriotic voice willing to meet in the middle and compromise. Nate's journey and manner have led to speaking engagements all over the USA, and somehow, despite all of this, he still manages to find time to run a nationwide veteran's charity.

I met him in its original LA branch. I was already an admirer of Nate from afar, and I had reached out to him on social media while I was visiting my Marine Corps friends in California. He invited me along to Unbreakable Perfomance in Hollywood where veterans get a chance to train alongside former NFL players and other athletes. The charity that he runs alongside NFL correspondent Jay Glazer is called Merging Vets and Players (MVP), and their message is clear – to help these groups of people find purpose after the uniforms or team jerseys have come off. By chance, the coordinator of the charity was a US marine who had served in the same area of operations as me. In 2010/11, his battalion lost twenty-five men during their deployment, and his experience had pushed him to drugs and a near successful suicide attempt through overdose – he was found on the beach by surfers and revived.

Like this marine, just being in Nate's presence did a lot to help push me away from drugs. The man had seen combat himself, but he hadn't reached for the powder. Perhaps, before I had started therapy, I would have taken this as evidence that I was unworthy. Now, having gone through those difficult sessions with NHS Veterans Wales, I took his example as one that I could follow.

What we see often determines our own actions. Growing up, we were told that soldiers and men do not discuss their feelings. If you have a problem, push it down, and hold it there with alcohol if you have to. Unhappy? Drink. Friend died? Drink. Girlfriend left you? Drink. Inevitably, as drugs have become far more easily obtainable, drinking has been supported or replaced with them.

Then there's what we see on the TV. Aren't all veterans broken? Entertainment's depiction of veterans is that we are damaged goods. If we are told that we must be men and we can't talk about what's going on inside of our heads and hearts, and if the only images of veterans we see on the TV are of suffering, then is it any wonder that many veterans cannot see a way out?

Maybe there will be people who look down on me for speaking openly about my weaknesses. I can't blame them for that, when I am still prone to doing it myself at times, but maybe – just maybe – the old breed 'didn't talk about it' because they were worried about what would happen if they did? That it was fear of shame as much as strength of pride that held tight the lips of some, while others were sent reaching for the bottle. I can't speak for them, I won't try and speak for them, but what I will say is that I've seen enough teary-eyed veterans of bygone battles to know that suffering after war is no recent phenomena. Some will disagree, and hate most of what I'm saying in these pages.

Well, fuck them.

Fuck their resentment and fuck their bitterness. I would rather be alive and perceived as weak than a miserable old cunt who drinks his whole life away and is consumed by cynicism. Of course, there's also the very likely chance that had I not admitted to suffering then I would be dead by now.

At Nate's charity, at the end of a training session, the attendees sit in a circle and discuss feelings, thoughts, and emotions. In that circle are infantrymen who saw some of the hardest tours of Iraq and Afghanistan, NFL players who were first-round picks, and decorated special forces soldiers. Talking in front of other warriors and admitting 'weakness' is daunting. In fact it is fucking terrifying. But if you had the balls to go to combat, then you can have the balls to talk about it – and not behind a mask of drugs and alcohol. You have to talk. To a friend, a therapist, your dog.

But fucking talk.

I was being interviewed for an American-based veteran's article by photojournalist Tim Kolczak, who had once served with the US Army in Iraq. We had walked along the beach, and now we sat on a bench set back by the dunes. I was watching the waves crash in as he asked me his questions.

'What pushed you to those darkest moments?' he said with a hint of Texas drawl. 'What pushed you to think about taking on your own life?'

I said nothing. I was watching the waves.

'I don't know,' I finally confessed. It was not an evasive answer, just honest. Seeing the last traces of a dying sunset bleeding out on the horizon, and hearing the crashing power of the ocean, it was as if I could not access that dark part of my mind or what dwelt there. Nature had blocked it out.

'I really don't know,' I told him again. 'Looking at this? How could I ever want to leave it?'

And that's the truth. It really fucking is. If there is a clue to managing PTSD, or any other darkness brought on by service, then I believe it is in nature. Woods, mountains, beaches. Walk them. Pay attention to them. Soak in the detail. Revel in it. For me, it has been the greatest ally I have discovered in the battle against myself.

And then there is the mentality of the last stand. A mindset that turns a soldier's difficulties into something challenging that his warrior spirit will be roused to take on, and defeat . . .

Any aspiring warrior grows up on last stands. What is more celebrated than 300 Spartans holding the Hot Gates of Thermopylae against a horde of a million Persians? Who is more heroic than the lightly armed paras who held the bridge at Arnhem against an SS Panzer Division? Who hasn't heard of Custer, or the Alamo? My own regiment held out against the Zulu in one of the most famous last stands of all, the Battle of Rorke's Drift, and so it is safe to say that I have been fed a healthy diet of fighting to the last round, washed down with the intention of taking as many of the enemy with you as you can.

The truth is, I often fantasized about being in one of these bleak situations where death or glory was the only outcome. I'm sure I'm not the only young soldier who pictured himself surrounded by enemy dead, his bayonet bloody, rifle now nothing but a club to beat back the heathen who tried in vain to bring him down. Those were the outrageous fantasies of course, but what of the realities? Last stands are not a thing of the past. I had the honour of writing *No Way Out*, the story of Easy Company in Musa Qala, where the Taliban threatened to overrun the tiny garrison for weeks. In the modern wars that followed 9/11, becoming a prisoner has never been an option. The militias of Iraq would not be merciful. The Taliban practically invented the practice of butchering captives on camera. Falling into their hands was unthinkable, and so as a soldier you consider what *you* would do if it came to it.

How would you do it? You're cornered. You're almost out of ammo. You know that they're going to get their hands on you, and you know what happens then – rape. By them, and by objects. Maybe they'll slit your throat quickly, or maybe they'll saw it off in long ripping strokes, like a lament on a violin. Maybe your eyes will be gouged out, or maybe you'll see what they're doing.

However it happens, you know that it will leave you wishing you'd stepped on an IED during your first week on tour. There is no fate worse than capture by this enemy, and so saving that last round or grenade for yourself isn't a cowardly act. It's just hastening the inevitable, and sparing your family the knowledge that there's a video of their son's final moments out there, his life reduced to a morbid curiosity for teenagers anxious to prove that they have a strong stomach.

But hey, here we are, veterans back on home soil. We're not surrounded by Taliban. We're not about to get overrun by the enemy. Funny then, that this is where most of us will fight our last stands. Last stands against our demons. Last stands against ghosts. Last stands against ourselves.

In these battles, there are no enemy on the compound walls or hammering at the gates. The Trojan horses and siege towers are drink and drugs that leak insidiously through our defences. We're surrounded by thoughts, not Taliban, but this darkness is just as lethal. It speaks to us. It tells us that life will never be the same. It tells us that we are weak, pathetic, and worthless for feeling the way that we do. It tells us that we are unworthy to be living. That we are burdens to our comrades – our friends and our family. There is no escape from this enemy, and so, as practically as if we were the last surviving member of an ambush, we're left with one choice – to kill ourselves, and escape the torture of the enemy that has infiltrated our minds.

I have fought a few of these last stands. I don't know what would have happened if I'd been left to hold off the enemy for another few hours alone. Fortunately for me, I had cavalry. Quick reaction forces. They came and dragged me out of the fight. They saved my life as literally as they could have done on any battlefield.

At the time, I was too drunk and high to see these events as 'last stands'. I kidded myself that they were just bumps in the road. Self-corrections of the mind. It was only when I was clear on the other side that I could look back and see that I was overrun. That the enemy were everywhere, and I was a 'grenade' or 'round' away from denying them their prize. In one instance, there was nothing figurative about the last bullet – my friend had a gun, and I wanted to use it.

It was an American Navy SEAL named Jocko Willink who first put the idea in my head that, as a soldier, I was looking at these last stands from the wrong direction. His podcast is something that every veteran should listen to, as it gives context to what we went through compared to warriors of the past, and on this occasion he beseeched veterans facing the last stand not to give in. Not to use that final round on ourselves, but against our enemy. Now out of the darkness, I can see that he was right.

We need to fight as hard as we did out there. We need to see what using the last round on ourselves really is – *a victory for our enemy*.

And I'm not talking about the enemy in our skulls. I'm talking about Iraqi militias. The Taliban. If we use the last round on ourselves, then we are doing their work for them. We're doing what they failed to do when we were in their backyards. Thinking about it like that, I'd rather suffer nightmares every night for the rest of my life than give those fuckers the satisfaction of knowing that they got me in the end. I worked my fucking bollocks off to stay alive on tour. My friends did the same for me. The enemy couldn't kill me there, and I'm not letting the cunts win now by default. Fuck them. There will be no bullet with my name on it. There will be no grenade clutched to my own chest, or yours – spit in the enemy's face instead. Push your thumbs into his eyes, and put your teeth into his throat.

Fight a last stand that lasts for decades. Make it worthy of the ones who went before you.

Of course, it's easier to think like this when I'm surrounded by friends and family. I'm in a fully manned castle now, as far from a last stand as I could imagine. I can only hope that next time I venture out the gates, and the ambush happens, that I remember all this. The enemy is always out there. It's the darkness, and it wants you to use the last round on yourself.

Don't give it what it wants. Fight to the last round, the last punch, the last breath.

However you do it, just fucking fight.

EPILOGUE

Brothers in Arms

The truth is that I don't speak to many of the men that I soldiered alongside. They used to bring back painful memories, or at least make me doubt that I should never have left the army. Through the rumour mill and social media, this is what I know of some. Others, like Jake, I talk to on a regular basis.

In the couple of years following the company's return from Afghanistan, drug use became rampant. The stats and research back up that soldiers returning from combat are more prone to misuse drugs and alcohol – huge fucking surprise – and the veterans of Iraq and Afghanistan handed the army a golden ticket in their mission to reduce the army's strength by over 20,000. No need to pay a soldier a redundancy package when you can catch him on a drugs test and let him go with no pension and no retraining package. Before the cuts that began in 2010, drug tests averaged out at about one a year. When the cuts came in, they could be almost weekly.

Without doubt there were people caught who deserved to be kicked out for breaking the rules, but there were also great soldiers who just needed help. Witness the four-tour NCO who finally mustered up the courage to visit the unit welfare officer and admit to his abuse of opiates – he was turned away for not shaving and subsequently went AWOL, selling drugs to support his habit. How was it that the army were allowed to cut these soldiers loose with no support? No rehab? I guess it's because they were a danger to others. That their staying on in the ranks could endanger the lives of their comrades.

But wait a minute – didn't the army offer the guys their jobs back as soon as they fell below the new manning minimum and were desperate for recruits?

Yeah, they fucking did.

Jake was one of those who fell to the drug tests. He was quite rightly decorated after the tour for staying in the fight when he was shot and returning to it when he was fixed up. His actions when he was blown up were commendable, but they counted for shit when he failed a drug test for steroids.

Steroids. Not coke. Not heroin. The career of a decorated three-tour NCO was cut short because he made the bad decision to take an athletic enhancer. Goodbye pension. So long retraining. Adios comrades, and hello driving a dairy-tanker, no one in the cab for company but his own angry thoughts. I didn't even laugh when he told me that he'd lost his shit with a farmer and drove the wagon into the man's Land Rover. There comes a point where this stuff just stops being funny. Hard to see the light side when you know your friend is medicating himself to sleep and on the constant edge of breakdown. Hard to forgive the military that told us we were part of a family, only to kick us onto the street at the first bad decision. Now that the army are struggling for numbers again, Jake has been offered his old job back – apparently the drug thing doesn't bother them, now. He told them to fuck off, of course. He's seen the myth of loyalty. It is as real as steel between brothers, but between the highest echelons and the rank and file, it has the strength of a wet paper bag.

It's hard for me to hide my disgust at the way men like Jake were treated by the green machine, but it is still a home for Danny and Toby. Toby has been through some hard times himself. His daughters have saved him; he couldn't leave them. Otherwise, he assures me, his post-Afghan divorce would have been the cherry atop the tragic-ending cake.

Danny is as much of a sharp-tongued sniper as ever, and recently transferred to a newly formed infantry unit that offers a higher chance of deployment. Like all of us, he just wants to be back on tour.

Maybe that will change now that he has twins with a beautiful lady he met in Paris and charmed with the help of Google Translate.

Jay was medically discharged from the army due to narcolepsy – which did a lot to explain his life as a mantress – and now lives with his family in South Wales. He's had his own rough patch, but he now looks fat and happy. We've promised that we'll reach out to each other should we ever have another dark day.

Nacho's services were no longer required by the army. The lawyers won't let me tell you why, but ask me over a pint. Thinking back on it, I let him down a lot during the tour. I should have been a much better leader. I see now that every mistake he made was the responsibility of his NCOs – me included – but back then we were young, headstrong, scared and angry.

The last I heard of Blake, he was no longer allowed to handle weapons. This was for the safety of other people as much as his own.

Gay Sam went on to win Mr Gay Wales. He was supported and cheered in his accomplishment by his comrades.

Emily is still serving with the army. I have often turned to her for advice with this book, including the painful decision to detail Hunt's injuries so that politicians cannot escape the effects of their decision making. I can't think of many other soldiers I know who are held in such universally high regard as this woman, but Johan would be one. The hard bastard from South Africa was medically discharged following his injuries, but he has overcome them to build a happy civilian life with his young family in Wales.

Owens, Corporal Rabbit, and Rhino are all working on the private security circuit. Be it Iraq, Afghanistan, or Africa, these men have now spent most of their adult lives in war zones. Like thousands of other veterans, they will one day have to leave their teammates behind and integrate into a society where weapon-handling and emergency first aid are not sought after competencies. I worry about that day. We need to prepare for it. We think our soldiers who fought in Iraq and Afghanistan have come home, but they haven't, not yet. That will happen when the security circuit spits them out, and then we will have thousands of life-long warriors returning to a culture that does not understand them. There is a lot to do to make this transition a peaceful one, both for the individuals, and society at large.

And what of those at home who lost loved ones on the other side of the world? They live daily with ghosts. Children grow up never having known their fathers. Some families are stoic, others are angry, but all have been robbed of that which was most precious. So too the Afghans whose homes and lives were 'collateral damage'. I would like to say that their suffering produced a better future for those same children who were sent in to collect the enemy dead, but in 2016, after almost a decade of constant fighting, the Taliban retook control of Musa Qala and the surrounding area. As I write this at the end of 2018, there is no sign of them giving up control. I imagine that any of those in the villages of Yatimchay and Chakaw who cooper-ated with us are long since beheaded. I think about the children who shouted 'smoke and a pancake', and I hope that they are happy and live without fear, though I know that under the Taliban such a thing is unlikely. Perhaps now they have themselves picked up a weapon, becoming my enemy, for as much as I hate how our war was fought, I do believe that the enemy was one worthy of killing. How does it make me feel, knowing that those smiling children could now hate the West? Hate my family? Hate me?

I try not to think about such things. There is no happy answer.

Such dark thoughts are part of the reason I have avoided re-unions, and cannot shed light on the current lives of more of my comrades. The possibility of becoming upset after a few drinks was real and shameful. Now that all of this is on the record and there can be no more denying, no more pretending that things were fine, I can take part in those things and be glad to. In fact, even in the process of editing this book I have rekindled connections with many brothers in arms. I hope this book shows that I have never forgotten the people I served alongside, and I never will. In these pages I endeavoured to write how I – and often, we – felt at the time. Now, almost a decade on from the tour, I have no anger or bitterness towards any members of my company – everyone was doing their best. Everyone was scared. I love them all and cliché be damned. We *were* that happy few. That band of brothers.

As for me, I will never soldier again.

Sometimes this truth leaves me angry. Sometimes it leaves me numb, sometimes empty, and sometimes in tears.

It has never given me joy.

What wires are so crossed in my brain that I should feel sadness and anger at being denied the one thing most people will go to the ends of the world to avoid?

The same ones that compelled me to it in the first place, of course. The wires that had me playing soldiers in the garden. The wires that had me punching the air with joy when I was eight years old and the first Gulf War started. Twenty-eight years later, it's fair to say that I'm no smarter than I was back then. In fact, now that I know what a terrible thing war is, then I am a bigger fool than ever.

But I am an honest fool. Honest enough to tell you – even as I curse myself for my stupid, selfish attitude – that I long to be back at war. I long to be back with the comrades who were everything to me.

And still are.

There is no convenient ending to this story, which I hope has done something to honour those I was so privileged to know. By the time that these words have gone from publisher to print, to bookshelf, some of us will have continued to thrive, but some of us will have fallen, and some more may have died by our own hands. Even when the last of us have gone, the short period of our lives spent at war will live on. The fear, the excitement, the anger – it may live on through our children, planted there by violence and bitter resentment. We can only hope – no, we must ensure – that these influences are matched by the assets that Afghanistan taught us – comradeship, selflessness, perspective. War wasn't all bad. I wouldn't want to be back there if it was.

So no, there is no ending to this story. Rather, there are

thousands of them. They will be acted out by all Afghanistan's soldiers, every story different, yet the same. They will be acted out by family, friends, and the strangers that the war touched.

If you are one of those soldiers, write your own ending so that it honours and remembers the sacrifice of your brothers. Write it so that, when you look back, the misery and the struggle melts away, and all that's left are the friends that you'd die for.

We will remember them.

APPENDIX

Operation Unfuck Your Head

This book is the total opposite of the one I saw myself writing as a young adult. I wanted to be as stoic as Eugene Sledge, as daring as Robert Mason, and as insightful as Robert Leckie. Instead I fumbled and grumbled my way through my tours, then succumbed to my circumstances. There is no excuse for that, and the blame is entirely my own.

Not the army's. Not the war's.

My own.

The choices were always mine to make, and more often than not I chose badly. The reason that I have told you about these decisions and where they led me is not because I want pity or a hug or a pat on the shoulder. It's because I want to tell you about the good choices that I've started to make. I want to tell you about them because they are choices that I think anyone is capable of making, and if you are suffering from PTSD or any other shit in your life, I think they can help you as much as they helped me. I'm not saying there's a silver bullet out there – I think the demons are only ever a slip-up away – but by making these changes I have gone from wanting to end my life on a daily basis to never wanting it to end at all. I don't believe there's such thing as a one-size-fits-all solution, but soldier, what's the worst that can happen if you try them?

PURPOSE

Above all else, a soldier – because let's not kid ourselves, we will be soldiers forever – must have purpose. He must have a mission. I grew up wanting to be a soldier, and then until the age of twenty-nine I was in uniform. Even working private security was a kind of military life – I was armed and worked almost exclusively with other squaddies. When I made the transition to writing full time late in 2016, I felt as though my reason for being was gone – I had been born to do something, that time had passed, and now I had the rest of my life ahead of me to see through without ever being truly engaged in it.

And think about that for a moment. After being a soldier, becoming a writer was my second dream. But it wasn't *the* dream, and as I turned thirty-four and passed the army's recruiting age limit, the reality that my true purpose in life had passed hit me like a burst of machine gun fire. I felt sick, lonely, and depressed. The knowledge that I was living out my second dream only pushed me down further.

I truly believe that soldiers are more often born than bred. Yes, in some times of need civilians will step up and become heroes on the battlefield, but a certain percentage of us seem to be born with it hardwired into our DNA. In centuries past, we likely wouldn't have lived long into our thirties – a constant thirst for battle would have seen to that – but now here we are, our genes praying for war, and society telling us that we must heed peace.

Regardless of the reason, the fact remains that we must regain purpose if we are to move on to happy and fulfilled lives *after* the military. That we must see those war days as a chapter in our lives and not the book. Yes, I understand the irony here, but this book is actually an illustration of that idea. With this work, I can try and tangibly close the cover on these stories of Afghanistan and move on to creating new ones in a new life, and the reason that I can do this is because I have refound *purpose*. I can no longer *be* a soldier, but that doesn't mean that I have to give up *thinking* about them. I can turn my new career into immortalizing heroic men and women from all wars, all countries, and all ages. I can put their stories into books and onto screens, so that their deeds will live on. This is my new-found purpose.

Every one of us has the capacity to find a new reason for being. It doesn't have to be a full-time job, or even a part-time one. One's rediscovered purpose could be to volunteer for a veteran's organization or to fundraise for anti-poaching groups in Africa. There are a million good causes that need time, money, and people, and I am confident there is one that will give purpose to any person out there who is struggling and in need of meaning to go on. If you are fighting for your life, and you see no reason to do so, then you will eventually lose the battle.

Find purpose.

WEAKNESS INTO STRENGTH

My friend Chris lost a leg in Iraq. He was only nineteen years old at the time. I don't think people would have held it against him had he retreated inside of himself and his home, and led his life away from curious stares and questions. Did he do that?

Did he fuck.

Chris took advantage of every opportunity his injury gave him. Numerous charities offered chances to travel the world and learn new skills. Chris took them, falling in love with sailing. It goes without saying that, as a squaddie, he embraced the one-legged pirate look. I can't think of many other people I know who are more active than this young man, and his achievement did not stop there. A few years ago, Chris wrote a Facebook post in which he fought back against hate-groups and highlighted how Muslims had been involved in his life-saving surgery and rehabilitation. Chris's post went viral, and is still being shared several years later.

Through his injury, Chris has become stronger as a person, and has experienced more by thirty than most people will in their entire lives. He has done this because he chose to turn a weakness into a strength, and though I would never compare PTSD to losing a leg, Chris's example – and that of hundreds of other wounded soldiers – has inspired me to do the same with my mental health problems. When I stopped looking at PTSD as something that held me back, and started looking it as an opportunity, the symptoms that I suffered from were severely reduced. True, I'm not about to go and put on my Tinder profile that I have PTSD and occasionally wake up screaming the house down, but I can embrace it by telling its story – good and bad – and hope that through sharing my own issues, others will follow. Just talking about it was the eventual difference between running myself into the dirt and embracing life once more.

DRUGS

In earlier edits of this book, I was adamant that you should avoid them. Now, having seen the research coming out on the positive effects that drugs like MDMA and cannabis can have on mental health disorders, I'm not so sure.

What I will say is this: do not see drugs as a flat-out alternative to other treatments, such as exercise and therapy. Respect drugs. Do not self-medicate. I know that they're tempting, and I know that a lot of the time they are enjoyable with no great consequence, but do you want to run that risk that the one time there *IS* a consequence that you don't get a second chance? Even though I had suicidal thoughts while sober, I never seriously considered following those thoughts through until I was either drunk or on drugs. I talked with a music producer and good friend of Chester Bennington, the lead man of Linkin Park who took his own life in 2017. The producer assured me that Chester always battled away his demons when sober, and for that reason he stayed that way. It just took one day – one slip-up – when Chester reached for the bottle, and then the actions of his impaired thinking were tragically irreversible for both him and his family.

Now, I won't be a hypocrite and tell you that I am teetotal, but ask yourself this – are you drinking because you're enjoying it or are you doing it to cover up emotions? To blunt pain? To forget? Without a doubt the answer will be clear to you. If it's anything less than having fun with friends, put the fucker down and go outside.

EXERCISE AND THE OUTDOORS

Before and during my time in the military I was a huge fan of the outdoors. I went running for hours and walking for days. Quite often this was alone, and without music. Like most of us, I wasn't living my life through my phone at that time.

It's only recently that I've made this effort to reconnect on some kind of level with nature. This doesn't mean that I pour soil down my underpants and hug trees, but simply that I get out there among it – be it a forest, beach, or mountain – and take in the detail. Marvel at life. Think of how small my problems really are in the context of the planet. If this sounds like hippie hocus-pocus then maybe it is, but it fucking works. I dare you to go out there, embrace it, and then tell me that it doesn't. Haven't you ever wondered why the cliché surfer is so chill? Why ramblers are always smiling even when it's pissing down with rain? There's a reason for it. Go find it. Without a doubt, when I have a down day, it is usually one where I have neglected to get outside, or at the very least visit the gym. On days where I have been outdoors AND hit the gym, my mind is bulletproof.

FRIENDS

'You are the sum total of the five people you spend the most time with' has become a common refrain in the business world after it was floated by motivational speaker Jim Rohn, and from experience I couldn't agree more. Just think about it. If you spend your time around miserable, angry people who see no solution to life's problems but drink and drugs, where do you think you'll end up? On the other hand, if you are surrounded by positive, active people who have purpose in their lives, don't you think that will rub off on you?

I knew I had to make changes in the people that I surrounded myself with. It doesn't mean you cut anyone out of your life, just that you shift the time you spend with people to better serve your-self. You *know* who are the positive influences in your life, and who are the ones leading you to dark places. Make the call.

THERAPY

My therapist Mark from NHS Veterans Wales is a big part of the reason I am still here today. I was under the impression that therapy would involve me lying on a sofa, talking away while the therapist watched the clock, but I was so wrong. Mark taught me new ways to process thoughts. Ways to challenge what my brain was telling me – assumptions I had made that were holding me back from switching out of war-fighting mode to peace. The simple act of catching a negative thought and assessing it for truth before acting on it is one of the biggest and most positive changes that I have been able to bring into my life. As a veteran, you have earned the right to see a therapist. Use that right. It won't cost you anything, so what is the worst that can happen? Maybe you'll cry, maybe you'll get angry. So what? What looks better? A crying veteran or a dead one?

Easy call. Go talk to a professional.

As I said, this book isn't what I thought it would be, and I know that I am straying from the domain of war memoir to self-help. I don't really care. Let's be honest, the whole act of writing it was self-help for me in the first place, and in that respect it has achieved its aim. I feel better for seeing it all on the page. I feel great for reread-ing my dark times and finishing with the light. I hope that at least one other veteran will benefit from what I have laid out here. I know that there will be others who despise me for it, and I don't hold that against them. So be it.

Now, enough of my stories. Set to work on your own. The road out of darkness is not an easy one, but if you wanted life to be easy then you wouldn't have become a soldier, would you?

So embrace the challenge for yourself.

March on for your family.

And fight the battles, for your brothers in arms.

Acknowledgements

First, thanks go to Terry Taliban. You tried to kill me. Instead you taught me a lot, and made me a stronger version of myself.

Of course, the real reason I survived Afghanistan is because of the people that I fought alongside. I'm grateful to all members of A Company, 2 Royal Welsh, and the wider cast of NATO Forces within Afghanistan. It's fun to take the piss out of REMFs, but everyone has their part to play.

Special thanks to my brothers in The Firm. You kept me alive and sane (ish). Thank you for letting me tell this story – our story.

Obviously, the war didn't stop when I got home. There are a lot of friends who have been there for me at some point. You know who you are. I would like to thank my family for the same, but they're not supposed to be reading this, so . . . if you got this far, let's just pretend you didn't. Deal?

My deepest gratitude to the strangers at Combat Stress and NHS Veterans Wales who helped me put my head back together. Diolch o galon.

As far as this book goes, it would never have happened without the trust and patience of Rowan Lawton, the team at Furniss Lawton, and Rory Scarfe. A million thank-yous to my editor Ingrid Connell for taking the book to the next level, and for coming up with the book's title, which I love. I'm grateful to the contribution of everyone at Pan Macmillan; even the lawyers! It's hard for me to get my head around all the moving parts that go into making the idea of a book a reality, but I'm indebted to everyone who has been a part of this journey; from my friends who read the earliest drafts, to those of you who have been kind enough to buy it and read this far!

When I was writing the dedication to this book, the obvious choice was the memory of those whose deaths are recorded in its pages. In the end, however, I decided that their dedication should be here, so that they are the men who have the final say in this story. Jamie and Corporal Bailey are both pseudonyms, but the men were real enough. I am grateful that I was able to call them friends, and comrades. So too many others who will always be remembered and honoured by their brothers in arms, and none more so than the two Welsh warriors of A Company who gave their lives that summer of 2009. My final, deepest gratitude is to Private Richard Hunt, and Private James Prosser.

Glossary

2 I/C	second in command of the company, usually a captain.
A-10	A-10 Thunderbolt II aircraft.
ACOG	Advanced Combat Optical Gunsight.
ANA	Afghan National Army.
AO	area of operations. Often centred around a town and its district centre, with smaller patrol bases and checkpoints pushed out as satellites. Usually a battle group of battalion size was allotted to each AO.
ATO	ammunition technician officer.
AWOL	absent without leave.
Barma team	the infantry team who look for IEDs at the head of a patrol.
bergen	a rucksack the size and weight of a house, in which an infantry soldier carries the things he needs to live and fight.
BFPO	British Forces Post Office.
CASEVAC	casualty evacuation.
CAT A	the most serious and grievous injuries, and the highest priority for evacuation.
CAT B	stretcher case injury.
CAT C	walking wounded.
chogis	locals.
claymore	an antipersonnel mine. Due to law and to avoid civilian

	casualties, British soldiers can only use these with the command-wire method of detonation.
colour man	the rank between sergeant and sergeant major. Equivalent to a staff sergeant in corps that aren't nails enough to be infantry.
cross deck	move to another unit/team/vehicle, i.e. cross decking a team from 1 to 2 Platoon for the duration of an operation.
CVRT	combat vehicle reconnaissance tank – also known as death traps.
dead ground	an area of ground that provides cover from view and fire. Often a home to IEDs.
dicker	a Taliban lookout. Also, dicked, dicking screen.
dismount	an infantry soldier who works out the back of a Warrior.
DC	district centre.
drop shorts	nickname for the Royal Artillery.
ECM	electronic counter measures (IED signal jamming for the rare bomb that wasn't victim operated).
EOD	explosive ordinance disposal.
FAC	forward air controller.
fire mission	air or artillery strikes.
FLET	forward line enemy troops. The front line held by the enemy.
FOB	forward operating base.
FOO	forward observation officer (Royal Artillery).
frag grenade	fragmentation grenade, designed to disperse lethal fragments on detonation.
FSG	fire support group. A group of soldiers with heavy weapons and bad intentions.
FST	fire support team.
gat	rifle.
gen	rumour.

green zone	the area of dense vegetation that runs along rivers and irrigated farmland.
GPMG or gimpy	general purpose machine gun, aka the pig, widow-maker, belt-fed murder machine.
head gone	go crazy/battle shock.
head shed	headquarters.
Hesco	flat-pack frames of metal and hessian. Opened up and filled with sand, they provide cover against small arms and blast. Invented by the same guy that came up with the Segway.
hexi blocks	small blocks of fuel that are probably really cheap to procure and bad for your health, and therefore perfect for soldiers to cook with.
H-hour	the time given to the beginning of an operation.
HLS	helicopter landing site.
HME	home-made explosive.
ICOM scanner	a VHF radio scanner that picks up the Taliban's un-secured frequencies.
IEDD team	improvised explosive device disposal team. i.e. heroes with giant balls.
illum-round	parachute flares of various sizes and deployed in vari-ous manners, from mortars to hand-held.
int	intelligence.
ISAF	International Security Assistance Force.
K-Kill	the catastrophic kill of an armoured vehicle, rendering it permanently irreparable.
laager	a circle of vehicles.
LMG	light machine guns; fully automatic and belt or maga-zine fed with 5.56mm ammunition.
Mastiff	a type of protective patrol vehicle developed post Iraq invasion. Unlike most vehicles in Helmand, getting blown up in a Mastiff wasn't a death sentence.
max units	the full amount of personal accident insurance a sol-dier could take out with PAX, a government-supported

	provider who were the only ones daft enough to offer us policies.
MERT	medical emergency response team i.e. heroes with giant balls and giant hearts.
MFC	mortar fire controller.
NBC	nuclear biological chemical.
NCO	non-commissioned officers.
nine-liners	casualty reports.
OC	officer commanding; the commander of a company, usually a major.
o-group	orders group. Could be anything from a quick heads up to a briefing spanning hours.
OMLT	operational mentoring and liaison team, pronounced omelette. A section strength of Brits embedded with elements of the Afghan National Army.
overwatch	a group providing cover to another unit, or watching an area of ground for enemy activity, i.e. overwatch on a heavily IED'd area to catch bomb layers.
Pedro	A Black Hawk helicopter deployed and equipped by the United States Air Force for the purpose of casualty evacuation, i.e. heroes with giant balls who say 'bro' and 'dude' a lot.
pink mist	being blown apart to the extent that all that's left of you is a pink mist hanging in the air. Also the name of one of our boys, because he was good at getting shot and blown up.
PKM	PK machine gun used by the Taliban and Afghan forces.
PX	convenience shop, short for post exchange.
QRF	quick reaction force; on this tour, usually two Warriors with one team of dismounts and a medic.
REME	Royal Electrical and Mechanical Engineers.
REMF	rear echelon motherfuckers, aka base-rats.
RSM	regimental sergeant major.
Rupert	officer.

sangars	a fighting position made of sandbags, or more permanent structures of hesco and steel. Excellent places to get shot at, wank in, and to contemplate a change in career.
full screw	corporal.
snap peg triggers	the method of detonation for an IED, often for targeting troops on foot.
stag	sentry duty.
sweats	veterans.
Terry	the Taliban.
UBAC	under body armour combat (it's a fucking shirt, but the army likes to complicate everything).
USMC	United States Marine Corps.
Vallon	a make of metal detector.
wadi	a dry river bed. Could vary greatly in size and depth. The places to pass across/through them were usually riddled with IEDs.
Warrior	a tracked armoured vehicle with a turret that houses a 30mm cannon and 7.62mm coaxial machine gun, with space in the back for a team of sweaty, angry infantry soldiers.
The Zoo	Two Platoon of our company.

Picture Acknowledgements

Page 16, *bottom*: © Courtesy of The Veterans Project

All other images are supplied by the author. Every effort has been made to identify the owners of copyright material reproduced in this book. The author would like to apologize for any omissions and will be pleased to incorporate missing acknowledgements in future editions.